QUALIFIED
Candidate Resumes and the Threshold for Presidential Success

QUALIFIED
CANDIDATE RESUMES AND THE THRESHOLD FOR PRESIDENTIAL SUCCESS

JAMIN SODERSTROM

iUniverse, Inc.
Bloomington

Qualified
Candidate Resumes and the Threshold for Presidential Success

iUniverse books may be ordered through booksellers or by contacting:

iUniverse
1663 Liberty Drive
Bloomington, IN 47403
www.iuniverse.com
1-800-Authors (1-800-288-4677)

ISBN: 978-1-4620-4541-9 (sc)
ISBN: 978-1-4620-4543-3 (e)
ISBN: 978-1-4620-4542-6 (dj)

Library of Congress Control Number: 2011914646

Printed in the United States of America

iUniverse rev. date: 9/23/2011

For my wife, Lisa

Using the tried and true resume submission process will be a new and better way to ensure that future presidents will be leaders who are qualified—by constitutional, historical, and practical standards—to hold the office once held by Washington, Lincoln, and Roosevelt.

CONTENTS

AUTHOR'S NOTE

Ideas can be life-changing. Sometimes all you need to open the door is just one more good idea.

— Jim Rohn

An idea not coupled with action will never get any bigger than the brain cell it occupied.

— Arnold H. Glasow

THE EVOLUTION OF AN IDEA

I BEGAN 2000 WITHOUT any real knowledge of or interest in politics or current events. But that same year I stopped playing college baseball and needed to find a new passion. Enter the now-historic presidential contest between George W. Bush and Al Gore. I became totally immersed, watching hours of daily campaign coverage, reading news magazines and newspapers, and eventually changing my major to broadcast journalism. The election was the first political event in which I took an active interest, and I enjoyed every minute of it.

Soon enough the drama of the disputed 2000 election faded, and my newfound passion took a detour from presidential elections to presidential history. Reading presidential biographies became my favorite pastime, and I started viewing politics and elections from a more historical perspective. Party affiliation, powerful speeches, and ideological stances on particular issues became less important to me than a candidate's basic qualifications and potential for presidential success. History taught me that becoming a successful president depended less on the best-laid plans in campaign speeches and more on the ability to adapt to ever-changing political circumstances.

Nearing the 2004 election, I knew that I had to pick one of the candidates, but none of the choices was very inspiring when viewed against the impressive presidential backdrop of Washington, Lincoln, and Roosevelt. About that same time, I started connecting the dots between my own school and job applications and the presidential election. It dawned on me that looking at resumes would help me easily compare the candidates' qualifications and make an informed voting decision. But try as I might, I could not find an official version of any candidate's resume. All the information I had to go on was whatever I could collect on my own. In the end, I was forced simply to guess which candidate I believed would become a more successful president.

By the time I entered law school in 2005, I planned on writing a book on presidential resumes, but I had not yet fleshed out the important details. Over the next three years I studied the Constitution, continued reading presidential and American history, and developed the eight basic categories that form the basis for all presidential resumes. I also developed an "intangibles" category to address the many non-quantifiable personal characteristics every president possesses. My vision was to create a tool to help voters compare presidential candidates with each other and with past presidents, and my thesis was that more qualified candidates become more successful presidents.

I was disappointed that I could not write *Qualified* before the 2008 election. It would have been a perfect contest in which to introduce my resume-based approach to selecting presidents. There was no heir apparent and each party had numerous contenders for the nominations, including well-known political figures and fresh political faces. But, alas, it was not to be. The election passed, Barack Obama became the forty-third American president (counting Grover Cleveland only once), and still no presidential resume was ever made public.

Between the 2008 election and publication of this book, I read biographies on every president along with many other historical works. My notes became detailed summaries of every president's qualifications, and the summaries became the presidential resumes. Standardized methodologies permitted each resume to be scored, ranked, and analyzed for any statistical correlations between a president's basic qualifications and presidential success. And the final result became the QUALIFIED THRESHOLD: the minimum resume score necessary for a candidate to have a very high probability of becoming an Average or better president.

THE GOALS OF *QUALIFIED*

Qualified has two primary goals: first, to educate readers on the most relevant and important presidential qualifications; and second, to challenge voters to help improve the current presidential selection process by insisting on seeing the 2012 candidates' resumes.

Tens of thousands of books have already been written about the successes and failures of the American presidents. Over 16,000 books have been written about Abraham Lincoln alone. But few books focus on the lives and experiences of presidents *before* they became president. Some books may offer explanations in retrospect as to why a president became a Great, Average, or Failed president, but they rarely reverse the analysis and determine without the benefit of hindsight whether a president was actually qualified to become president.

This book attempts to fill that academic void without supporting or opposing any particular partisan ideology, political party, or presidential candidate (past or present). It ignores presidential successes and failures and focuses instead on the experiences and abilities each president brought into office. Only when analyzing the results and drawing conclusions does it consider a president's actual success, and it does so simply by comparing each president's qualifications with an historical presidential ranking determined by an ideologically-neutral group of presidential scholars and historians.

And with education comes a greater duty to participate. Keeping that in mind, this book challenges readers to begin insisting that every presidential candidate release an official resume before the 2012 election so his or her basic qualifications can be evaluated by the American public. By accepting this "resume challenge," readers will have already participated in the presidential election process in a meaningful way.

While writing *Qualified*, one thing has become clear to me: it is *nice* for a candidate to have a five-step plan for solving every political problem, but it is *necessary* for a candidate to have enough relevant experiences and abilities that he or she can actually deliver positive results and become a successful president. Presidential qualifications as presented on a resume, not hopeful rhetoric as presented in a campaign speech, are what are really needed in the Oval Office.

Jamin Soderstrom
Houston, Texas

PREFACE

Politics, it seems to me, for years, or all too long, has been concerned with right or left instead of right or wrong.

> – Richard Armour

THERE IS NO MORE important decision an American voter can make than selecting who will become the next President of the United States. The reason is simple. The moment a president takes office, he or she immediately becomes the central figure in American government and the *de facto* leader of the free world. There is literally no more powerful or influential position a person can hold. Yet even with the stakes so high, the Constitution provides few presidential eligibility requirements and no formal guidelines for determining whether a candidate is qualified to become president.

With this in mind, *Qualified* begins with a simple premise: American voters should not be forced to guess whether a candidate is qualified to become president. The problems America now faces, and those it will continue to face in the coming decades, are too large to risk electing or re-electing an unqualified president in 2012, 2016, or 2020. Only qualified presidential leadership—leadership based on relevant experiences and abilities rather than partisan rhetoric and impractical promises—can meet the many difficult challenges that lay ahead.

EXCESSIVE PARTISANSHIP

One of the underlying problems that America now faces—and perhaps the single most important reason that electing qualified presidents is so critical—is the excessive partisanship coming from all sides of the political spectrum. Over 200 years ago, George Washington warned in his *Farewell Address* of the "constant danger of excess" in party spirit, and of America's natural tendency toward partisanship. And in years past, excessive partisanship has indeed driven Americans to vicious words and sometimes to violence. It has also scarred the country in ways that have taken decades or more to heal (e.g., slavery, segregation, Watergate). Thankfully, only once has it actually torn the nation apart and threatened its existence through civil war.

With a combination of strong founding principles and qualified presidential leadership, America has survived each period of extreme political discord and has emerged stronger and more united. The relative peace and prosperity America has experienced over two centuries is largely founded upon the moderation of its politics and the quality of its leaders. The partisan pendulum swings slightly left and then slightly right, and America remains balanced in the middle.

The best way to prevent or overcome these harmful periods of excessive partisanship is for American voters to elect highly qualified presidents. Without qualified presidents, other experienced and enlightened political leaders, and an informed and involved electorate, there is no guarantee that America will retain its top place in the world.

Historic Extremes

Excessive partisanship in America is not new. Strained political passions have threatened national unity several times before, but great political leaders rose to the challenge and led America back towards unity and prosperity.

The first American decade weathered epic political debates and bitter personal rivalries in a contest to define the meaning and purpose of the American Revolution and to put into action the words and principles written in the Constitution. At that time it was by no means certain that the American experiment in representative government would succeed. Alexander Hamilton and Thomas Jefferson were men of great ability and great vision, and were the clear leaders of the early partisan disputes. But ultimately, neither man's vision conquered the other. Due in large part to the excellent presidential leadership of George Washington (and to a lesser extent John Adams), America emerged from the 1790s with a balance of the best values and core virtues championed by both political parties. In fact, each of the first six presidents had great qualifications, placing America's early years in good hands and enabling it to survive the partisan excesses of the era.

Much of the nineteenth century was also filled with excessive partisanship and ideological extremism. In the decades leading up to the 1860 election there was an absence of highly qualified presidents, and only strong congressional leadership successfully pulled the nation back from the brink of disunion and war. Finally, when disunion became inevitable, the long and bloody Civil War ensued and over 600,000 soldiers died. But during those darkest days of American history between 1861 and 1865, President Abraham Lincoln (the second most highly qualified president elected between 1828 and 1900) was able to preserve the Union and end slavery. Without his strong and enlightened leadership, the nation never would have survived.

The Progressive Era of the 1900s and the Depression Era of the 1930s were also profound periods in American history, but they were not known for excessive partisanship. The partisan and ideological divisions of the country were passionate to be sure, but they were not excessive. This could be due to the fact that three highly qualified presidents served during those eras—Theodore Roosevelt, Woodrow Wilson, and Franklin Roosevelt—each of whom managed the nation's domestic and international affairs quite well.

The next truly extreme partisan era was the 1960s and the Watergate period of the 1970s. President John F. Kennedy was assassinated in 1963. Then President Lyndon Johnson's domestic Great Society programs re-wove the political fabric of the nation (many believe for the better), while his international and military policies simultaneously created a new tear. More assassinations came—including Martin Luther King, Jr. and Robert Kennedy in 1968—the highly qualified but ethically challenged Richard Nixon rose to the presidency, and partisan rhetoric, protests, riots, and other public violence dominated the American political scene. At the peak of the Watergate affair, Nixon resigned the presidency and left a battered and bruised nation with political wounds that only time could heal. Even today, four decades later, many of the scars from this last excessively partisan era remain visible.

The Modern Era

Most of the time America's political spirit, its well-intentioned political disagreements, and its passionate debates over important issues are strengths of the democratic system, not weaknesses. These conflicts—in moderation—eventually help to forge political compromise and public consensus on the difficult issues of the day. They also help to create a feeling of indivisible national unity. Bitterness and animosity have never been hallmarks of the normal American political dynamic.

But ever since the 2000 election, and even more so since the 2008 election, the volume of partisan bitterness and ideological animosity has risen continuously with no end in sight. Political leaders seem fundamentally opposed to compromise, and are deeply divided on many national and international issues. There is a palpable unwillingness from people at all ends of the political spectrum to listen respectfully to those with whom they disagree. Those who look different, sound different, have a different background, or espouse different political beliefs are despised on arrival.

The political issues of the day may not have the same moral foundations as slavery, or the same disgraceful catalysts as political assassinations and Watergate, but collectively they are profound enough to strain the nation to its breaking point. A short list of some of the divisive political issues that need to be addressed over the next decade (or sooner) includes:

- the resolution of the Iraq and Afghanistan Wars and America's overall involvement and approach in the Middle East;
- the continuing threat of terrorism;
- the rising fiscal deficits and national debt;
- the rising prices for necessities like food, gas, and healthcare;
- the solvency, availability, and effectiveness of the Medicare, Medicaid, and Social Security programs;
- the high unemployment and underemployment rates;
- the lingering effects from the financial collapse and bailouts;
- the weakening U.S. dollar vis-à-vis other global currencies; and
- the illegal immigration and border security problems.

But as the list gets longer and each of the problems gets ever more serious, politicians and protesters alike choose to score points by calling their opponents "fools" or "liars" or "un-American," casting blame and pointing fingers rather than seeking reasonable common ground, political compromise, public consensus, and workable solutions. Maintaining the status quo of excessive partisanship will almost certainly lead to bigger problems and fewer and less palatable solutions in the coming years.

THE MEDIA'S ROLE

Particularly in the modern era of 24-hour cable news and endless political chatter on the Internet, excessive partisanship is smothering proper government. The full-throated bickering from the extreme ends of the political spectrum is now so pervasive that it nearly drowns out any moderate voice. Soon the public discussions and debates will become unintentional parodies of what true political discourse should be. It would be unsurprising if the great leaders of American history would not even recognize the modern trend of "gotcha" questions, sound bites, and simple slogans lacking substance.

The media is always in the mix. Regrettably, many popular news outlets and well-known (and in some cases very talented) public commentators have become predictable, unoriginal, and wholly unimpressive in their news reporting and political analysis. Viewers simply turn to Fox News for a conservative perspective and recitation of the Republican or Tea Party talking points. They flip over to MSNBC to hear ranting against Fox News and a well-rehearsed liberal/progressive agenda. Newspaper readers subscribe to *The New York Times* or *The Wall Street Journal* to find a view that supports their political perspective and completely contradicts their opponents' perspective. And tech-savvy people religiously follow a specialized blog or other Internet website to receive their "news" and get their marching orders. Media outlets like CNN—those that seem to diligently seek nonpartisan and unbiased analysis—suffer in comparison with poor ratings and diminished influence due to a perceived lack of passion and an actual lack of shouting.

But the fault neither starts nor stops with the news stations, newspapers, Internet bloggers, and other members of the media. They are simply the messengers. They are salesmen sent out by politicians and the chattering class of political professionals to sell financially profitable partisanship. Just like any other successful enterprise, they cater to their customers' appetites and happily serve whatever the public wants to eat. They aggressively try to monopolize the viewership or readership of niche markets (e.g., Fox News = conservative Republicans;

MSNBC = progressives; *The New York Times* = traditional liberals). The more polemic and juicy their political dishes, the more customers they attract.

Ultimately it is the public's appetite for news and politics—guided and manipulated by the politicians who serve the spiciest partisan dishes—that permits the excessively partisan political menu that is widely available today. The media simply helps sell the soup.

Confirmation Bias Soup

The most popular item on America's current political menu is a steaming portion of confirmation bias soup. *Confirmation bias* is a person's tendency to seek out or interpret information in a way that helps confirm his or her previously held beliefs. It is a phenomenon that causes people to make errors in the way they evaluate certain information and evidence in order to permit them to maintain the beliefs they already have. If new information favors their previous assumptions, they accept it and weigh it heavily. However, if new information tends to disprove their preconceptions, they give it little weight or ignore it altogether. Often the accuracy or truth of the evidence matters little; if it supports their preconceptions, they believe it, and if it opposes what they believe, they avoid, ignore, or seek to discredit it. And whenever the information or evidence is ambiguous or neutral, anyone eating confirmation bias soup simply interprets it in favor of his or her own existing beliefs.

Politicians and other newsmakers have become masters of playing to viewers', readers', and voters' natural tendencies towards confirmation bias. They trumpet their own beliefs in unhesitatingly confident tones (the more cocksure, the more convincing). They preach only to their own political choirs, all the while knowing they will have a receptive and nonjudgmental audience. And they fling fire and brimstone down upon the heads of opponents who spout views contrary to their own political gospel. When the politicians and newsmakers are finally caught in hypocrisies, exaggerations, and misstatements, they ask forgiveness for the logs in their own eyes while refusing to forgive their political opponents for the specks in theirs.

Partisan Labels

To make uncompromising partisanship more palatable for widespread consumption, every popular political movement and media outlet has adopted a euphemistic name. Just like the car industry—the Dodge *Intrepid*; the Jeep *Liberty*; the Ford *Explorer*—a good name sells the product. Some popular American political labels include:

- Conservative (meaning traditional and reliable);
- Liberal (meaning generous, open-minded, and tolerant);
- Progressive (meaning progress-seeking and forward-moving);
- Independent (meaning nonpartisan and free-thinking);
- Bipartisan (meaning having support from multiple parties);
- Libertarian (meaning favoring personal freedom); and
- Green (meaning favoring the environment).

Of course, equally partisan opponents twist around the positive connotations of each political label to make them sound derogatory (e.g., conservative = intolerant; liberal = socialist; independent = disloyal).

The more moderate, reasonable, or nuanced a perspective is—generally one that takes longer than a bumper-sticker slogan to explain and does not conform to a specific label—the more likely it will be dismissed offhand, marginalized with a derogatory political label, or drowned out by the cacophony of partisan screaming.

NEXT STEPS

All of the recent excessive partisanship and political rancor finally prompts the question: How can American voters elect future presidents who have the experience, ability, and temperament to rise above the fray and become historically successful presidents? *Qualified* humbly suggests the answer is to evaluate every presidential candidate's resume in order to determine whether he or she is actually qualified to become president.

ONE
The Resume Challenge

You cannot escape the responsibility of tomorrow by evading it today.
— Abraham Lincoln

If you call failures experiments, you can put them in your resume and claim them as achievements.
— Mason Cooley

The Modern Resume

LEGEND HAS IT THAT Leonardo da Vinci created the first professional resume back in the late fifteenth century. However, the more likely historical antecedent to the modern resume is the traditional practice of using letters of introduction, which dates back to feudal England and the Middle Ages.

Over the centuries, letters of introduction have slowly evolved into what is now considered the American-style resume. The modern resume is simply a short summary (one or two pages) of a person's relevant professional experiences, education, and abilities. In recent decades, improved technology has helped resumes become highly useful tools on both sides of the job search process. Resumes now help companies find and compare qualified candidates with each other and with specific job-related criteria. They also help candidates to demonstrate their interest in and qualifications for any open positions. Today, every professional job applicant must have an up-to-date professional resume in order to be marketable and successful, and every employer requires candidates to submit a resume at the beginning of the hiring process.

One reason why the resume submission process is so widely used is that it is simple, straightforward, and produces excellent results. It spans the fields of education, business management, journalism, medicine, financial services, government, and law, among many others. The simplicity and usefulness it brings to an otherwise unwieldy job search/

1

candidate search process makes a well-drafted professional resume perhaps the most valuable tool in a candidate's toolbox, and the most helpful document for an employer to review. By requiring a candidate to provide an easy-to-read summary of his or her qualifications, and by permitting an employer to easily compile and compare the resumes of the most qualified candidates, the resume submission process significantly raises the probability that the most qualified candidate will be offered the position.

It is safe to say that almost every professional who has successfully applied for a job in the last decade used a resume. In fact, most probably have an up-to-date resume on file for any future employment searches. This reality spans every profession and every professional . . . except politics and politicians.

PRESIDENTIAL RESUMES
Collectively, American voters are without a doubt the world's most important hiring managers and employers. They are always searching for candidates for local, state, and national political positions, and they spend big money doing it. Their search results help to hire mayors, members of city councils and state assemblies, governors, representatives and senators, and, most importantly, vice presidents and presidents.

Nevertheless, voters are still forced to compile for themselves—using the Internet, the media, candidate speeches and interviews, and any other available sources—whatever information they can find that they think may be relevant to their voting/hiring decisions. No simple, standardized system is used to help evaluate all of the potential candidates for political office *at the beginning* of the hiring process and to help weed out any unqualified candidates.

The current election process skips the crucial step of reviewing a candidate's basic qualifications (as would be summarized on a resume) and moves straight to the later step of interviewing the candidates. Voters and the media ask which candidates are "most liked" or "most agreed with" (or "least disliked") rather than which candidates are most qualified. Fancy campaign advertising and polished presentations in debates, interviews, and stump speeches seduce voters and the media alike. But come Election Day, all any voter can do is guess whether one candidate's qualifications are better or worse than the others'.

As recently as the 2008 election, the American voters/employers still used a backwards hiring proces. And to date, no presidential candidate has ever followed the most basic job search requirement by proactively distributing an official resume to his or her prospective employer, the American voters. With all that can be gained from evaluating a candidate's professional resume, there is no good reason why voters are not already insisting that all presidential candidates submit their official resumes to the American public prior to the 2012 election.

The Advantages

Many of the advantages of insisting that presidential candidates publicly release their official resumes are obvious. It will streamline the early stages of presidential campaigns, caucuses, and primaries. It will enable voters to carefully analyze and quickly dismiss any candidates who are clearly unqualified. And it will help voters to better compare candidates with each other.

Using a resume submission process will also give greater historical context to every presidential election, helping voters compare the basic qualifications of current presidential candidates with those of past presidents (both successful and unsuccessful). Making accurate comparisons between current and future candidates and past presidents becomes dramatically easier when using standardized resumes that are based on every president's constitutional, historical, and practical responsibilities.

Moreover, insisting on reviewing presidential resumes has no drawbacks. Resumes will never replace stump speeches, press interviews, public debates, or campaign advertisements. They may help narrow the field more quickly than usual, but that has a net positive effect provided that the remaining candidates are all qualified. And if an unqualified presidential candidate is able to gain enough public support despite his or her lack of qualifications, he or she is welcome to continue campaigning just as vigorously as if he or she was the most qualified candidate in history.

The media and the opposing campaign staffs will undoubtedly perform a thorough fact-check of every candidate's resume and will certainly broadcast whether a resume contains mistakes, falsities, half-truths, or exaggerations. This built-in and public vetting process will help to ensure honesty and accuracy in every presidential resume.

In the end, the resume process will save money and eliminate the fringe and grossly unqualified candidates at an early stage in the election cycle. Once all of the presidential candidates have survived the resume vetting process and have showed that they are qualified to become president, the biggest winner will be the American voters.

THE RESUME CHALLENGE

Every four years, the Constitution vests in the American voters a crucial decision with profound national and global implications. They must select who will serve as the next American president. Every presidential election is a momentous occasion, regardless of the current state of the Union. Every election has potential either to keep America on the current course (good or bad), or to take America in a brave new direction.

The bad news is that the problems America is now facing, and will continue to face over the next decade and beyond, are large and are mounting. These problems include war, deficits, debt, immigration, tax revenues, healthcare, and terrorism, among many others. Each is important to the future of the nation, and each has been consistently demagogued by excessively partisan politicians, media personalities, newsmakers, and voters. Without leaders who possess a willingness to listen, to seek common ground, to find compromise—indeed, a willingness to be friends with those with whom they disagree—none of these issues will be resolved soon or in an acceptable manner. The failure to solve the problems in one's own generation unfairly burdens future generations, and is a failure of leadership on all sides of the political spectrum.

The good news is that history often repeats itself in a positive way. America has quite frequently found strong and enlightened leaders in times of crisis. Under the leadership of highly qualified presidents and other political leaders, America has generally held a steady course and has continued to pursue the collective American dream of life, liberty, and the pursuit of happiness. America can be brought back from the partisan precipice at which it now stands because it has been brought back before under the leadership of great presidents.

Selecting qualified presidents is the collective responsibility (and should be the fundamental goal) of professional politicians, the media, and the American voters in each presidential election. As the results of this book's resume analysis demonstrate, more qualified candidates become more successful presidents. This leads naturally to the resume challenge:

Voters should insist that every presidential candidate submit an official resume to the American public prior to the 2012 election and every election thereafter.

Using the tried and true resume submission process will be a new and better way to ensure that future presidents will be leaders who are qualified—by constitutional, historical, and practical standards—to hold the office once held by Washington, Lincoln, and Roosevelt.

Obviously, requiring resumes from presidential candidates is not an earth-shattering proposal. But it is unquestionably a sensible step in the right direction. Candidates who can show from the outset of their campaigns that their basic qualifications—the sum of their experiences and abilities as would be listed on a resume—make them qualified to become president deserve serious consideration by the American voters. Candidates whose resumes show that they are unqualified for the presidency do not deserve such serious consideration.

RESUME PREVIEWS

The resume challenge and the underlying analysis of the most relevant presidential qualifications are the most important parts of this book. The concept of the QUALIFIED THRESHOLD is the most important result. But the most interesting and useful pieces of information contained in this book appear in the appendices.

Appendix A provides forty-three presidential resumes, each of which describes in exacting detail (based on exhaustive historical research) every president's qualifications upon first taking office. Some of the most interesting (and surprising) presidential resumes include:

- the resumes of the ten presidents who took office with Great qualifications, most of whom became successful presidents;
- the resumes of the biggest presidential overachievers (Abraham Lincoln, Grover Cleveland, and Lyndon Johnson) and

underachievers (Richard Nixon, John Quincy Adams, and Herbert Hoover); and

- the resumes of the most recent presidents, including Barack Obama (Average qualifications), George W. Bush (Below Average qualifications), and Bill Clinton (Near Great qualifications).

Perhaps even more interesting than the past presidents' resumes provided in Appendix A are the sample presidential resumes provided in Appendix B.

In an attempt to prompt public discussion of presidential qualifications, and to convince one or more current or potential presidential candidates to accept the resume challenge and release an official resume, Appendix B provides resumes for seventeen of the top or most talked about contenders in the 2012 presidential field. Unsurprisingly, the candidates' qualifications range from Great to Poor, and their personal backgrounds are equally diverse.

Some of the most interesting (and surprising) current candidate resumes include:

- Hillary Clinton's and Condoleezza Rice's resumes, which demonstrate that they are by far the most qualified potential candidates in the 2012 election;
- Sarah Palin's, Michele Bachmann's, and Chris Christie's resumes, which show that each of them is clearly unqualified to become president (at least in 2012); and
- Ron Paul's and Newt Gingrich's resumes, which show that they are each highly qualified but also that they have certain intangible characteristics that may harm their electability (e.g., old age, partisanship, past indiscretions).

Most of the other candidates' resumes are clustered in or near the Average and Above Average resume rankings. This simply indicates that in order for one of these candidates to emerge as the most qualified (and most electable) candidate and become the Republican nominee, he or she needs to differentiate himself or herself from the other candidates based on intangible characteristics rather than basic qualifications.

In the end, only qualified presidents can meet the political challenges of today and help ensure a brighter tomorrow. This book shows that there are several qualified (even highly qualified) contenders in the current candidate field who could become successful presidents. It also shows that President Obama was just barely qualified in 2008, and that he is vulnerable against a qualified challenger in what is certain to be a referendum election in 2012. It will be fascinating to see whether the Republican Party ultimately nominates qualified candidates for president and vice president, respectively, and whether President Obama is capable of fending off a pair of strong challengers.

Next Steps

Any candidate can submit a resume and cover letter for any position, including positions for which the candidate is unqualified. This is as true with candidates aspiring to the presidency as it is with any other professional candidate for any other professional position. Therefore, American voters need to know what qualifications actually make a candidate qualified to become president. Describing and analyzing the constitutional eligibility requirements and presidential responsibilities and qualifications is precisely what the rest of this book does.

The Constitution is the guide which I will never abandon.
— George Washington

The Constitution of the United States was made not merely for the generation that then existed, but for posterity—unlimited, undefined, endless, perpetual posterity.
— Henry Clay

THERE ARE TWO THRESHOLD measurements that should be used to determine whether a candidate is qualified to become president. The first determines whether a candidate is constitutionally eligible to become president: the CONSTITUTIONAL THRESHOLD. The second determines whether a candidate is, in all other relevant respects, qualified to become president: the QUALIFIED THRESHOLD.

Most of this book is devoted to providing an in depth analysis of the specific, relevant experiences and abilities that form the basis of the QUALIFIED THRESHOLD. But meeting the CONSTITUTIONAL THRESHOLD is the unavoidable first step in the presidential election process. Therefore, this book first discusses the six basic constitutional requirements that form the basis of the CONSTITUTIONAL THRESHOLD. The rest of the book then discusses the analysis and application of the other presidential qualifications which form the basis of the QUALIFIED THRESHOLD.

THE SIX REQUIREMENTS
The six requirements that form the basis of the CONSTITUTIONAL THRESHOLD are non-negotiable. If any presidential candidate fails to fully satisfy them, he or she does not meet the CONSTITUTIONAL THRESHOLD and is ineligible to become president regardless of his or her other qualifications.

Constitutional Requirements 1, 2, and 3

Article II, Section 1, Clause 5 of the Constitution establishes the first three constitutional eligibility requirements:

> *No person except a natural born Citizen, or a Citizen of the United States, at the time of the Adoption of this Constitution, shall be eligible to the Office of President; neither shall any person be eligible to that Office who shall not have attained to the Age of thirty-five Years, and been fourteen Years a Resident within the United States.*

Clause 5 makes three things clear.

1. **Every presidential candidate must be a "natural born Citizen."**

The ratification of the Fourteenth Amendment to the Constitution in 1868 guaranteed that every person born in the United States is a "natural born Citizen." Based on this requirement, every presidential candidate must have been born in one of the United States or in a location that is considered to be the sovereign soil of the United States.

This constitutional language has never been tested by a formal legal challenge over a presidential candidate's citizenship, but it has been raised several times in American history. Most recently it was raised in the 2008 presidential election where there were questions concerning the birthplace of both of the major candidates: Barack Obama and John McCain.

Barack Obama. In 2008, rumors surrounded Barack Obama's birthplace. Obama consistently maintained that he was born in Hawaii in 1961 and that he therefore met the "natural born Citizen" requirement. Prior to the election, Obama released his short-form certificate of live birth which seemed to settle the matter. However, "birther" conspiracies continued to circulate in the press and in the public arena for several years. In April 2011, in response to increased attention to the issue, President Obama released his long-form certificate of live birth which also showed that he was born in Hawaii in 1961. This seems to have finally put the issue to rest. There appears to be no evidence—other than speculation and conspiracy theories—that any formal legal challenge to his eligibility to become president based on his birthplace could ever be successful.

10

John McCain. At the same time rumors were swirling around with respect to Barack Obama's birthplace, concerns were also raised over John McCain's birthplace. McCain was born on a United States military installation in the Panama Canal Zone in 1936. Presumably, the military base would be considered sovereign United States soil for purposes of the "natural born Citizen" requirement, but no formal legal challenge was ever made. Because there have been so few judicial decisions raising this relatively obscure issue, constitutional scholars and lawyers have simply opined (without making any formal legal determination) that McCain met the "natural born Citizen" requirement and was eligible to become president based on his birthplace.

Other examples. During the 1884 election, it was rumored that Chester A. Arthur had been born in Canada and therefore that he was not a "natural born Citizen." However, no evidence has ever substantiated such a rumor, and it is widely accepted that Arthur was born in Vermont.

2. **Every presidential candidate must have "attained to the Age of thirty-five Years."**

No person can become president without having first "attained to the Age of thirty-five Years." In other words, every presidential candidate must be at least 35 years old when he or she becomes president.

It is theoretically possible that a 34-year-old candidate could be elected president and then turn 35 before taking the oath of office, but it is highly unlikely that this would ever happen. Section 3 of the Twentieth Amendment to the Constitution may apply in these types of situations, where it states:

> . . . *if the President elect shall have failed to qualify, then the Vice President elect shall act as President until a President shall have qualified; and the Congress may by law provide for the case wherein neither a President elect nor a Vice President elect shall have qualified, declaring who shall then act as President, or the manner in which one who is to act shall be selected, and such person shall act accordingly until a President or Vice President shall have qualified.*

However, it is impossible to be certain how Congress and the federal courts would act in such an unusual circumstance.

A similar issue arose once in the 1934 senatorial election in West

Virginia. The constitutional minimum age for senators is 30 years old and the victorious candidate, Rush Holt, was only 29 years old on Election Day. Holt pledged to wait six months until he turned 30 to be sworn in, and the Senate ruled that the constitutional age requirement applied at the time of oath-taking and therefore that he could be elected at 29 years old and be sworn in late and begin serving his term after he turned 30.

There has never been a serious presidential candidate who was 35 years old or younger. The youngest major candidate was William Jennings Bryan, who was 36 years old in his first campaign for president in 1896, but even he met the constitutional minimum age requirement by more than one-and-a-half years. With respect to the age requirement, voters must be mindful that all or most of the federal officeholders in the line of succession (Vice President, Speaker of the House of Representatives, President Pro Tempore of the Senate, Secretary of State, etc.) should also be at least 35 years old to be eligible to serve as president if necessary. Because senators need only be 30 years old and representatives need only be 25 years old, and because there is no minimum age for cabinet officers, it is possible that someone in the presidential line of succession could be too young to become president.

3. **Every presidential candidate must have "been fourteen Years a Resident within the United States."**

The constitutional language that a president must have "been fourteen Years a Resident within the United States" prevents otherwise eligible presidential candidates from becoming president if they have never or only briefly been residents within the United States. This requirement was due to the Founding Fathers' fear that a royal monarch or other powerful member of European aristocracy would come to America and try to be elected president immediately. The Constitution prevented that possibility.

Modernly, this requirement has not raised any concerns, but someday it could. For instance, Barack Obama, a "natural born Citizen" of the United States, moved with his mother to Indonesia in 1967 when he was 6 years old. If he had only returned to reside in the United States in 2001 instead of 1971, he would not have been eligible to become

12

president because he would not have been a "Resident within the United States" for at least fourteen years.

Constitutional Requirements 4, 5, and 6

In addition to the eligibility requirements set forth in Article II, Section 1, Clause 5 of the Constitution, specific language in several other parts of the Constitution create three additional requirements which every presidential candidate must satisfy in order to meet the CONSTITUTIONAL THRESHOLD.

4. **Every presidential candidate must be willing to take the oath of office.**

Article II, Section 1, Clause 8 provides:

Before he enter on the Execution of his Office, he shall take the following Oath or Affirmation: "I do solemnly swear (or affirm) that I will faithfully execute the Office of President of the United States, and will to the best of my Ability, preserve, protect and defend the Constitution of the United States."

To date, all presidents have been willing to take the oath of office, and it is reasonable to expect that all future presidential candidates will also be willing to do so. The following are some interesting facts about the presidential oath-taking.

- Franklin Pierce chose to affirm instead of swear the oath of office in 1853.
- Several presidents placed their hands on books other than a Bible. For instance, John Quincy Adams swore on a book of law and Lyndon Johnson swore on a Roman Catholic missal.
- Other presidents placed their hands on multiple Bibles (e.g., Dwight Eisenhower, Harry Truman, and Richard Nixon).
- Some presidents simply responded "I do" or "I will" rather than repeat the oath verbatim (e.g., Chester A. Arthur and Herbert Hoover).
- Many presidents beginning with George Washington, but not all presidents, have added "So help me God" at the end of their recitation of the oath.

5. **The presidential candidate and vice presidential candidate must be residents of two different states.**

The Twelfth Amendment to the Constitution provides:

The Electors shall meet in their respective states and vote by ballot for President and Vice-President, one of whom, at least, shall not be an inhabitant of the same state with themselves.

The Twelfth Amendment thus provides that a president and vice president cannot be residents of the same state. Because this issue has never formally arisen, the answer to how such a situation would be legally or politically resolved is uncertain. Presumably, the presidential candidate would meet the requirement and be eligible to become president, while the vice presidential candidate would not meet the requirement, be deemed ineligible to become vice president, and need to be replaced.

There have been several potential residency conflicts in American history, but none was ever realized. For instance, George Washington, Thomas Jefferson, James Madison, and James Monroe were all residents of Virginia and therefore could not have served together as president and vice president. Richard Nixon and Ronald Reagan were both California residents in the 1960s and could not have joined together on a presidential ticket (Nixon became a New York resident by the 1968 presidential election, however). And current candidates Tim Pawlenty and Michele Bachmann are both residents of Minnesota. The Twelfth Amendment would not permit them to serve together as president and vice president as long as they remain residents of the same state.

The Twelfth Amendment also provides that "no person constitutionally ineligible to the office of President shall be eligible to that of Vice-President of the United States," meaning that vice presidential candidates must themselves satisfy the each of the six constitutional eligibility requirements and meet the CONSTITUTIONAL THRESHOLD. This raises an interesting and important question about how much focus should be given to the constitutional eligibility for the presidency of those officials in the presidential line of succession. The line of succession, created by federal statute, includes in the following order: Speaker of the House; President Pro Tempore of the Senate; Secretary of State; Secretary of the Treasury; Secretary of Defense; Attorney

General; Secretary of the Interior; Secretary of Agriculture; Secretary of Commerce; Secretary of Labor; Secretary of Health and Human Services; Secretary of Housing and Urban Development; Secretary of Transportation; Secretary of Energy; Secretary of Education; Secretary of Veterans Affairs; and Secretary of Homeland Security. Attempting to answer this difficult question is outside of the scope of this book, however.

6. **The presidential candidate must not have already been elected president twice or have already served as president for more than six years.**

The Twenty-Second Amendment to the Constitution provides:

No person shall be elected to the office of the President more than twice, and no person who has held the office of President, or acted as President, for more than two years of a term to which some other person was elected President shall be elected to the office of the President more than once.

Pursuant to the Twenty-Second Amendment, no candidate is eligible to become president if he or she has already been elected president twice, or if he or she has been elected president once but served more than two years of his or her predecessor's elected term.

The Twenty-Second Amendment was ratified in 1951. It would have affected two former presidents had it been ratified fifty years earlier, and it continues to affect two other former presidents.

- Theodore Roosevelt served more than three years of President William McKinley's term after McKinley was assassinated in 1901. Roosevelt was himself elected president in 1904. Had the Twenty-Second Amendment then existed, Roosevelt would have been prevented from becoming president had he wanted to run in the 1908 election or had he won the 1912 election.
- Franklin Roosevelt was elected president in 1932 and 1936, and therefore would have been prevented from being re-elected in 1940 and 1944 had the Twenty-Second Amendment then existed.
- Harry Truman served more than three years of President Franklin Roosevelt's fourth term after Roosevelt died in office in 1945. Truman was himself elected in 1948. The Twenty-Second Amendment specifically carved out an exception that

15

permitted him to be re-elected in 1952 had he chosen to run again, but he chose not to run.

- Both Bill Clinton and George W. Bush have already been elected president twice and therefore are no longer eligible to serve as either president or vice president.

THE NEXT STEP

In most presidential elections, all major candidates will satisfy the CONSTITUTIONAL THRESHOLD and be constitutionally eligible to become president. Therefore, it is the second step—determining whether a presidential candidate is actually qualified to become president—where most of the drama, controversy, and fun occurs in presidential campaigns and elections.

THREE
RESUME CREATION AND ANALYSIS

Under democracy one party always devotes its chief energies to trying to prove that the other party is unfit to rule—and both commonly succeed and are right.

— H.L. Mencken

When I was a boy I was told that anybody could become President; I'm beginning to believe it.

— Clarence Darrow

AFTER A PRESIDENTIAL CANDIDATE shows that he or she is legally eligible to become president by satisfying the CONSTITUTIONAL THRESHOLD, voters should then move to the crucial second step: determining whether the candidate is actually qualified to become president. This step leads directly to the QUALIFIED THRESHOLD. The QUALIFIED THRESHOLD is the minimum resume score necessary for a candidate to have a very high probability of becoming an Average or better president.

Simply put, candidates who are qualified will meet the QUALIFIED THRESHOLD and have a high probability of becoming successful presidents (i.e., an Average or better historical ranking). Such candidates deserve voters' serious consideration. Candidates who score below the QUALIFIED THRESHOLD are unqualified to become president and do not deserve the same serious consideration.

CREATING THE RESUMES
In order to perform the first comprehensive analysis of every American president's basic qualifications upon taking office, *Qualified* creates forty-three presidential resumes (provided in Appendix A), each of which is based on every president's constitutional, historical, and practical responsibilities. Such an analysis is possible because even with all of the changes in American government that have occurred over the past

17

two centuries, the core responsibilities of the presidency have remained the same since 1789.

The resumes of thirty-four presidents are drafted as of the day the president was elected (e.g., George W. Bush's resume is drafted as of November 2000, and Barack Obama's resume is drafted as of November 2008).

For the nine presidents who ascended to the presidency mid-term due to the death or resignation of their predecessors, their resumes are drafted as of the day they were elected vice president (or, in the case of Gerald Ford, the day he was nominated to become vice president by President Richard Nixon). This slight adjustment is necessary because American voters did not have another opportunity to re-evaluate the vice president and reconsider their voting decision between election or nomination to the vice presidency and ascension to the presidency. Thus, these nine presidents' experiences serving as vice president are not included on their resumes.

The nine presidents who fall into this subset include:

Election	President	Reason for Ascension
1840	John Tyler	W.H. Harrison died
1848	Millard Fillmore	Taylor died
1864	Andrew Johnson	Lincoln was assassinated
1880	Chester A. Arthur	Garfield was assassinated
1900	Theodore Roosevelt	McKinley was assassinated
1920	Calvin Coolidge	Harding died
1944	Harry Truman	F. Roosevelt died
1960	Lyndon Johnson	Kennedy was assassinated
1973*	Gerald Ford	Nixon resigned

*Note: Gerald Ford was appointed, not elected, in 1973

Using the same standardized resume templates and scoring/ranking methodologies, this book also creates sample resumes for seventeen current or potential presidential candidates, each of which is provided in Appendix B. Each of these resumes is drafted as of the start of the presidential election season formally beginning in January 2012.

SCORING AND RANKING METHODOLOGY

Each resume is divided into eight resume categories that are directly related to every president's constitutional, historical, and practical responsibilities. The categories and their possible score ranges are:

Resume Category	Minimum Score	Maximum Score
Legislative Experience	0	15
Executive Experience	0	15
Military Experience	0	15
Foreign Experience	0	15
Private Work Experience	0	10
Education/Intellect	0	10
Writing Ability	0	10
Public Speaking Ability	0	10
Total	**0**	**100**

The within-category rankings of the first four categories with a maximum possible score of 15 are:

Category Score	Category Rank
13–15	Great
10–12	Above Average
6–9	Average
3–5	Below Average
0–2	Poor

The within-category rankings of the second four categories with a maximum possible score of 10 are:

Category Score	Category Rank
9–10	Great
7–8	Above Average
4–6	Average
2–3	Below Average
0–1	Poor

Chapters Four through Eleven provide the complete results of the analysis with respect to each of the eight resume categories, along with detailed summaries of each of the president's particular experiences and abilities in each category. The summaries are intended to provide precise historical information about each president's specific experiences and abilities, and justification for each president's particular score in every resume category and overall.

Based on the possible scores in each of the resume categories, a president's maximum possible resume score is 100. The overall resume rankings are calculated as follows:

Resume Score	Resume Rank
55 or higher	Great
50–54	Near Great
45–49	Above Average
40–44	Average
35–39	Below Average
34 or lower	Poor

Due to temporal and physical limitations, no president or presidential candidate will ever come close to a "perfect" score of 100. In fact, a score 55 or higher is considered Great, and no president has received a score of 70 or higher.

It is unlikely that many (if any) future presidential candidates will receive total resume scores of 70 or higher. There are only so many positions a person can hold in any given year, and there are only so many experiences a person can gain in any one position. For example, a secretary of state can accrue executive experience and foreign experience at the same time, but cannot at the same time accrue private work experience. And an attorney can accrue private work experience and improve his or her public speaking and writing abilities, but cannot at the same time accrue meaningful military experience. Even if a future presidential candidate does gain so many experiences and have such impressive abilities that he or she receives a score of 70 or higher, he or she will likely be fairly old by that time and may be disqualified by many voters based on the intangible personal characteristic of age.

WEIGHTING METHODOLOGY

A choice needed to be made as to the maximum possible resume and category scores. So why is 100 the maximum possible resume score?

And why do four resume categories have a maximum possible score of 15, while four have a maximum possible score of only 10? The answers are relatively simple and should not be overly controversial.

Total Resume Score

The maximum possible resume score is 100 for purposes of simplicity, ease of calculation, and potential for meaningful differentiation between presidents. The first two purposes are self-evident.

The third purpose is slightly more nuanced. If the maximum total resume score was 50, it would have forced the results to fit within a fairly narrow scoring range and it would create a less exact scoring system. For example, a president's public speaking ability would then need to be scored between 0 and 5 rather than between 0 and 10, creating fewer possible individual scores. This would mean that a president who is noticeably better than a 4 but worse than a 5 (as compared to the other forty-two presidents) would be forced into a score that does not precisely describe his public speaking ability. The opportunity for meaningful differentiation between presidents or presidential candidates with slightly different experiences and abilities would be lost.

Additionally, if the maximum total resume score was 500, it would have provided a possible scoring range that would be too large. It would create the sort of absurd system of a school which gave grades ranging between A and Z. What exactly would the grades H, P, and U signify? With too many grade possibilities, the meanings of specific grades lose significance. For example, if the two presidents with the most executive experience would each normally score a 15, is there a good reason to force differentiation between them and give one a score of 74 and the other a score of 73? Probably not. A maximum total resume score of 100 provides enough meaningful differentiation between presidents or candidates without forcing unnecessary distinctions.

Individual Category Scores

The reason why the first four resume categories received a maximum possible score of 15 while the second four received a maximum possible score of only 10 is the precise language used in the Constitution. The Constitution specifically vests every president with legislative, executive, military, and foreign responsibilities. The first four categories are directly related to these four "core" presidential responsibilities. Chapters Four through Seven explain in great detail that presidents are required by the Constitution to be closely involved in, if not primarily responsible for, (i) proposing, signing, and vetoing legislation, (ii) enforcing federal laws and performing other executive duties, (iii) acting as Commander in Chief of the American military, and (iv) serving as Head of State and chief diplomat responsible for foreign relations and policy. As these are the core presidential responsibilities, it makes sense that directly relevant experiences would be weighted more heavily than experiences and abilities that are only indirectly relevant.

Chapters Eight through Eleven explain in great detail how private work experience, education/intellect, writing ability, and public speaking ability are complementary (but still very important) to a president's core constitutional responsibilities but are not themselves core responsibilities.

As the results of the statistical correlation analysis show, there is generally a weak or very weak correlation between any particular resume category score and presidential success. This simply means that a candidate who has a high score in any one particular resume category does not have a significantly higher probability of becoming a successful president than a candidate who has a low score in that same category. There is a much more significant statistical correlation between a candidate's total resume score and presidential success.

PRESIDENTIAL RANKINGS BENCHMARK

For a presidential resume to be not only an interesting historical document but also a useful tool for making future election decisions, a benchmark was needed against which the resumes could be evaluated and compared. The most applicable benchmark was one that permitted comparisons between resume qualifications and actual presidential success. A fairly recent and widely-accepted historical presidential ranking was the natural choice.

There have been a number of historical studies and presidential rankings published over the last six decades. The historian Arthur M. Schlesinger, Sr. conducted one of the first comprehensive presidential surveys in 1948, and repeated the survey in 1962. His son, Arthur M. Schlesinger, Jr., conducted a similar survey in 1996. Organizations such as the Siena Research Institute also publish periodic presidential ranking survey results.

Some rankings include the most recent presidents (such as George W. Bush and Barack Obama) and those presidents who served only a very short time in office (such as William Henry Harrison and James Garfield). Other rankings do not. Those that include the most recent presidents tend to be more controversial, in part because the presidents' supporters and detractors are still living and are still making concerted efforts to help shape history's final assessment. Moreover, many presidential decisions are not shown to be good or bad for many years, making any ranking within the first decade after a presidency ends somewhat premature.

This book uses the historical presidential ranking contained in *Presidential Leadership: Ranking the Best and the Worst in the White House* as the benchmark for its analysis and discussion of resume qualifications and presidential success. *Presidential Leadership* is a widely-accepted study based on an October 2000 presidential ranking survey. The survey participants were an "ideologically balanced group of 132 prominent professors of history, law, and political science." The survey specifically sought to balance the number of "liberals" and "conservatives" participating in the survey in order to create an ideologically neutral ranking. Notably, the survey's results were "remarkably similar" to the 1996 Schlesinger poll which was considered by many to have a liberal slant.

The results of the *Presidential Leadership* survey relevant for these purposes were as follows:

Historical Ranking	President	Rank
Great	George Washington	1
	Abraham Lincoln	2
	Franklin Roosevelt	3
Near Great	Thomas Jefferson	4
	Theodore Roosevelt	5
	Andrew Jackson	6
	Harry Truman	7
	Ronald Reagan	8
	Dwight Eisenhower	9
	James K. Polk	10
	Woodrow Wilson	11
Above Average	Grover Cleveland	12
	John Adams	13
	William McKinley	14
	James Madison	15
	James Monroe	16
	Lyndon Johnson	17
	John F. Kennedy	18
Average	William Howard Taft	19
	John Quincy Adams	20
	George H.W. Bush	21
	Rutherford B. Hayes	22
	Martin Van Buren	23
	Bill Clinton	24
	Calvin Coolidge	25
	Chester A. Arthur	26
Below Average	Benjamin Harrison	27
	Gerald Ford	28
	Herbert Hoover	29
	Jimmy Carter	30
	Zachary Taylor	31
	Ulysses S. Grant	32
	Richard Nixon	33
	John Tyler	34
	Millard Fillmore	35
Failure	Andrew Johnson	36
	Franklin Pierce	37
	Warren G. Harding	38
	James Buchanan	39

Four presidents were not included in this ranking. William Henry Harrison and James Garfield were not included due to their deaths early in their presidencies, and George W. Bush and Barack Obama were not included due to the fact that they had not yet become president when the survey was conducted.

Readers should note that Bill Clinton was near the end of his second presidential term when the *Presidential Leadership* survey was conducted. As was previously discussed, the inclusion of recent presidents in historical rankings is somewhat controversial due to the fact that history has not yet been able to reach any sort of consensus on their presidential successes and failures. Readers should keep this in mind when evaluating President Clinton's historical ranking.

In the following chapters, whenever this book compares a president's total resume score or resume category score with his actual presidential success, it is specifically referring to the historical presidential ranking as compiled in October 2000 and as documented in *Presidential Leadership*. And for simplicity and to avoid confusion, this book uses the same categories used by *Presidential Leadership*—Great, Near Great, Above Average, Average, Below Average, and Failure—when ranking the presidential resumes.

Interestingly (and not unexpectedly), the overall resume rankings and the historical presidential rankings are fairly evenly balanced across each of the six ranking categories.

Resume Ranking Category	Number of Presidents in Category	Historical Presidential Ranking Category	Number of Presidents in Category
Great	10	Great	3
Near Great	3	Near Great	8
Above Average	7	Above Average	7
Average	9	Average	8
Below Average	8	Below Average	9
Poor	6	Failure	4
Total	**43***		**39***

*Note: this discrepancy is because only thirty-nine presidents were included in the historical presidential ranking while *Qualified* ranks the qualifications of all forty-three presidents.

DISCLAIMERS

Readers should be aware of several things before continuing.

Objectivity

First, in a social science field such as political science, it is impossible to have completely objective data. It is therefore also impossible to have completely objective evaluations of and conclusions based upon such data. *Qualified* acknowledges this fact and attempts to present the historical facts in the most objective manner possible, and then to make its evaluations and draw its conclusions in the most objective manner possible. Like a scientific experiment, the goal is for the analysis and results to be reproducible by others who evaluate the same historical facts.

Historical Research

And second, none of the historical facts used in this book are based on original research. Every historical fact provided as the basis for the analysis and conclusions was found in one or more presidential biographies, or in another presidential or historical publication or set of materials. Of course, the purpose of this book is not to present original research, but rather to take commonly known and widely accepted historical facts and extrapolate new theories and ways of evaluating such information.

Any incorrect or incomplete factual information was either: (i) incorrect in the original source; or (ii) not found in an original source. For example, it is possible that certain presidents traveled outside of the United States more times than is described in those presidents' foreign experience qualifications simply because no biographer or other historical source found such trips relevant or otherwise important. These potential inconsistencies were unavoidable.

LEGISLATIVE EXPERIENCE RANKINGS

Rank	Score	President	Historical Ranking
Great	15	James Madison	Above Average
		Lyndon Johnson	Above Average
	14	James K. Polk	Near Great
		Gerald Ford	Below Average
	13	John Adams	Above Average
		John Tyler	Below Average
		Andrew Johnson	Failure
		James Garfield	Not Ranked
		William McKinley	Above Average
Above Average	12	Thomas Jefferson	Near Great
		Martin Van Buren	Average
		James Buchanan	Failure
		John F. Kennedy	Above Average
	11	Franklin Pierce	Failure
	10	Richard Nixon	Below Average
		Harry Truman	Near Great
Average	9	James Monroe	Above Average
		Millard Fillmore	Below Average
	8	George Washington	Great
		Warren G. Harding	Failure
	7	William H. Harrison	Not Ranked
	6	John Quincy Adams	Average
		Benjamin Harrison	Below Average
		George H.W. Bush	Average
		Barack Obama	Not Ranked
Below Average	5	Andrew Jackson	Near Great
		Abraham Lincoln	Great
	4	Calvin Coolidge	Average
	3	Jimmy Carter	Below Average
Poor	2	Rutherford B. Hayes	Average
		Theodore Roosevelt	Near Great
	1	Franklin Roosevelt	Great
		Bill Clinton	Average
	0	Zachary Taylor	Below Average
		Ulysses S. Grant	Below Average
		Chester A. Arthur	Average
		Grover Cleveland	Above Average
		William H. Taft	Average
		Woodrow Wilson	Near Great
		Herbert Hoover	Below Average
		Dwight Eisenhower	Near Great
		Ronald Reagan	Near Great
		George W. Bush	Not Ranked

FOUR
LEGISLATIVE EXPERIENCE

Suppose you were an idiot, and suppose you were a member of Congress; but I repeat myself.

— Mark Twain

There is but one way for a president to deal with Congress, and that is continuously, incessantly, and without interruption. If it is really going to work, the relationship has got to be almost incestuous.

— Lyndon Johnson

THE FIRST RESUME CATEGORY is Legislative Experience. It is first in both the constitutional sense (Article I of the Constitution defines a president's legislative responsibilities) and the practical sense (a law must be enacted before a president can enforce it).

Legislative experience can be exceedingly useful for a president. For example, Lyndon Johnson was perhaps the greatest legislator in American history (certainly one of the greatest) before he became president. The skills he developed and the experiences he collected while serving in the House of Representatives and as Majority Leader of the Senate helped him tremendously when as president he proposed and successfully passed his Great Society legislative agenda. Whether one loves or hates the content of the Great Society programs, one cannot argue with the fact that President Johnson's legislative leadership in 1964 and 1965 was masterful.

Presidents who scored Great in the Legislative Experience resume category not only had long careers in one or more federal legislative bodies, but also were very effective in exercising legislative influence. But legislative experience is not an absolute necessity for a candidate to become a successful president, even a legislatively successful president. Franklin Roosevelt serves as a prime example. Roosevelt had a Legislative Experience resume score of 1 when he was elected president, but he was very successful in passing his New Deal legislative agenda, the most sweeping legislation in American history, between 1933 and 1935. Woodrow Wilson is another example. He had no legislative experience prior to taking office but had significant legislative accomplishments as president. There is a wide range of previous legislative experiences (and other experiences and abilities as described in the following chapters) among the presidents. This is completely unsurprising, as every president has taken a unique path to the White House.

LEGISLATIVE RESPONSIBILITIES

Every president has certain legislative responsibilities, which include constitutional responsibilities and historical and practical responsibilities. Constitutional responsibilities are specifically provided for in the text of the Constitution and are required to be performed for the government to function properly. Historical and practical responsibilities are not specifically provided for in the text of the Constitution but are nevertheless performed by some or all presidents.

Constitutional Responsibilities

Several provisions in the Constitution vest the president with specific legislative responsibilities.

Article I, Section 7, Clause 2 of the Constitution provides:

Every Bill which shall have passed the House of Representatives and the Senate, shall, before it become a Law, be presented to the President of the United States; If he approve he shall sign it, but if not he shall return it, with his Objections to that House in which it shall have originated, who shall enter the Objections at large on their Journal, and proceed to reconsider it. If after such Reconsideration two thirds of that House shall agree to pass the Bill, it shall be sent, together with the Objections, to the other House, by which it shall likewise be reconsidered, and if approved by two thirds of that House, it shall become a Law. . . . If any Bill shall not be returned by the President within ten Days (Sundays Excepted) after it shall have been presented to him, the Same shall be a Law, in like Manner as if he had signed it, unless Congress by their Adjournment prevent its Return, in which Case it shall not be a Law.

Clause 2 is the basis for "Bicameralism and Presentment," the principle that both the House of Representatives and the Senate must pass a bill and the president must sign the bill (or wait more than ten days without vetoing it while Congress remains in session) for the bill to become law. The only two exceptions are (i) a veto "override" by a two-thirds vote of both Houses of Congress, and (ii) a "pocket veto," where the president fails to sign a bill and Congress adjourns before ten days have passed.

Since 1789, presidents have vetoed 1,498 congressional bills and Congress has overridden only 110 vetoed bills (approximately 7% of the vetoed bills). Several other quick facts about vetoes and overrides (excluding pocket vetoes) include:

- seven presidents never vetoed a bill (J. Adams, Jefferson, J.Q. Adams, W.H. Harrison, Taylor, Fillmore, and Garfield);
- Andrew Johnson vetoed twenty-one bills, and fifteen were overridden (approximately 71%, the highest override percentage of any president);
- the three presidents who vetoed the most bills (by far) were Franklin Roosevelt (372 vetoes, nine overridden), Grover Cleveland (304 vetoes in his first term alone, two overridden), and Harry Truman (180 vetoes, twelve overridden); and
- thirteen presidents who vetoed bills never had a veto overridden (the most was Lyndon Johnson with sixteen vetoes).

Several of the most successful presidents from a legislative perspective (e.g., William McKinley, Lyndon Johnson) were excellent at getting Congress on board with a bill before it was ever introduced or debated. This maximized the possibility of passing a bill by finding compromise positions early in the process and limiting later public disagreements.

Article II, Section 3 of the Constitution provides:

[The President] shall from time to time give to the Congress Information of the State of the Union, and recommend to their Consideration such Measures as he shall judge necessary and expedient; he may, on extraordinary Occasions, convene both Houses, or either of them, and in Case of Disagreement between them, with Respect to the Time of Adjournment, he may adjourn them to such Time as he shall think proper
. . . .

Section 3 anticipates and expects for presidents to recommend to Congress legislation which they believe to be important. Thus, the modern trend of presidents taking a lead role in drafting legislation and submitting it to Congress is a constitutionally correct process and wholly unsurprising.

Section 3 also provides that the president may call Congress into a special session on "extraordinary occasions." Presidents have done so twenty-seven times in American history, but no president has called a special session of Congress since Harry Truman did in 1948. The best example (from a legislative perspective) of calling a special session is Franklin Roosevelt's first 100 days in 1933, when he called a special session of Congress and eventually passed much of his historic New Deal legislative agenda.

Historical and Practical Responsibilities

Many decades in American history are known for congressional dominance over the executive branch. For instance, during much of the nineteenth century Congress was very strong and had brilliant leaders (e.g., Henry Clay, Daniel Webster, John C. Calhoun) whose influence often surpassed the era's comparatively weak (and unqualified) presidents. The simplistic phrase "Congress proposes and the president disposes" was frequently true until the turn of the twentieth century when presidents began to more aggressively assert their legislative prerogatives and more passionately and publically champion their own legislative agendas.

One of President John Adams's acts provides a great example of "majoritarianism," the prevailing mindset during America's first century. In 1798, he famously deferred to the Federalist-dominated Congress when he signed into law the Alien and Sedition Acts. He believed that he should not stand in the way if a majority of the people, speaking through their elected representatives, wanted a particular law. This view that Congress represented the true will of the people was unremarkable at the time and widely held by members of both parties. Only with the development of mass communication techniques (e.g., radio, television, the Internet) were presidents able to more easily reach national audiences and see themselves as the true representative of the people.

Modernly, presidents have taken an increasing (sometimes dominant) role in proposing legislation and pushing it through Congress. The more popular a president is, and the larger a majority the president's party has in Congress, the more legislative influence a president can wield.

Presidents now frequently submit already drafted legislation to Congress to be tinkered with or even passed in full. Franklin Roosevelt's New Deal and Lyndon Johnson's Great Society are two great examples of situations where popular presidents dictated their wills to Congress.

There are also many practical reasons why previous legislative experience is valuable for presidents. It can help a future presidential candidate develop personal relationships and friendships with other members of Congress which may later help to improve the working relationship between the executive and legislative branches and attract future congressional votes. It can also help develop a working knowledge of parliamentary procedure and other congressional rules, making it easier to guide legislation through Congress. And in some circumstances it can provide a president with some additional credibility in proposing an aggressive legislative agenda.

QUICK FACTS

The following are some quick facts about the presidents' legislative experiences upon taking office.

20   Presidents who served in a state legislature (Jefferson, Madison, Monroe, J.Q. Adams, Van Buren, W.H. Harrison, Tyler, Polk, Fillmore, Pierce, Buchanan, Lincoln, A. Johnson, Garfield, T. Roosevelt, Harding, Coolidge, F. Roosevelt, Carter, and Obama). Only Pierce and Theodore Roosevelt had formal leadership positions.

19   Presidents who were members of the U.S. House of Representatives (Madison, J.Q. Adams, Jackson, W.H. Harrison, Tyler, Polk, Fillmore, Pierce, Buchanan, Lincoln, A. Johnson, Hayes, Garfield, McKinley, Kennedy, L. Johnson, Nixon, Ford, and G.H.W. Bush). Only Madison, Polk, Garfield, and Ford had formal leadership positions.

16   Presidents who were members of the U.S. Senate (Monroe, J.Q. Adams, A. Jackson, Van Buren, W.H. Harrison, Tyler, Pierce, Buchanan, A. Johnson, B. Harrison, Harding, Truman, Kennedy, L. Johnson, Nixon, and Obama). Only Lyndon Johnson had a formal leadership position.

5   Presidents who served as vice president and were later elected president (J. Adams, Jefferson, Van Buren, Nixon, and G.H.W. Bush).

5   Presidents who served in the Continental Congress or Confederation Congress (Washington, J. Adams, Jefferson, Madison, and Monroe).

2   Presidents who served as a delegate to the Constitutional Convention (Washington and Madison).

11   Presidents who had no formal legislative experience at any level (Taylor, Grant, Arthur, Cleveland, Taft, Wilson, Hoover, Eisenhower, Reagan, Clinton, and G.W. Bush).

METHODOLOGY

The scoring and ranking methodology for the Legislative Experience resume category is as follows:

1. Any person who served in any legislative capacity receives a minimum of one point regardless of length of service (1 year in a state assembly = 1 point).

2. Any person who served in a local or state legislative capacity receives approximately one point for every three years of service (9 years in state senate = 3 points).

3. Any person who served in a federal legislative capacity receives one point for every year of service (8 years in the U.S. Senate = 8 points). This includes experience as vice president before 1953 when the vice presidency became much more of an executive branch position.

4. Any person who held a legislative leadership position or otherwise effectively exercised substantial legislative influence (Speaker of the House, very influential senators or state assembly leaders, etc.) may receive additional points.

5. No person will be ranked Great, regardless of length of service, unless he or she demonstrated substantial influence or held an important leadership position.

This methodology (and each of the scoring and ranking methodologies used in the following chapters) seeks simplicity, fairness, accuracy, and repeatability. The goal is for readers to be able to use the same historical information and accurately reproduce a presidential resume with the same (or very similar) scoring.

LEGISLATIVE EXPERIENCE SUMMARIES

The following summaries provide specific details on every president's legislative experience prior to taking office. They are listed in descending order based on the president's individual score, with earlier presidents appearing first within the same score. Each of these summaries and those in the following chapters provide readers with a precise historical and factual record on which to evaluate every president's qualifications and resume scores.

GREAT

JAMES MADISON   15

James Madison was on the Committee of Safety for Orange County, Virginia, from 1774 to 1775. He was then a delegate to the Virginia Constitutional Convention in 1776 but played only a modest role. He then served on the Virginia Council of State (an eight member advisory committee) under governors Patrick Henry and Thomas Jefferson from 1778 to 1779.

Madison became a delegate to the Confederation Congress from 1779 to 1783, quickly becoming very effective. He served in the Virginia General Assembly from 1784 to 1786.

Madison was a leader at the Annapolis Convention in 1786 where it was determined that the Articles of Confederation needed to be substantially revised. He was the most influential delegate at the Constitutional Convention in 1787, presenting the "Virginia Plan" for the new form of government and often leading the debates. He then collaborated with Alexander Hamilton and John Jay in New York in 1788 to write many of THE FEDERALIST essays before returning to Virginia to lead the fight for ratification. He became known as "Father of the Constitution."

Madison was floor leader in the U.S. House of Representatives from 1789 to 1797, while at the same time becoming one of President Washington's closest advisers. As political parties began forming in the early 1790s, he became one of the first leaders of the Democratic Republican Party which opposed the Federalist Party.

In his last legislative post, Madison served once more in the Virginia General Assembly from 1799 to 1801, helping to secure Thomas Jefferson's election as president.

LYNDON JOHNSON   15

Lyndon Johnson was possibly the most dominant and effective legislative leader in American history. His powers of personal persuasion and his ability to take "burdensome" duties and turn them into tools to exercise greater influence were legendary.

Johnson's father was a Texas state legislator and Johnson used to accompany him to the state capitol in Austin, Texas, and wander the halls watching and listening to the legislative action. He grew to love politics and always wanted to be a legislator.

Johnson was a legislative aide to Texas Congressman Richard Kleberg from 1931 to 1935. He quickly mastered the ins-and-outs of the Washington political scene and gained a reputation as a smart legislative operator. He accepted additional positions which many would have considered menial (messenger boy, doorman to the House chambers), and turned them into positions where he could better learn the political process.

Johnson served in the U.S. House of Representatives from 1937 to 1949. He had modest influence for a junior congressman, but his ambition was to become a senator. He found a close friend and great mentor in the legendary Speaker of the House Sam Rayburn who helped Johnson rise to power in the U.S. Senate.

Johnson then served in the U.S. Senate from 1949 to 1960. He became what biographer Robert Caro accurately described as the "Master of the Senate." He was minority whip from 1951 to 1953, Minority Leader from 1953 to 1955, and Majority Leader from 1955 to 1960. As Majority Leader, he accumulated powers that previous majority leaders had not had (the committee chairmen were the most powerful figures in the Senate at that time). He accepted the "burdens" of previously avoided tasks, making them tools of influence. Among other things, he assigned office space, granted committee assignments, managed the bill steering committee, ran the Democratic caucus, scheduled votes on bills and other matters, and directed Democratic campaign finances. No other Senate leader has ever wielded so much legislative power.

JAMES K. POLK   14

James K. Polk was clerk of the Tennessee Senate from 1819 to 1823, managing the paperwork and learning the nuances of parliamentary procedure. He then was a member of the Tennessee House of Representatives from 1823 to 1825.

Polk served in the U.S. House of Representatives from 1825 to 1839, quickly gaining influence and a national reputation. He was chairman of the powerful Ways and Means Committee before serving as Speaker of the House from 1835 to 1839. He was called "Old Hickory's Boy" due to his close and long-time relationship with President Jackson. He also became known as a policy wonk. He did not seek re-election in 1839, instead becoming Governor of Tennessee.

GERALD FORD   14
Gerald Ford served in the U.S. House of Representatives from 1949 to 1973. Throughout his twenty-four-year legislative career he was a kind, approachable, conscientious, and hard-working public servant. He was a loyal Republican, but well-liked on both sides of the aisle.

Ford had a goal to become Speaker of the House and steadily increased his influence by serving in Republican leadership positions. He gained some prominence in 1950 by getting a seat on the appropriations committee. He was chairman of the Republican conference (the third leadership position behind minority leader and minority whip) from 1963 to 1965. He also served from 1963 to 1964 on the Warren Commission which investigated the Kennedy Assassination.

Ford was Minority Leader from 1965 to 1973. He maintained strict party loyalty and rarely lost a Republican on a party-line vote. He also became a master of public relations. As a politician he was unspectacular but very effective, showcasing to good effect his plainspoken, humble, common sense manner and his personal integrity.

JOHN ADAMS   13
John Adams served as selectman (a member of the local governing committee) in Braintree, Massachusetts, in 1766, and then as a representative in the Massachusetts colonial legislature from 1768 to 1774. In 1774, Adams served as a delegate to the First Continental Congress, where nothing much of substance was accomplished. Adams was a delegate to the Second Continental Congress from 1775 to 1778 and was the Congress's most active and influential leader. He served on at least twenty-six committees including the committee that drafted the Declaration of Independence. He was also the head of the Board

of War. As the most outspoken advocate for independence during the many floor debates, Thomas Jefferson called him the "Colossus of Independence."

Adams was a delegate to the Massachusetts Constitutional Convention when he returned from Europe in 1779. He worked as a sub-subcommittee of one and was the primary drafter of the Massachusetts Constitution.

Adams later served as the first Vice President from 1789 to 1797 after returning from Europe. He was frustrated with the vice presidency, calling it the "most insignificant office that ever the invention of man contrived or his imagination conceived." Nevertheless, he played an important role in the early Congress, presiding daily over the U.S. Senate and casting more tie-breaking votes (31) than any other vice president in history.

JOHN TYLER   13
John Tyler served in the Virginia General Assembly from 1811 to 1815, quickly becoming an influential member. He then served on the Virginia Council of State from 1815 to 1816.

Tyler was a member of the U.S. House of Representatives from 1816 to 1822. He soon became an outspoken advocate for states' rights and strict construction of the Constitution (i.e., protecting slavery and opposing the national bank). He spoke often and well, but was not as oratorically gifted as some of his illustrious colleagues.

Tyler again served in the Virginia General Assembly from 1823 to 1825, before resigning to become Governor of Virginia in 1826.

Tyler then served in the U.S. Senate from 1827 to 1836. He broke with the Democratic Party over issues relating to the national bank and joined the new Whig Party in 1834. He resigned his seat in 1836 when he refused to follow voting instructions from the Virginia legislature.

Tyler once more served as a member of the Virginia General Assembly from 1838 to 1839, and was unanimously elected Speaker.

ANDREW JOHNSON   13
Andrew Johnson was an alderman in Greeneville, Tennessee, from 1829 to 1833. He then served in the Tennessee State Assembly, first from 1835 to 1836 and again from 1839 to 1841. He also served in the Tennessee Senate from 1841 to 1843.

Johnson later served in the U.S. House of Representatives from 1843 to 1853. He was considered a "maverick," but overall he was a loyal Democrat. He endlessly championed an eight-hour work day for federal employees and a homestead law for the western territories.

Johnson served in the U.S. Senate from 1857 to 1862. He was adamantly pro-slavery, but more adamantly pro-Union. In 1861, he became a nationally-known figure as the only senator from a seceding state to remain loyal to the Union.

JAMES GARFIELD   13

James Garfield served in the Ohio Senate from 1859 to 1861. He impressed his colleagues with his extraordinary speaking talents, but lost some of his effectiveness by speaking on almost every matter, a habit he struggled with for his entire legislative career.

Garfield resigned from the Union Army to serve in the U.S. House of Representatives from 1863 to 1880. He became a protégé of Treasury Secretary Salmon P. Chase and was part of the radical Republicans during the Reconstruction Era. In his early years, he frustrated many of his congressional colleagues with his lack of party discipline, tact, and overconfidence.

His influence steadily increased, however, and by the 1870s he was one of the leading Republicans in Congress. He served as chairman of the appropriations committees for four years, but never succeeded in becoming Speaker of the House or chairman of the powerful Ways and Means Committee.

WILLIAM MCKINLEY   13

William McKinley served seven terms in the U.S. House of Representatives from 1877 to 1891. He became a Republican leader and chairman of the powerful Ways and Means Committee, but was never successful in his pursuit of the Speakership. He soon developed a national reputation and became quite effective.

McKinley thrived in Congress. His supremely courteous and friendly nature made him popular with both Republicans and Democrats. He was a peacemaker by nature and sought to broker deals behind the scenes so as to avoid contentious public debates. His dedication to committee work and his attention to detail gave him a great understanding of the legislative process.

ABOVE AVERAGE

THOMAS JEFFERSON   12

Thomas Jefferson served in the Virginia House of Burgesses from 1769 to 1775. He was the protégé of two powerful legislators, Peyton Randolph (his uncle) and Edmund Pendleton.

Jefferson was the youngest delegate from Virginia to the Second Continental Congress from 1775 to 1776. His role was modest, taking no part in the debates. He was typically assigned the task of drafting committee reports such as the *Declaration of the Causes and Necessity for Taking Up Arms* in 1775, and the *Declaration of Independence* in 1776.

Jefferson was an influential leader in the newly-created Virginia General Assembly from 1776 to 1779. He drafted many laws attempting to eliminate injustices and establish a well-ordered republican government, but not all of his forward-thinking laws were adopted by his less visionary colleagues. He was then a delegate to the Confederation Congress from 1783 to 1784.

Jefferson served as Vice President from 1797 to 1801, presiding daily over the U.S. Senate and having no executive responsibilities.

MARTIN VAN BUREN   12

Martin Van Buren served in the New York Senate from 1812 to 1815 (the second youngest member ever elected). He soon gained influence by being outspokenly anti-British during the War of 1812. Overall, he was a moderate populist who was a supremely gifted backroom legislator and an expert at counting votes. He resigned in 1815 to become Attorney General of New York.

Van Buren was a delegate to the New York State Constitutional Convention in 1821, helping make the state's political systems more democratic. He was known for favoring "sober second thought" over "temporary excitement" in decision-making.

Already the undisputed master of New York state politics, Van Buren served in the U.S. Senate from 1821 to 1828. He brought his same organizational skills to the national stage. He was very popular in the Washington social scene, one of his keys to building the powerful political organization now known as the Democratic Party.

Van Buren served as Vice President from 1833 to 1837. He performed his constitutional duties by presiding over the U.S. Senate, but he also was one of the few vice presidents prior to the 1950s who had some executive influence due to his close relationship with President Jackson.

JOHN F. KENNEDY   12

John F. Kennedy served in the U.S. House of Representatives from 1947 to 1953. He won his seat due to a combination of his father's great wealth and political connections, and his own status as a war hero and good-looking young man. His office was effective in serving his Massachusetts constituents (his father bankrolled most of the staff members so he had far more aides than most congressmen), but legislatively he had few accomplishments. Mostly he used his seat as a stepping stone to higher office.

Kennedy then served in the U.S. Senate from 1953 to 1960. He had slightly more influence as a Senator, but was still better known for being a "celebrity politician" with a glamorous life, fashionable wife, and famous family name. He did start making a name for himself as a foreign policy "expert" due to his foreign travels and his service on the foreign relations committee beginning in 1957, but he never gained significant influence over foreign policy.

JAMES BUCHANAN   12

James Buchanan served in the Pennsylvania State Assembly from 1814 to 1820 as a member of the Federalist Party. He then served in the U.S. House of Representatives from 1821 to 1831, switching parties in 1929 and becoming a Democrat.

Buchanan served as U.S. Senator from Pennsylvania from 1834 to 1845, and became the acknowledged leader of the state Democratic Party, particularly in his influence over federal patronage. Nationally, however, he had only modest influence, taking a back seat to colleagues such as Henry Clay, Daniel Webster, and John C. Calhoun. Throughout his career he never sponsored an important bill that became law.

FRANKLIN PIERCE   11

Franklin Pierce served in the New Hampshire House of Representatives from 1828 to 1832. He was immediately a prominent member (his father was governor of New Hampshire several times) and served as Speaker from 1831 to 1832.

Pierce served in the U.S. House of Representatives from 1833 to 1837, but his contributions were modest. He then served in the U.S. Senate from 1837 to 1842. He had some influence in the Democratic Party, but no legislation he sponsored ever succeeded in passing.

Pierce presided over a New Hampshire Constitutional Convention for several months in 1850 and 1851. Ultimately, the voters rejected the new state constitution the convention drafted.

HARRY TRUMAN   10

Harry Truman served in the U.S. Senate from 1935 to 1944. In the early years he was called the "Senator from Pendergast" due to his close ties to the corrupt political bosses of western Missouri. He was, however, scrupulously honest in every matter and became one of the best liked and most popular senators in Washington. He was only moderately influential, however, and was largely ignored by President Franklin Roosevelt.

Truman was a hard-working and effective Senator, and a loyal Democrat. He disliked public speaking and rarely spoke to introduce or support a bill or to enter a debate. He loved to go out of his way to do favors for his colleagues, a habit which earned him many friends and great respect. He headed the special committee to investigate the national defense program during World War II (his brainchild which became known as the Truman Committee). He was universally praised for his assiduous and fair leadership of this committee, which did good work documenting and attempting to prevent waste and mismanagement. Although the committee had members of both parties, impressively, each of the more than fifty reports that were issued was unanimous.

RICHARD NIXON   10

Richard Nixon served in the U.S. House of Representatives from 1947 to 1951. He quickly became one of the most effective Republican legislators. He was one of the principal authors of the Taft-Hartley Act which counteracted some of the overreaches of labor unions, and he served on the House Un-American Activities Committee, becoming the only effective and distinguished member of that dangerous and abusive committee. Ultimately, he became one of the most recognizable members of Congress due largely to his investigations of accused communist Alger Hiss.

Nixon next served in the U.S. Senate from 1951 to 1953. He remained one of the most visible Republicans in Congress, an ardent but not radical anti-communist, and a politician who generally favored liberal goals through conservative means. He was the logical choice as the Republican nominee for the vice presidency.

Nixon served as Vice President from 1953 to 1961. For several of those years he was the tie-breaking vote in the U.S. Senate. Along with his executive responsibilities, he was one of the Eisenhower administration's most effective liaisons with Congress.

Although his service in Congress was relatively short, Nixon's skills as a legislator were substantial. He likely would have become one of the most effective legislators of his generation had he served longer in Congress.

AVERAGE

JAMES MONROE   9

James Monroe served on the Virginia Council of State from 1782 to 1783. He was then a delegate to the Confederation Congress from 1783 to 1786. He resigned his seat in 1786 to start a private law practice in Virginia and improve his finances.

Monroe served in the Virginia General Assembly from 1787 to 1788. He was also a delegate to Virginia's ratification convention in 1788 where he joined the anti-federalist movement and voted against ratifying the Constitution. After losing the election for the U.S. House of Representatives to his friend James Madison, he was appointed to the U.S. Senate and served from 1790 to 1794. His friendly personality and growing confidence helped him steadily increase his political effectiveness. He resigned his seat in 1794 to become Minister to France.

Monroe again served in the Virginia General Assembly in 1810 before becoming Governor of Virginia for the fourth time.

MILLARD FILLMORE   9

Millard Fillmore served in the New York State Assembly from 1829 to 1832 as a member of the Anti-Mason Party. He was purposefully inconspicuous at first due to a lack of experience and self-confidence, but he soon became more comfortable and gained some influence. He chose not to stand for re-election in 1832, but he did serve on the committee that drafted the City of Buffalo's charter.

Fillmore served in the U.S. House of Representatives from 1833 to 1835 as part of the disintegrating Anti-Mason Party. He declined to run for office in 1834, but he helped to found the new Whig Party and returned to the U.S. House of Representatives from 1837 to 1843 as a Whig. He was chairman of the Ways and Means Committee from 1841 to 1843.

GEORGE WASHINGTON   8

George Washington served in the Virginia House of Burgesses from 1759 to 1775. He became a leader in 1769 when he called for a boycott of British goods.

Washington was a delegate to the First Continental Congress in 1774 but played only a small role. He was then a delegate to the Second Continental Congress in 1775, this time playing a more substantial role until his selection as Commander in Chief of the Continental Army and his departure to war.

Washington was the "indispensable man" at the Constitutional Convention in 1787. He was unanimously elected president of the Convention and presided daily over the historic proceedings.

WARREN G. HARDING   8

Warren G. Harding served in the Ohio Senate from 1900 to 1903. His friendly nature and tendency toward bipartisanship won him many friends. He was somewhat influential by 1903, mostly because few Ohio state legislators were ever elected to more than one term in that era, making him one of the only legislative veterans. He then served as the Lieutenant Governor from 1904 to 1906, presiding over the Ohio Senate.

Almost a decade later, Harding served in the U.S. Senate from 1915 to 1920. He was one of the most popular people on Capitol Hill, but never desired to rise to higher office. He enjoyed being well-liked and relatively non-partisan.

WILLIAM HENRY HARRISON   7

William Henry Harrison served as a delegate to Congress from the Northwest Territory from 1799 to 1800. As a delegate, he convinced Congress to pass two bills, one of which divided the Northwest Territory into the Ohio and the Indiana Territories.

Harrison served in the U.S. House of Representatives from 1816 to 1819. He then became a member of the Ohio Senate from 1819 to 1821. He later served the remainder of a term in the U.S. Senate from 1825 to 1828. He never took a leadership role in any of his legislative positions.

JOHN QUINCY ADAMS   6

John Quincy Adams served in the Massachusetts state legislature from 1802 to 1803. He then served in the U.S. Senate from 1803 to 1808. Like his father, he was a very independent politician. His superb education and facility with language led him to insist that legislation be written using proper spelling and grammar, making him a nuisance to many other senators with less intellectual polish and poor writing abilities. He resigned in 1808 because he refused to vote as instructed by the Massachusetts state legislature.

BENJAMIN HARRISON   6

Benjamin Harrison served in the U.S. Senate from 1881 to 1887. He was a competent legislator and loyal Republican, but never served in a legislative leadership position. He was a champion of providing federal aid to education, particularly to the largely illiterate South. He was popular with his Republican colleagues because he was a great public speaker who could expound party doctrine in the U.S. Senate and on the campaign trail.

GEORGE H.W. BUSH   6

George H.W. Bush served in the U.S. House of Representatives from 1967 to 1971. He naturally sought moderation and compromise. He became an effective politician and a rising star in the Republican Party.

Bush served as Vice President from 1981 to 1988. While the position had evolved by that time to include many more executive responsibilities, he still presided over the U.S. Senate and had some legislative duties.

BARACK OBAMA   6
Barack Obama served in the Illinois Senate from 1997 to 2004. He started out idealistic and somewhat naïve on the issues, but soon became a more pragmatic politician. When Democrats became the majority party in 2003, he had his name on most of the bills that were passed through the legislature due largely to his close relationship with the Democratic leader of the Illinois Senate. He was generally bored as a state legislator and began campaigning for the U.S. Senate in 2003.

Obama then served in the U.S. Senate from 2005 to 2008. He was a "celebrity politician" from the start, due to his historic status as a black senator and his well-received speech at the 2004 Democratic convention. He was a loyal Democratic vote, but was never a legislative leader. He was similarly bored in the U.S. Senate and started campaigning for the presidency in 2007.

BELOW AVERAGE

ANDREW JACKSON   5
Andrew Jackson was a delegate to the Tennessee Territory Constitutional Convention in 1796. His role was modest, but he vigorously supported the constitution during the ratification process.

Jackson served in the U.S. House of Representatives from 1796 to 1797, but resigned his seat in 1797. Several months later he was elected to the U.S. Senate and served from 1797 to 1798. He resigned again in 1798.

More than two decades later, Jackson again served in the U.S. Senate from 1823 to 1825. He resigned once again after losing the 1824 presidential election.

ABRAHAM LINCOLN   5
Abraham Lincoln served in the Illinois House of Representatives from 1834 to 1842. He became a prominent Whig leader.

Lincoln later served in the U.S. House of Representatives from

1847 to 1849, still as a member of the fracturing Whig Party. His most notable speech in his one term in Washington was the *Spot Resolutions Speech* where he challenged President Polk to provide specific facts justifying the Mexican-American War.

CALVIN COOLIDGE 4
Calvin Coolidge was a Republican committee ward member and councilman for Northampton, Massachusetts, from 1897 to 1900. He then served in the Massachusetts State Assembly from 1907 to 1909. He steadily gained influence due to his close connection with one of the state's most powerful political bosses.

Coolidge then served in the Massachusetts Senate from 1912 to 1916. He was very effective and served as Senate President from 1915 to 1916.

JIMMY CARTER 3
Jimmy Carter served on the Sumter County school board from 1956 to 1962, becoming chairman in 1961. He then served in the Georgia Senate from 1963 to 1967. At first he worked hard but had little influence. By 1966, however, he was voted by his colleagues as one of the most effective state senators.

POOR

RUTHERFORD B. HAYES 2
Rutherford B. Hayes served in the U.S. House of Representatives from 1865 to 1867. He disliked being a congressman and entered only one minor debate, even though the momentous Reconstruction issues were before him. He resigned after starting his second term to become Governor of Ohio.

THEODORE ROOSEVELT 2
Theodore Roosevelt served in the New York State Assembly from 1882 to 1884. He immediately made a name for himself by being an aggressive and vocal advocate for governmental reform and moderately progressive legislation. His political influence was almost immediate, introducing many bills and masterfully using the press to champion his causes. He became Minority Leader in 1883 and continued to

throw his considerable political weight around, never hesitating to challenge his political opponents who included the corrupt Tammany Hall politicians. He lost the election for Speaker in 1884. After three years he had already developed a national reputation.

FRANKLIN ROOSEVELT   1
Franklin Roosevelt served one term in the New York Senate from 1911 to 1913. Unlike his colleagues, he chose to move to Albany full-time and become a professional politician (he maintained no other career). He became known for his outspoken contest against "bossism," and had modest influence in the state senate, though he was not well liked by his colleagues.

BILL CLINTON   1
Bill Clinton served as a student clerk on the Senate Foreign Relations Committee under Senator J. William Fulbright from 1966 to 1968. He received a practical congressional and foreign policy education, becoming comfortable roaming the halls of Congress and discussing the Vietnam War and other national political issues.

ZACHARY TAYLOR   0
Zachary Taylor never served in any legislative capacity.

ULYSSES S. GRANT   0
Ulysses S. Grant never served in any legislative capacity.

CHESTER A. ARTHUR   0
Chester A. Arthur never served in any legislative capacity.

GROVER CLEVELAND   0
Grover Cleveland never served in any legislative capacity.

WILLIAM HOWARD TAFT   0
William Howard Taft never served in any legislative capacity.

WOODROW WILSON   0
Woodrow Wilson never served in any legislative capacity.

HERBERT HOOVER 0

Herbert Hoover never served in any legislative capacity.

DWIGHT EISENHOWER 0

Dwight Eisenhower never served in any legislative capacity.

RONALD REAGAN 0

Ronald Reagan never served in any legislative capacity.

GEORGE W. BUSH 0

George W. Bush never served in any legislative capacity.

EXECUTIVE EXPERIENCE RANKINGS

Rank	Score	President	Historical Ranking
Great	15	Dwight Eisenhower	Near Great
		Herbert Hoover	Below Average
	14	Bill Clinton	Average
	13	Theodore Roosevelt	Near Great
		Franklin Roosevelt	Great
Above Average	12	James Monroe	Above Average
	11	John Quincy Adams	Average
	10	William H. Harrison	Not Ranked
Average	9	Ulysses S. Grant	Below Average
		Richard Nixon	Below Average
		Ronald Reagan	Near Great
		George H.W. Bush	Average
		George W. Bush	Not Ranked
	8	George Washington	Great
		Thomas Jefferson	Near Great
		James Madison	Above Average
		William Howard Taft	Average
	7	Andrew Johnson	Failure
		Rutherford B. Hayes	Average
		Chester A. Arthur	Average
		Jimmy Carter	Below Average
	6	Martin Van Buren	Average
		Woodrow Wilson	Near Great
Below Average	5	Andrew Jackson	Near Great
		Zachary Taylor	Below Average
		William McKinley	Above Average
		Calvin Coolidge	Average
		Harry Truman	Near Great
	4	James Buchanan	Failure
	3	John Adams	Above Average
		John Tyler	Below Average
Poor	2	James K. Polk	Near Great
		Grover Cleveland	Above Average
		Warren G. Harding	Failure
		Lyndon Johnson	Above Average
	1	Franklin Pierce	Failure
		Millard Fillmore	Below Average
		James Garfield	Not Ranked
		Benjamin Harrison	Below Average
		John F. Kennedy	Above Average
		Gerald Ford	Below Average
	0	Abraham Lincoln	Great
		Barack Obama	Not Ranked

FIVE
EXECUTIVE EXPERIENCE

It was settled by the Constitution, the laws, and the whole practice of the government that the entire executive power is vested in the President of the United States.
       – Andrew Jackson

The best executive is the one who has sense enough to pick good men to do what he wants done, and self-restraint to keep from meddling with them while they do it.
       – Theodore Roosevelt

THE SECOND RESUME CATEGORY is Executive Experience. Previous executive experience has often been hailed by candidates and commentators as the most important presidential qualification.

There are numerous jobs in which a presidential candidate can gain valuable executive experience. They include:

- federal cabinet secretaries and other high-ranking federal officials;
- state governors or other high-ranking state officials;
- city mayors or other city or county officials;
- business executives or hands-on business owners; and
- military officers.

In early American government there were relatively few executive positions, but modernly there are hundreds of top federal officials, fifty states with their own executive officers, thousands of businesses with executive management, and thousands of high-ranking military officers.

In 1789, George Washington entered the presidency with high-ranking military experience and long-time management over his extensive properties and business interests. Five of the next seven presidents (Thomas Jefferson, James Madison, James Monroe, John Quincy Adams, and Martin Van Buren) served as Secretary of State, and three served as state governors (Thomas Jefferson, James Monroe, and Martin Van Buren). Clearly, voters sought presidents with prior executive experience from the nation's very beginning.

EXECUTIVE RESPONSIBILITIES

Every president has certain executive responsibilities which can be categorized as constitutional responsibilities and historical and practical responsibilities.

Constitutional Responsibilities

Several provisions in the Constitution vest the president with executive responsibilities. Article II, Section 1 provides:

> *The executive Power shall be vested in a President of the United States of America.*

Known as the "Vesting Clause," Section 1 is intentionally ambiguous. Unlike Congress's many specific and enumerated powers found in Article I, Section 8 (e.g., powers to tax, spend, provide for an Army and Navy, declare war, and regulate interstate and international commerce), there are few enumerated executive powers. For over two centuries this constitutional ambiguity has been frustrating for many judges, lawyers, politicians, and citizens seeking to determine the exact scope of a president's executive power. It has also been liberating for presidents who sought to exercise expansive executive powers.

So what is the precise scope of the "executive Power"? The short answer is simply that it largely depends on the current president. When a president is strong, his or her executive powers are expansive, but when a president is weak, his or her executive powers are minimal. The only definite parameters are those established by historical precedent or by legal precedent as announced by the Supreme Court. In every case, the president's executive powers are subject to the checks and balances of the legislative and judicial branches.

Article II, Section 2, Clause 3 provides:

> *[The President] may require the Opinion in writing, of the principal Officer in each of the executive Departments, upon any subject relating to the Duties of their respective Offices, and he shall have Power to Grant Reprieves and Pardons for Offenses against the United States, except in Cases of Impeachment.*

The first part of Clause 3 simply states that the president oversees the top officials in each of the executive departments and can require them to submit reports and otherwise follow his orders. This includes the officials in each of the cabinet departments and the many smaller administrative agencies.

The second part of Clause 3 vests the president with the "Pardoning Power," permitting him or her to grant pardons (releases from legal consequences) and reprieves (delays of punishment) for any federal crime. Some presidents have granted many pardons, the most being Franklin Roosevelt (3,687), Woodrow Wilson (2,480), Harry Truman (2,044), Calvin Coolidge (1,545), Herbert Hoover (1,385), and Ulysses Grant (1,332). Others have used the pardoning power sparingly, including George Washington (16), John Adams (21), George H.W. Bush (77), and George W. Bush (176). There are few parameters surrounding the president's Pardoning Power.

Article II, Section 2, Clauses 2 and 3 provide:

[2][The President] shall nominate, and by and with the Advice and Consent of the Senate, shall appoint Ambassadors, other public Ministers and Consuls, Judges of the supreme Court, and all other Officers of the United States, whose Appointments are not herein otherwise provided for, and which shall be established by Law; but the Congress may by Law vest the Appointment of such inferior Officers, as they think proper, in the President alone, in the Courts of Law, or in the Heads of Departments. [3] The President shall have Power to fill up all Vacancies that may happen during the Recess of the Senate, by granting Commissions which shall expire at the End of their next Session.

Clauses 2 and 3 grant the president the "Appointment Power." The Appointment Power is a significant political and administrative power, permitting the president to choose his or her top officers and to fill all federal judicial vacancies, subject only to approval by a majority of the Senate. It is also a significant burden, however, as making appointments takes up a great deal of every president's time and resources.

The Appointment Power comes with the complimentary and inherent "Removal Power." The Supreme Court has held that unless Congress specifically places a restriction on the president's Removal Power for certain "independent" positions—those which exercise quasi-legislative and quasi-adjudicative functions as well as executive functions, and which require "good cause" to remove (e.g., top officials of the Federal Reserve Board, Federal Election Commission, and Securities and Exchange Commission)—the president is able to remove (i.e., fire) any executive officer at any time without cause.

Article II, Section 3 provides:

> *[The President] shall take Care that the Laws be faithfully executed, and shall Commission all the Officers of the United States.*

The first part of Section 3 requires the president to enforce— to "faithfully execute"—all federal laws. This includes everything from protecting the individual rights provided in the Constitution, to enforcing federal drug laws, immigration and border laws, environmental regulations, and anti-discrimination statutes. Many federal executive agencies are used to help enforce federal laws, including the Environmental Protection Agency, the Federal Bureau of Investigation, and many other executive departments, agencies, and bureaus.

The second part of Section 3 requires simply that the president must actually commission (i.e., formally hire) each executive officer once the Senate has confirmed the nominee.

Historical and Practical Responsibilities

Historians acknowledge that the president's role as America's chief executive officer was designed with George Washington specifically in mind. Every person who signed and ratified the Constitution knew that Washington would serve as the first president. Deference to Washington's experience and judgment probably made the president's ambiguous "executive Power" more acceptable to the anti-aristocrats of the Founding Era.

Since 1789, the presidency's intentionally ambiguous executive responsibilities have been subject to wide-ranging interpretations. Those presidents whom historians call "strong" have interpreted their executive prerogatives broadly and have exercised great influence over a wide array of domestic and international affairs. Those presidents whom historians call "weak" have been more subservient to the dictates of Congress and have had their executive prerogatives sharply curtailed by legislative and judicial checks and balances.

History shows that a president's approach to exercising executive power is determined by a variety of considerations, including:

- political assertiveness;
- national popularity;
- ability to work with (or to dominate) Congress;
- whether the matter is international (where presidential power is substantial) or domestic (where presidential power is subject to stronger congressional checks and balances); and
- whether the Supreme Court has specifically identified a limit to executive power in a particular circumstance.

In a practical sense, the president is the head of the federal bureaucracy and has all of the administrative responsibilities that come therewith. The president, through the executive bureaucracy, exerts some level of control over many areas and industries of American society. The executive branch of government has grown from fewer than 1,000 employees in 1789 to fifteen cabinet departments and almost 2.8 million federal non-military employees as of 2009. Today more than ever, the president acts as a chief executive officer who sets high-level policy priorities and goals for a sprawling network of diverse departments and agencies.

Finally, one of the most important executive decisions a president makes is the selection of cabinet officers who head each of the executive departments. Historically, the president's cabinet was made up of significant American statesmen who met with the president frequently (often daily) for serious policy discussions. George Washington's first cabinet—made up of Secretary of State Thomas Jefferson, Treasury Secretary Alexander Hamilton, Secretary of War Henry Knox, Attorney General Edmund Randolph, and Postmaster General Samuel Osgood—set a high bar for excellence which has never been matched. Modernly, cabinet officials are still very important, but cabinet meetings have become more ceremonial than operational.

QUICK FACTS
The following are some quick facts about the presidents' executive experiences upon taking office.

9   Presidents who served as a cabinet secretary (Jefferson, Madison, Monroe, J.Q. Adams, Van Buren, Buchanan, Grant, Taft, and Hoover).

6   Presidents who served as Secretary of State (Jefferson, Madison, Monroe, J.Q. Adams, Van Buren, and Buchanan).

3   Presidents who served as Secretary of War (Monroe, Grant, and Taft).

1   Presidents who served as Secretary of Commerce (Hoover).

5   Presidents who served in other high-ranking federal positions (Arthur, T. Roosevelt, F. Roosevelt, Taft, and G.H.W. Bush).

4   Presidents who served as Vice President when that office had increased executive responsibilities (post-1950) (Nixon, L. Johnson, Ford, and G.H.W. Bush).

20 Presidents who served as a state (or territory) governor (Jefferson, Monroe, Jackson, Van Buren, W.H. Harrison, Tyler, Polk, A. Johnson, Hayes, Cleveland, McKinley, T. Roosevelt, Taft, Wilson, Coolidge, F. Roosevelt, Carter, Reagan, Clinton, and G.W. Bush).

5   Presidents who served as a statewide official other than governor (Van Buren, Fillmore, Harding, Coolidge, and Clinton).

5   Presidents who served as a city mayor or other city or county executive (A. Johnson, Cleveland, T. Roosevelt, Coolidge, and Truman).

2   Presidents with no executive experience (Lincoln and Obama).

METHODOLOGY
The scoring and ranking methodology for the Executive Experience resume category is as follows:

1. Any person who served in a local executive position receives one point for approximately every three years of service (6 years as a small town mayor = 2 points).

2. Any person who served in a major city executive position, statewide executive position, or high-ranking federal executive

position receives one point for every year of service (5 years as state attorney general = 5 points).

3.   Any person who had executive responsibilities in a role already covered by another resume category (e.g., military, foreign, private) may receive some additional points in this category depending on (i) the level of the position, and (ii) the length of service.

4.   No person will be ranked Great, regardless of length of service, unless his or her executive performance was truly excellent and included supervising or commanding large numbers of employees or troops.

EXECUTIVE EXPERIENCE SUMMARIES

The following detailed summaries are listed in descending order based on the president's individual score, with earlier presidents appearing first within the same score.

GREAT

HERBERT HOOVER   15

Herbert Hoover served as the head of the Commission for Relief in Belgium (CRB) from 1914 to 1917 during the early years of World War I. Most of Belgium and much of Western Europe was starving due to the war, and Hoover and the CRB organized a massive food relief program that saved millions of lives. As the head of the CRB, he had a German passport that permitted him access to all parts of Europe and provided that "this man is not to be stopped anywhere under any circumstances." In his position he interacted with many world figures and heads of state.

Once America entered World War I, Hoover served as the chief U.S. Food Administrator from 1917 to 1920, overseeing all aspects of the domestic food industry, including imports and exports, production, pricing, consumption, and rationing.

Hoover then served as Secretary of Commerce from 1921 to 1928. He transformed the department from a small assortment of bureaus into a well-organized operation intent on promoting, guiding, and protecting American economic development. He was the most influential and effective Commerce Secretary in history.

Hoover also had substantial executive experience as an international businessman and mining expert.

DWIGHT EISENHOWER   15
Dwight Eisenhower had extensive executive responsibilities as a career military officer from 1915 to 1952 and rose to the rank of 5-Star General and Supreme Allied Commander. He also had executive duties as president of Columbia University from 1948 to 1950.

He had an effective executive leadership style, similar to that of a great sports coach. He was very well organized. He knew how to absorb details quickly without losing sight of the big picture. He was always concerned about morale but was strict on rules and performance standards. He was willing to delegate broadly but never shied away from taking ultimate responsibility for a decision made under his command. Much of his leadership style was taken from the best qualities of three renowned generals under whom he served: Fox Conner, Douglas MacArthur, and George C. Marshall.

BILL CLINTON   14
Bill Clinton served as Attorney General of Arkansas from 1977 to 1979. He spent his time traveling the state giving speeches and making legal policy decisions. As the state official with the most ties to the Carter administration, he was frequently invited to the White House and consulted on federal appointments in Arkansas.

Clinton then served five terms as Governor of Arkansas, first from 1979 to 1981 and again from 1983 to 1992. After failing to be re-elected due to a somewhat disorganized and overambitious first term and the anti-Carter wave, he returned to the governorship. Over the next decade he became a more reassuring and responsible state official. He showed political flexibility, combining idealism with pragmatism. He was also skilled at using polling to help develop effective public communications strategies. In 1986, he assumed the chairmanship of the National Governors Association, and in 1990, he became chairman of the politically moderate Democratic Leadership Council. By 1992, he was the longest serving governor in the country and a nationally recognized political figure.

THEODORE ROOSEVELT   13

Theodore Roosevelt was one of three federal Civil Service Commissioners from 1889 to 1895, and immediately became the *de facto* leader. The Civil Service Commission's purpose was to reform the long-standing and corrupt political patronage system, and he made it a strong and effective force.

Roosevelt next served as Commissioner of the New York City Police Department from 1895 to 1897. In that era, the NYPD was rife with corruption and bribery. In two years he significantly reformed the department, getting it to neutrally enforce laws, to become de-politicized and de-ethnicized, and to reduce corruption.

Roosevelt then served as Assistant Secretary of the Navy from 1897 to 1898. He assumed as much authority as the position allowed and was an effective and industrious administrator. He personally drafted the detailed report *Naval Policy of America as Outlined in Messages of the Presidents of the United States from the Beginning to the Present Day*, which served as the official manual for political-naval operations.

When Roosevelt returned from Cuba, he served as Governor of New York from 1898 to 1900. His daily press conferences were unprecedented and enabled him to effectively champion and pass progressive legislation, including civil service and labor reforms.

Roosevelt also had some executive responsibilities as a military officer.

FRANKLIN ROOSEVELT   13

Franklin Roosevelt served as Assistant Secretary of the Navy (his cousin Theodore Roosevelt's former position) for eight years from 1913 to 1920. Only 31 years old when he was appointed, he was the youngest assistant secretary in history. In that position, he worked with the White House (often directly with President Wilson) on naval policy matters; he worked closely with Congress to secure naval funding; he negotiated contracts with contractors for naval projects; and he worked closely with the naval military leaders to manage and supervise the American fleet. Throughout World War I, he was intimately involved with all American naval mobilization efforts and military activities in the Atlantic Ocean and in Europe.

Roosevelt served four years as Governor of New York from 1929 to 1932. As Governor, he developed effective administrative habits:

informality in meetings, hosting evening drinks with important guests, political flexibility regardless of the moment's crisis, willingness to make and accept responsibility for decisions, and setting an optimistic tone while speaking directly to the people. He was the first governor who realized the severity of the Great Depression and quickly moved to use government to alleviate suffering and joblessness. Many of his state government programs were unprecedented and laid the groundwork for future national programs.

Roosevelt's leadership style as an executive was straightforward but always with a twist of political nuance. He was a great delegator who was willing to accept ultimate responsibility for every decision made. He was decisive, energetic, optimistic, and flexible in dealing with ever-changing circumstances. He disliked paperwork, but had a great ability to quickly absorb and understand great amounts of information. He was also a master at persuasion and at stroking the egos of legislators whose support or votes he needed.

ABOVE AVERAGE

JAMES MONROE   12

James Monroe served as Governor of Virginia from 1799 to 1802. Prior to his service, the governorship had little executive power except for being Commander in Chief of the Virginia Militia. However, he transformed the position into one of substantial state and national influence, advocating government reforms, establishing state-supported public education and road maintenance, and strengthening the militia. Under his administration, the Virginia governorship became America's second most powerful office, and he became a prominent national leader.

A decade later, Monroe started his fourth one-year term as Governor of Virginia in 1811. He resigned when he was appointed Secretary of State. He served as Secretary of State from 1811 to 1816, during the end of the American trade embargo and throughout the War of 1812. During the war, he also served as Acting Secretary of War twice (from 1812 to 1813 and from 1814 to 1815) on top of his duties as Secretary of State. With President Madison badly shaken after Washington was burned in 1814, Monroe was the figure exercising the most control over the executive branch of government through the 1816 presidential elections.

Monroe also had some executive responsibilities as a foreign minister and a military officer.

JOHN QUINCY ADAMS 11

John Quincy Adams served as Secretary of State from 1817 to 1825. Although President Monroe struggled with delegating responsibility, Adams managed his department very competently and was President Monroe's most effective advisor. His accomplishments included negotiating the Treaty of 1818 with Great Britain over the northwestern boundary with Canada, negotiating the Transcontinental Treaty of 1819 with Spain, and being the main proponent of the Monroe Doctrine (the principle that the United States would not permit further European intrusion into and colonization of the Western Hemisphere).

Adams also had some executive responsibilities as a foreign minister.

WILLIAM HENRY HARRISON 10

William Henry Harrison served as Secretary of the Northwest Territory from 1798 to 1799. The Northwest Territory then included parts of what are now Ohio, Indiana, Illinois, Michigan, Wisconsin, and Minnesota.

Harrison then served as Governor of the Indiana Territory from 1801 to 1812. During that period the free white man population grew from about 5,000 settlers to over 25,000 residents. His responsibilities were to draft and enforce local laws, negotiate land treaties with local Indian tribes in order to help expand the United States territories without war, and to organize and command the territorial militia.

Harrison had some executive responsibilities as a foreign minister and a military officer.

AVERAGE

ULYSSES S. GRANT 9

Ulysses S. Grant served as Acting Secretary of War as well as General-in-Chief from 1866 to 1868. He was widely acknowledged to be the second most influential person in the nation (some thought him even more influential than President Johnson). He directly oversaw the governance of the southern states while they were divided into five military districts during the early stages of Reconstruction.

Grant also had considerable executive responsibilities as a military officer from 1843 to 1854, and again from 1861 to 1868. His executive leadership style was a simple, principled, "big picture" approach, not overly concerned with details.

RICHARD NIXON   9

Richard Nixon served as an administrator of the rubber branch of the federal Office of Price Administration during 1942. He was an excellent organizer and efficient administrator, creating new systems to improve the unwieldy bureaucratic communications process. Soon he was promoted to acting chief of the rationing coordination unit.

Nixon served as Vice President under President Eisenhower from 1953 to 1961. He was the first Vice President to have formal executive responsibilities within the executive branch. Among other things, he was made chairman of the President's Committee on Government Contracts. He also became President Eisenhower's constant fact-finder and goodwill ambassador to dozens of foreign nations. For eight years he was also a very active and influential political advisor to President Eisenhower and his cabinet.

Nixon also had executive duties as a military officer.

RONALD REAGAN   9

Ronald Reagan served as Governor of California from 1967 to 1975. His tenure in the governor's office included dealing with crises surrounding university student sit-ins and rebellions, race riots, and anti-Vietnam War protests. He was considered a successful governor, largely avoiding the radical wing of the Republican Party and seeking political compromise. He was able to unite the mass of California citizens who were uncomfortable with the radical student protesters and political activists who were visible and vocal throughout the state. He found a way to balance the state budget which was in a severe deficit (he was forced to raise taxes), and also started reforming the state welfare system.

GEORGE H.W. BUSH   9

George H.W. Bush served as Director of the Central Intelligence Agency from 1976 to 1977. When he took over the agency was in crisis. He was an effective manager and leader who brought much needed stability and order.

Bush served as Vice President from 1981 to 1988. He had significant executive responsibilities including: daily national security briefings, weekly meetings with President Reagan, chairing the National Security Council's Crisis Management Center, chairing the national security planning group in charge of developing foreign policy options, and chairing the task force on combating terrorism beginning in 1985. By 1988, he had been the Vice President with the most executive branch responsibilities in American history.

GEORGE W. BUSH   9

George W. Bush served as Governor of Texas from 1995 to 2000. He started calling his approach to governance "compassionate conservatism." As Governor he pushed for implementing tax cuts while focusing more government funds on education and teacher salaries. He also passed more strict criminal laws and tort reform. In 1998, he won a landslide re-election and soon became a potential presidential candidate.

Bush also had significant executive responsibilities as a business owner and executive.

GEORGE WASHINGTON   8

George Washington married widow Martha Dandridge Custis in 1759 and immediately became one of Virginia's wealthiest landowners. He then left military service for business management. From 1759 through 1775 and again from 1784 to 1788, he pursued full-time his business interests, closely managing his extensive properties and commercial dealings. Unlike many of his neighbors, he was watchful over his holdings and investments and protected his economic interests with great assiduousness.

Washington also had extensive executive responsibilities as a high-ranking military officer from 1754 to 1759, and again from 1775 to 1783. His executive leadership both as a businessman and military officer evolved over four decades. He became a great delegator of important responsibilities, maximizing his overall control while distancing himself from relatively minor details. He also had an impressive eye for talent.

Thomas Jefferson   8

Thomas Jefferson served as Governor of Virginia from 1779 to 1781. During those years, the governorship had few powers except as Commander in Chief of the Virginia Militia.

Returning from France, Jefferson served as the first Secretary of State from 1790 to 1794. His service was somewhat tainted due to his passionate disagreements with Treasury Secretary Alexander Hamilton, his abiding love of all things French (and his corresponding hatred for all things British), and his personal and political falling-out with President Washington. His service was still very competent, however, if not highly distinguished.

Jefferson also had some executive responsibilities as a foreign minister.

James Madison   8

James Madison served as Secretary of State from 1801 to 1809. He and President Jefferson (in collaboration with the brilliant Treasury Secretary Albert Gallatin) were largely co-architects and co-executors of the new Democratic-Republican Party's policies. As an executive, he was often indecisive until he had the opportunity to carefully study and reflect upon the question before him.

As Secretary of State, Madison presided over the Louisiana Purchase from France, headed American diplomacy during the Napoleonic Wars, negotiated with Spain over the Florida territory, and helped design and support America's disastrous embargo policy. Ultimately, Madison's service was quite effective, although in foreign affairs he often attempted to act with more strength and international influence than America actually possessed.

William Howard Taft   8

William Howard Taft served as president of the Philippine Commission in 1900, traveling to the Philippines to help establish a civilian government under the auspices of American sovereignty. He was soon appointed Governor of the Philippines and served from 1901 to 1904.

As Governor, he used his talents as a lawyer and judge to draft and enforce new laws, including a criminal code, an internal revenue code, a corporations code, and a land use and settlement code. His warm demeanor and love for the Filipino people made him a popular leader in the Philippines, and his effective administration earned him respect back home in America.

Returning to America in 1904, Taft was appointed Secretary of War and served from 1904 to 1908. A close friend of President Theodore Roosevelt, he soon became a jack-of-all-trades advisor, as President Roosevelt preferred to manage the military himself. Due to his extensive knowledge and experience in foreign affairs, he was occasionally sent on foreign trips as President Roosevelt's personal representative. He was a capable administrator, though he had a hands-off approach to his department.

ANDREW JOHNSON   7

Andrew Johnson was mayor of Greeneville, Tennessee, in 1834 and again in 1837.

Many years later, Johnson served as Governor of Tennessee from 1853 to 1857. During that time, the governorship was not very powerful, but he used the office to make the most of his appointment powers and to advance his future ambitions. At President Lincoln's request, Johnson resigned his seat in the U.S. Senate to become Military Governor of East Tennessee from 1862 to 1864 after it was reclaimed by the Union Army. He recruited new Union troops, shut down pro-Confederate newspapers and encouraged pro-Union ones, and appointed well-known Unionists to prominent Tennessee positions. He had difficulties working with the Union generals and beginning the Reconstruction efforts in Tennessee, but overall he performed moderately well.

RUTHERFORD B. HAYES   7

Rutherford B. Hayes was Governor of Ohio from 1867 to 1871 and again from 1875 to 1876. He enjoyed being Governor, although the position had limited powers. He prided himself in always appearing dignified and in being bipartisan or nonpartisan. The primary issues he faced were black suffrage and civil service reform. Overall, he was a good but not a great Governor.

Hayes also had executive responsibilities as a military officer.

CHESTER A. ARTHUR 7

Chester A. Arthur served as Collector of the New York Customhouse from 1871 to 1877. As Collector, he was responsible for the revenue collection and management of by far the largest revenue collection office in the nation, collecting over $100 million in revenue annually in the 1870s. Arthur was generally considered a capable administrator.

But Arthur was in complete agreement with the customs of having public agencies exercise political influence through a system of salary assessments directed to the political party in power, and of public officials wielding power through spoils and patronage. He was suspended by President Hayes in 1877 after an investigatory commission's hearings focused upon allegations of widespread corruption, inefficiencies, and excessive political partisanship in the New York Customhouse.

Arthur also had executive responsibilities as a military officer.

JIMMY CARTER 7

Jimmy Carter was Governor of Georgia from 1971 to 1975. He successfully reorganized the state government which, under his predecessors, had often been poorly managed. He worked hard and was a competent and detail-oriented administrator, but he struggled to work with the legislature, particularly with those who tended to oppose his agenda. His unwillingness to "wheel and deal" with legislators made it difficult for him to win supporters through compromise. As an administrator, Carter disliked meetings. He preferred to work with individual staff members and make up his mind on a strategy or direction after listening to many different people separately. This helped him remain intimately involved in administrative details, but it often led to disorganized official and campaign operations.

Carter also had executive responsibilities as a small business owner and as a naval officer.

MARTIN VAN BUREN 6

Martin Van Buren served as Attorney General of New York from 1815 to 1819. During that time he created a sophisticated political organization, but was removed in 1819 by his rival, New York Governor DeWitt Clinton.

Van Buren served several months as Governor of New York in 1829, before resigning to become Secretary of State from 1829 to

1831. He became a close friend and advisor to President Jackson and was his constant companion and confident. While inexperienced in international affairs, he was a successful administrator and diplomat. He resigned in 1831.

Van Buren was Vice President from 1833 to 1837 and was one of the few vice presidents who had any executive influence prior to the 1950s.

WOODROW WILSON   6

Woodrow Wilson served as Governor of New Jersey from 1911 to 1912. He was very successful in his first year, gaining a national reputation by passing several major bills. For a man without prior government experience, he was surprisingly adept at working with the legislature and communicating with voters.

Wilson also had significant executive responsibilities as President of Princeton University.

BELOW AVERAGE

ANDREW JACKSON   5

Andrew Jackson served as Military Governor of the Florida Territory, which he had helped seize from Spain, in 1821. He also had extensive executive responsibilities as a high-ranking military officer, particularly from 1812 to 1820.

ZACHARY TAYLOR   5

Zachary Taylor had many executive responsibilities as a military officer. He served in the Army for forty years, steadily rising up through the ranks to become a Major General in 1846 during the Mexican-American War. Throughout his career, he regularly commanded more than 1,000 soldiers and was generally considered a competent leader and administrator.

WILLIAM MCKINLEY   5

William McKinley was Governor of Ohio from 1892 to 1896. In that era the governorship was not a very powerful position, but he worked closely with the legislature and became an effective executive. One of the major issues he dealt with was the intense relationship between labor and capital. In 1894, he called out militia troops to halt violence that erupted during mineworker strikes. His simple and straightforward manner and appeal helped him to connect with voters and resulted in a landslide victory in his second election. Particularly in his second term, he started using his gubernatorial office as a national platform from which he could speak on national issues.

McKinley had some executive responsibilities as a military officer.

CALVIN COOLIDGE   5
Calvin Coolidge was mayor of Northampton, Massachusetts from 1909 to 1912. He was a capable executive and administrator who believed strongly that it was more important to enforce the current laws than to pass new laws for every new political situation. He was fairly progressive in the Theodore Roosevelt mold.

Coolidge then served as Lieutenant Governor of Massachusetts from 1917 to 1919. The position was a stepping stone to the governorship, but had few executive powers or responsibilities. He was then Governor of Massachusetts from 1919 to 1920. He gained national attention and respect for his able handling of the Boston police strike in 1919, calling out the Massachusetts National Guard to break the strike while still supporting employment and civil service reforms.

HARRY TRUMAN   5
Harry Truman served as one of three "judges" in Jackson County, Missouri (which included Kansas City), first from 1923 to 1925, and again from 1927 to 1935. The position of "judge" was actually the county's top administrative position, not a judicial position. The last eight years he was the presiding judge, essentially acting as the chief executive of the county. He was responsible for a $7 million budget and 700 county employees, which included the county treasurer, county sheriff, health officials, road construction crews, administrative clerks, courthouse personnel, etc. He was universally praised for being an outstanding administrator who was scrupulous with county finances and hands-on and detail-oriented with every county project.

Truman was also the Missouri Director of the Federal Reemployment Service from 1933 to 1935, helping to channel over 100,000 unemployed workers into contract jobs. He also had some executive responsibilities as a military officer.

JAMES BUCHANAN   4

James Buchanan served as Secretary of State from 1845 to 1849. President Polk made each of his cabinet secretaries promise not to use the position to campaign to become his presidential successor in 1849. His four years of service were eventful, dealing with the annexation of Texas, the Mexican-American War, British claims over parts of the Oregon Territory, and foreign trade tariffs. He was a competent administrator, even though President Polk was a micro-manager who made all of the large decisions.

Buchanan also had some executive responsibilities as a foreign minister.

GROVER CLEVELAND   3

Grover Cleveland served as Mayor of Buffalo, New York, in 1882. He was elected in a landslide as a Democrat in a largely Republican county, and was known for scrupulous honesty and straightforwardness. He proved he would veto any measure that he did not think was in the public good.

Cleveland, unknown outside of Buffalo prior to 1882, became Governor of New York in another landslide election in 1882. He served as Governor from 1883 to 1884, and quickly became a national phenomenon due to his willingness to veto measures and his emphasis on reform. As Governor, he developed a good working relationship with then-State Assemblyman Theodore Roosevelt, a conservative-progressive Republican.

WARREN G. HARDING   3

Warren G. Harding had some executive responsibilities as owner and publisher of a small town newspaper.

POOR

JOHN ADAMS   2

John Adams had no executive responsibilities as Vice President. He did have some executive responsibilities as a foreign minister.

JOHN TYLER 2
John Tyler served as Governor of Virginia from 1826 to 1827. At that time, the position had little executive power, and he exercised little influence over the state legislature.

JAMES K. POLK 2
James K. Polk served as Governor of Tennessee from 1839 to 1841. In the midst of the Whig Party's boom years, he was unsuccessful in his re-election campaigns in both 1841 and 1843.

LYNDON JOHNSON 2
Lyndon Johnson was the Texas Director of the National Youth Administration (NYA) from 1935 to 1937. The NYA was a New Deal program focused on getting jobs for out-of-work youth. As the state director, he helped put nearly 20,000 young people to work on local building and improvement projects. He was the youngest state director appointed, and he proved to be the most effective director in the country.

MILLARD FILLMORE 1
Millard Fillmore served as Comptroller of New York in 1848. The comptrollership was one of New York's most powerful offices, and he was a capable administrator.

FRANKLIN PIERCE 1
Franklin Pierce had some executive responsibilities as a military officer.

JAMES GARFIELD 1
James Garfield had some executive responsibilities as a military officer.

BENJAMIN HARRISON 1
Benjamin Harrison had some executive responsibilities as a military officer.

JOHN F. KENNEDY 1
John F. Kennedy had some executive responsibilities as a military officer.

GERALD FORD   1
Gerald Ford had some executive responsibilities as a military officer.

ABRAHAM LINCOLN   0
Abraham Lincoln never served in any executive capacity.

BARACK OBAMA   0
Barack Obama never served in any executive capacity.

Rank	Score	President	Historical Ranking
Great	15	George Washington	Great
		Ulysses S. Grant	Below Average
		Dwight Eisenhower	Near Great
Above Average	12	Andrew Jackson	Near Great
		Zachary Taylor	Below Average
	11	William H. Harrison	Not Ranked
Average	8	James Garfield	Not Ranked
		Benjamin Harrison	Below Average
	7	James Monroe	Above Average
		Rutherford B. Hayes	Average
	6	William McKinley	Above Average
		Franklin Roosevelt	Great
		John F. Kennedy	Above Average
		Richard Nixon	Below Average
		Gerald Ford	Below Average
		George H.W. Bush	Average
Below Average	5	Theodore Roosevelt	Near Great
		Harry Truman	Near Great
		Jimmy Carter	Below Average
	4	Franklin Pierce	Failure
		Andrew Johnson	Failure
		Chester A. Arthur	Average
	3	Ronald Reagan	Near Great
		George W. Bush	Not Ranked
Poor	2	John Adams	Above Average
		Thomas Jefferson	Near Great
		Abraham Lincoln	Great
		William Howard Taft	Average
		Herbert Hoover	Below Average
		Lyndon Johnson	Above Average
	1	James Madison	Above Average
		James K. Polk	Near Great
	0	John Quincy Adams	Average
		Martin Van Buren	Average
		John Tyler	Below Average
		Millard Fillmore	Below Average
		James Buchanan	Failure
		Grover Cleveland	Above Average
		Woodrow Wilson	Near Great
		Warren G. Harding	Failure
		Calvin Coolidge	Average
		Bill Clinton	Average
		Barack Obama	Not Ranked

MILITARY EXPERIENCE RANKINGS

SIX
MILITARY EXPERIENCE

To be prepared for war is one of the most effectual means of preserving peace.
– George Washington

I have never advocated war except as a means of peace.
– Ulysses S. Grant

Together we must learn how to compose differences, not with arms, but with intellect and decent purpose.
– Dwight Eisenhower

THE THIRD RESUME CATEGORY is Military Experience. Particularly in times of war and other military conflicts, a president's prior military service or experience may provide a certain amount of credibility for his or her decisions when acting in the constitutional role of Commander in Chief. Voters have relished selecting military heroes as president multiple times in American history, although sometimes the word "hero" was used very generously.

As Commander in Chief, presidents are responsible for every action conducted by the American military at home and abroad. Since 1789, there have been multiple wars and many other military conflicts in which America was engaged, including:

- the War of 1812 (1812 to 1815);
- the Mexican-American War (1846 to 1848);
- the Civil War (1861 to 1865);
- the Spanish-American War (1898);
- the Philippine-American War (1899 to 1902);
- World War I (1917 to 1918);
- World War II (1941 to 1945);
- the Cold War (1945 to 1991);
- the Korean War (1950 to 1953);
- the Vietnam War (1964 to 1975);

- the Persian Gulf War (1990 to 1991);
- the Iraq War (2003 to 2010);
- the War on Terror (2001 to present); and
- the Afghanistan War (2001 to present).

Many American soldiers have been killed in the service of the nation and at the direction of the president. Estimated American casualties (combat and other war-related deaths) include:
- 20,000 during the War of 1812;
- 13,000 during the Mexican-American War;
- 625,000 during the Civil War (North and South);
- 116,000 during World War I;
- 405,000 during World War II;
- 58,000 during the Vietnam War;
- 4,400 during the Iraq War; and
- 1,400 during the Afghanistan War.

Certainly, acting as Commander in Chief is every president's most solemn responsibility.

The three presidents with the greatest prior military experience are George Washington, Ulysses S. Grant, and Dwight Eisenhower. Their military leadership and wartime heroics made each of them both nationally and internationally famous (and deservedly so). Each of them rode his military successes all the way to the presidency. A number of other presidents have also used prior military service to gain public notice and as a stepping stone to high political office.

MILITARY RESPONSIBILITIES

Similar to a president's legislative and executive responsibilities, every president has certain military responsibilities as Commander in Chief that can be classified as constitutional responsibilities and historical and practical responsibilities.

Constitutional Responsibilities

Article II, Section 2, Clause 1 of the Constitution provides:

The President shall be Commander in Chief of the Army and Navy of the United States, and of the Militia of the several States, when called into the actual Service of the United States.

In 1789, this included commanding the U.S. Army and Navy, and the various state militias when called into federal service. This has been interpreted modernly to include all of the other "branches" of the military including the U.S. Air Force, Marine Corps, Coast Guard, and the various state national guards (descendants of the state militias) when called into federal service.

It is probable that the Framers of the Constitution simply used the same terminology as they had during the Revolutionary War and as several of the first state constitutions had already used—Commander in Chief—even though the presidency is in fact a civilian office. The Commander in Chief title confers presidential authority over all military commanders, not an actual military rank. George Washington established an early and important precedent during the Revolutionary War of always deferring to civilian authority over the military while acting as Commander in Chief.

Historical and Practical Responsibilities

Perhaps the most important responsibility of every president is to act as Commander in Chief. George Washington was the Commander in Chief of the Continental Army throughout the Revolutionary War from 1775 to 1783. He remained the highest ranked military officer in the country under the Articles of Confederation through 1789. All of the Founders knew that he would become the first president and Commander in Chief. But even their consummate faith in him did not allow them to trust the creation of a standing army. In their minds, too many wars had occurred in Europe due to massive standing armies to risk keeping a large number of regular troops armed and ready for battle. Following this early peacetime tradition, America had no large and permanent standing army until after World War II.

Sometimes presidents have overseen only a small military establishment during peacetime. For example, the size of the U.S. Army was:
- about 12,000 at the start of the War of 1812;
- about 16,000 at the start of the Civil War;
- about 108,000 at the start of World War I; and
- about 175,000 at the start of World War II.

But the size of the Army grew exponentially after the start of each of those wars, to:
- about 35,000 in the War of 1812;

- about 2.2 million in the Civil War (Union Army only);
- about 4.3 million in World War I; and
- about 16 million in World War II.

Today, the annual military budget is almost $700 billion, and there are almost 1.5 million active duty military personnel and another 850,000 in the reserves. These troop levels are still lower, however, than during the Korean and Vietnam Wars.

As a practical matter, the president's authority over the military is generally exercised through the Department of Defense (formerly the Department of War and the Department of the Navy). With such vast domestic and foreign military operations, and the fact that America is the world's only remaining military superpower able to project massive force into any global theater, it is important for a president to understand the functions and capabilities of the U.S. military. And in an age of nuclear weapons where the president's finger is always "on the button," military experience, knowledge, and discretion become even more important.

Many voters believe that it is important for a president to have served in the military. Low-ranking combat experience is important and honorable, but high-ranking military leadership during times of war is most similar to a president's duties as Commander in Chief. Such experience provides a birds-eye view of the overall military operations and carries with it the burden of having to order solders into engagements where some will be killed. Such high-ranking experience also often involves working closely with foreign leaders and military officers, another very valuable presidential experience.

QUICK FACTS

The following are some quick facts about the presidents' military experience upon taking office.

23   Presidents with wartime service (Washington, Monroe, Jackson, W.H. Harrison, Taylor, Pierce, Lincoln, Grant, Hayes, Garfield, Arthur, B. Harrison, McKinley, T. Roosevelt, Truman, Eisenhower, Kennedy, L. Johnson, Nixon, Ford, Reagan, G.H.W. Bush, and G.W. Bush). Lincoln, Arthur, Reagan, and George W. Bush did not see combat.

10   Presidents who were generals (Washington, Jackson, W.H. Harrison, Taylor, Pierce, Grant, Hayes, Garfield, B. Harrison, and Eisenhower).

16   Presidents with no military service (J. Adams, Jefferson, J.Q. Adams, Van Buren, Tyler, Fillmore, Buchanan, Cleveland, Taft, Wilson, Harding, Coolidge, Hoover, F. Roosevelt, Clinton, and Obama).

METHODOLOGY

The scoring and ranking methodology of the Military Experience resume category is as follows:

1. Any person with any military service (state or federal) receives at least one point, regardless of length of service or combat experience.
2. Any person may receive additional points for: (i) quality of military training; (ii) length of service; (iii) extent of combat experience; (iv) any combat wounds; (v) receipt of medals or commendations; (vi) commanding a significant number of troops; and (vii) overall quality of leadership.
3. No person will be ranked Above Average without significant military leadership experience at a high level.
4. No person will be ranked Great, regardless of length of service or rank, unless he or she demonstrated excellent military leadership for an extended period of time.
5. Any person without actual military training or experience but who was indirectly part of any military operations may receive points depending on the role and extent of leadership.

MILITARY EXPERIENCE SUMMARIES

The following detailed summaries are listed in descending order based on the president's individual score, with earlier presidents appearing first within the same score.

GREAT

GEORGE WASHINGTON   15

George Washington first served as a military officer from 1754 to 1759. He began as second in command—a Lieutenant Colonel—of a 300-

man Virginia Militia regiment. He commanded 160 troops in his first combat experience, presiding over what is now known as a massacre of French soldiers at Jumonville Glen. He also was in command at Fort Necessity when his troops were slaughtered by French and Indian soldiers. In 1755, he became a Captain in the British Army, serving as aide-de-camp to British General Braddock. General Braddock was soon killed during fighting in the Monongahela Valley, and Washington became known for his bravery in rallying the surviving troops and directing an orderly retreat. From 1755 to 1759, he served as Colonel of a newly formed Virginia Militia regiment, commanding up to 1,000 men.

Years later, Washington was unanimously elected Commander in Chief of the Continental Army. He served eight years in the field from 1775 to 1783. He was in direct command of up to 16,000 soldiers, and had twenty-eight generals serve under him. He was not a military genius, but he educated himself by studying military books and by learning from his somewhat frequent mistakes. Prior to 1775, he had no experience deploying artillery or maneuvering cavalry, and had no background in engineering skills to construct defensive positions or conduct sieges. He eventually settled on a defensive "Fabian" strategy of retreating whenever his army's fate was at risk, but he still lost more battles than he won. He was the heart and soul of the Continental Army.

ULYSSES S. GRANT   15

Ulysses S. Grant graduated from West Point Military Academy and was commissioned a Second Lieutenant in the Army, serving from 1843 to 1854. In his early career he tolerated military life but never loved it. After several postings in the southern states, he was sent to Texas and then to Mexico from 1846 to 1848 to serve first under General Zachary Taylor and then under General Winfield Scott during the Mexican-American War. He was Quartermaster in charge of supply train logistics, an organizational position at which he excelled and which served him extremely well later as a top general. He fought in about as many battles as was possible during the war. He remained in the Army for several more years after the war, serving most of those years as a Captain stationed in California. He resigned in 1854.

At the outbreak of the Civil War in 1861, Grant became an Illinois

Militia volunteer and was placed in charge of a local regiment. He was soon promoted to Brigadier General in the regular Union Army. From 1861 to 1865, he found success on the battlefield unparalleled by any other Union commander and was steadily promoted up to a 4-Star General (the first in American history). His major victories over the Confederate Army, many of which were commanded with brilliance, boldness, improvisation, and originality, included the battles at Fort Henry, Fort Donelson, Shiloh, Vicksburg, the Wilderness, Petersburg, and finally Appomattox, where he accepted Confederate General Robert E. Lee's unconditional surrender.

By 1865, Grant was General-in-Chief of the Union Army, responsible for over 500,000 troops. After the Union victory he continued to be General-in-Chief, overseeing the five military districts into which the Southern states were divided during the early years of Reconstruction. In his whole career, Grant never lost a battle or ran from a fight. His victories were due to more than just having a superior number of troops; in fact, his casualty ratio in battle was noticeably lower than General Lee's. He was a military genius who brought strategic clarity and simplicity to warfare. He combined great battlefield flexibility with a willingness to risk defeat in order to win victory. He was the leader who developed the strategic military doctrines of complete war, overwhelming force, and unconditional surrender.

Dwight Eisenhower 15

Dwight Eisenhower was commissioned a Second Lieutenant after graduating from West Point Military Academy, and he served in the Army from 1915 to 1952. He quickly impressed every officer under whom he served with his natural leadership abilities and his intelligence. He was promoted to Captain by 1917 and was training officer candidates when America entered World War I. He never served in Europe during World War I, however. In 1918, he was promoted to command a tank warfare training camp in Pennsylvania. It bothered him that he missed the action in the greatest war in history up to that point. He continued to serve stateside until 1922.

Eisenhower then served in the Panama Canal Zone as the executive officer of the 20th Infantry Brigade under the highly respected General Fox Conner from 1922 to 1925. Service under Conner was great informal training in military history and leadership, an experience he compared to an operational graduate school in military affairs.

Eisenhower graduated first in his class of 275 officers from the Army's Command and General Staff School in 1926, and was sent to the War Department in Washington. For the next two years he attended the Army War College and prepared a history of the U.S. Army in France, traveling to France to study the various terrains and battlegrounds.

Eisenhower returned to Washington from France in 1929 and became a top aide to General Douglas MacArthur, then the Army Chief of Staff. From 1929 to 1935, he served directly under MacArthur in Washington, learning from (and often clashing with) the brilliant, flamboyant, and headstrong General. MacArthur then took him to the Philippines (then an American commonwealth) from 1935 to 1939 to help organize and train a new Philippine military. Because MacArthur's style was wholly big-picture, most of the details were left to Eisenhower. MacArthur considered Eisenhower to be the best officer in the Army, even though he had not yet been promoted beyond Lieutenant Colonel as of 1939.

Eisenhower returned to Washington and served in multiple positions from 1940 to 1941, including as an executive officer in the 15th Infantry Regiment, commander of the 1st Battalion, and chief of staff of the Third Army where he organized the largest military maneuvers prior to America's entry into World War II. In 1941, he was reassigned to be a top aide to the brilliant Army Chief of Staff General George C. Marshall. He greatly impressed Marshall and was given increasing amounts of responsibility, with over 100 officers serving directly under him by mid-1942.

Eisenhower was sent by Marshall to become the top American general in the European Theater in 1942, with his headquarters in London. He interacted with all of the top Allied commanders and many world leaders, getting along very well with most of them. In 1943 he was named Supreme Allied Commander in charge of all Allied military operations in Europe.

During Eisenhower's European command he was responsible for major military operations, including: Operation Torch (the invasion of North Africa and the Mediterranean in 1942); Operation Overlord (the invasion of France in 1944, including D-Day); Operation Market Garden (the invasion of Belgium and the Netherlands in 1944, including the Battle of the Bulge); and ultimately obtaining the unconditional surrender of Germany in May 1945.

Eisenhower returned from Europe in 1945 a world-famous military leader. He then served as Army Chief of Staff from 1945 to 1948 and declined entreaties to run for the presidency in 1948. He continued to be a military advisor to President Truman from 1948 to 1950 while he served as President of Columbia University. He then became the first Supreme Allied Commander in Europe of the newly formed North Atlantic Treaty Organization (NATO) which was attempting to compete against the Soviet Union's huge military build-up at the start of the Cold War.

Eisenhower continued to be NATO's Supreme Allied Commander and the top-ranking American general until 1952 when he resigned his commission during the presidential campaign.

ABOVE AVERAGE

ANDREW JACKSON   12

Andrew Jackson, without any previous military training or experience, was elected Major General of the Tennessee Militia in 1801 and served in that position until 1814. Most of that time was peaceful, so he simply commanded the annual muster of militia and oversaw the sporadic training of militia troops.

When the War of 1812 started, Jackson led approximately 2,500 members of the Tennessee Militia on a long march southward, but they returned after failing to see any action (but to great public fanfare). In late 1813 and 1814, he commanded several engagements between Tennessee Militia and the Creek Indians. They could more accurately be described as massacres (several thousand militia troops against less than 1,000 Indians with a casualty ratio of 10-to-1).

Jackson received a commission as Major General in the U.S. Army in 1814 and became commander of the Southern Military District, giving him the highest active military rank in the country only eighteen months after his first military campaign. In 1814, he negotiated the Indians' cession of the land encompassing much of what is now Georgia and Alabama, and commanded several minor engagements with British troops. On January 8, 1815, he commanded close to 8,000 troops to victory over British troops in the Battle of New Orleans, where the British had close to 2,000 casualties and the Americans had only thirteen casualties. The victory was a massacre due to the poor British approach route and strong American entrenchments.

After the War of 1812 was over, Jackson led approximately 5,000 troops into the Florida territory and succeeded in claiming it from Spain. He resigned his officer's commission in 1820 after having spent approximately three years between 1812 and 1820 in the field commanding troops.

Zachary Taylor   12

Zachary Taylor was commissioned a First Lieutenant in the U.S. Army in 1808 and served from 1808 to 1848. He was promoted to Captain in 1810, Major in 1816, Lieutenant Colonel in 1819, Colonel in 1832, Brigadier General in 1837, and Major General in 1846. He served during the War of 1812, the Indian Wars in Florida from 1837 to 1839, and the Mexican-American War from 1846 to 1848.

Before and during the War of 1812, Taylor participated in several skirmishes with Indian tribes but never saw large-scale combat. During peacetime between 1815 and 1837, he was assigned various commands and focused on building new forts and roads and recruiting troops. From 1837 to 1839, he commanded close to 1,000 troops (regulars and militia) in Florida and fought in the Battle of Lake Okeechobee against the Seminole Indians.

Taylor commanded the U.S. Army of Occupation in Texas and Northern Mexico from 1846 to 1848. He fought in the Battle of Palo Alto, the Battle of Resaca de la Palma, and the Battle of Monterrey (each in 1846), and the Battle of Buena Vista (1847). Many considered the battles to be American victories, but Taylor never defeated the Mexican Army or conquered any Mexican stronghold.

Taylor was not a great military leader. He displayed no killer instinct or tactical or strategic brilliance. His military successes were usually due to having better trained and more capable subordinates. He was generally a competent military leader.

WILLIAM HENRY HARRISON   11

William Henry Harrison was commissioned an Ensign in the U.S. Army and served in the Northwest Territory frontier from 1791 to 1799. He was promoted to Lieutenant in 1793 and served as aide-de-camp to General "Mad" Anthony Wayne. He participated in multiple skirmishes with Indian warriors and was cited for gallantry at the Battle of Fallen Timbers in 1794. He was promoted to Captain in 1797 and commanded Fort Washington near Cincinnati during peacetime until resigning in 1799.

As Governor of the Indiana Territory from 1801 to 1812, Harrison organized and commanded the local militia. This included twice-annual musters where the troops assembled, marched and drilled. In that era militia members supplied their own weapons and training typically took a backseat to drinking and talking politics and farming.

Harrison served as a General before and during the War of 1812 from 1811 to 1814. In 1811, he led approximately 1,000 militia troops to fight against approximately 700 Indian warriors commanded by Chief Tecumseh. On November 7, 1811, at the Battle of Tippecanoe, he commanded what was considered a partial victory where Indian warriors attacked his camp and were repulsed, but he still lost over 200 troops.

Harrison was then commissioned into the U.S. Army and promoted to Brigadier General in 1812 and Major General in 1813. He commanded between 1,000 and 5,000 troops in several battles, including defending the Siege of Fort Meigs in 1812, and winning the Battle of Thames River in 1813, which effectively sealed the Canadian border from British attacks. He resigned his commission in 1814 due to a disagreement with then-Secretary of War John Armstrong. President Madison appeased Harrison by appointing him Peace Commissioner to the Indian tribes from 1814 to 1815.

AVERAGE

JAMES GARFIELD   8

James Garfield helped raise troops for a volunteer Ohio regiment at the outbreak of the Civil War in 1861. The regiment was filled with his former students at Hiram College, and he was rewarded with a commission as a Lieutenant Colonel. He was soon promoted to

Colonel and placed in charge of a brigade (about 1,500 soldiers) in the Army of the Cumberland commanded by General Don Carlos Buell. He participated in several minor battles (including at Paintville and Sandy Valley) where the Union Army recaptured Eastern Kentucky. His contributions were small, but he became a war "hero" in Ohio. He was the commanding officer in charge of Eastern Kentucky for several months during the early days of Reconstruction.

Garfield was promoted to Brigadier General and then Major General in 1862 and 1863, respectively. He eventually became the chief of staff to General William Rosecrans. The largest battle in which he participated was at Chickamauga Creek, where he successfully disassociated himself from a tragically unsuccessful morning fight by riding to "assist" in another part of the battle which was ultimately successful.

Garfield was the quintessential "political general." He made no military decisions without first considering the political impact. He had no formal military training but despised regular Army soldiers and West Point officers, preferring the patriotism of volunteer soldiers. His leadership was unimpressive from a military standpoint.

BENJAMIN HARRISON   8
Benjamin Harrison was commissioned a Second Lieutenant in the Union Army in 1862 and recruited an Indiana volunteer regiment. He was quickly promoted to a Colonel. He and his troops became part of the Army of the Cumberland and later joined General William T. Sherman in the Atlanta Campaign and March to the Sea in 1864. Surprisingly for a small and reserved man, he showed strong leadership abilities and was singled out by his superiors for promotion. He fought in multiple battles, including the Battle of Resaca and the Battle of Golgotha Hill in 1864, where he showed particular valor. He resigned his commission in 1865 with the rank of Brigadier General.

JAMES MONROE   7
James Monroe aborted his studies at the College of William and Mary and enlisted in the Virginia infantry in 1776. He was made a Lieutenant in the Virginia sharpshooters. He fought in the Battle of Long Island and the Battle of Trenton. At the Battle of Trenton, he was severely wounded and was later cited for conspicuous gallantry. When he had

sufficiently healed ten weeks later, he was promoted and served as a Major and aide-de-camp to General Lord Stirling. His service under Lord Stirling broadened his knowledge from frontline tactics to larger battlefield strategies. The last action he saw was at the Battle of Monmouth Courthouse. He resigned his commission in 1778.

Due to his battlefield valor, Monroe was appointed a Lieutenant Colonel by Virginia's legislature in 1779, but was unable to recruit a company of soldiers to lead. In 1780, Governor Jefferson appointed him Colonel and Virginia Military Commissioner to the southern Continental Army then fighting in South Carolina. He saw no more action in the Revolutionary War and returned to Virginia in 1780 to study law.

From 1812 to 1813 and again from 1814 to 1815, Monroe served as Acting Secretary of War. When Washington was attacked and burned by British soldiers in 1814, Monroe took to the battlefield and commanded troops as would an Army general. As Acting Secretary of War—and with a passive President Madison—he was essentially in charge of overseeing America's military. He resigned as acting Secretary of War after the War of 1812 ended in 1815.

RUTHERFORD B. HAYES 7

Rutherford B. Hayes drilled with an Ohio Militia regiment for a short time in 1846, but withdrew due to medical issues and never served in the Mexican-American War.

At the outbreak of the Civil War, Hayes joined the Union Army in 1861 as a Major and was steadily promoted until resigning as a Major General in 1865. He fought in several minor battles including those at South Mountain and Cedar Creek. He was wounded in battle several times and as a result ended up missing the historic and bloody Battle of Antietam.

WILLIAM MCKINLEY 6

William McKinley enlisted in an Ohio volunteer regiment and served from 1861 to 1865. He started out as a Commissary Sergeant and was steadily promoted to Lieutenant and finally to Major. His diligence and earnestness earned him a place on the staff of future President Hayes when Hayes was still a Union general. He fought in many battles, including the Battle of South Mountain, the Battle of Opequhan, the Battle of Fisher's Hill, and the Battle of Cedar Creek.

FRANKLIN ROOSEVELT 6

Franklin Roosevelt never served in any military capacity. However, from 1913 to 1920, and throughout World War I, he was second in command in the Department of the Navy when he served as Assistant Secretary (a civilian office). During this time, he worked closely with military commanders and oversaw American naval operations at home and abroad.

JOHN F. KENNEDY 6

John F. Kennedy joined the U.S. Navy as an Ensign in 1941. For the first year of America's entry into World War II, he served stateside in Washington in the Navy's foreign intelligence office. In 1942, he attended a midshipman's school and became a junior officer on a patrol-torpedo (P-T) boat. He spent seventeen months in the Pacific Theater on patrols near the Solomon Islands. On August 1, 1943, his P-T boat was rammed by a Japanese destroyer (either a freak accident or poor military performance). He managed to lead his crew to safety by swimming several miles while towing two injured men to a small island and then signaling for help. He was singled out as a war hero after the incident and used for public relations purposes to help support the war effort. He took several months to recuperate from his own injuries and then left the Navy in early 1945.

RICHARD NIXON 6

Richard Nixon joined the U.S. Navy in 1942 and was commissioned a Lieutenant. He set sail for the South Pacific in 1943. His role was as an air transport command officer, an important logistical position directing the movements of Marines. He remained just behind the front lines and thus did not see much direct combat. In late 1943 he was promoted to head of the air transport operation, a position which commanded a staff of about twenty men. He became beloved by his troops, and was eventually commended and promoted to Lieutenant Commander. He resigned in early 1946.

GERALD FORD   6

Gerald Ford joined the U.S. Navy as an Ensign in 1942. For the first year, he was a physical fitness specialist who ran conditioning drills for troops stateside. Then he was promoted to Lieutenant, sent to gunnery training, and became a junior officer in charge of an anti-aircraft gun crew aboard the U.S.S. Monterey light aircraft carrier. He also was director of the ship's physical training. He served in the Pacific Theater for a year from 1943 to 1944, during which time he received ten battle stars and a promotion to the reserve rank of Lieutenant Commander.

GEORGE H.W. BUSH   6

George H.W. Bush enlisted in the U.S. Navy as soon as he turned 18 years old in 1942 and became the youngest pilot in the Navy. He flew a torpedo bomber in the Pacific throughout 1944, making many dangerous bombing runs in Wake Island and Chichi Jima. On September 2, 1944, he was shot down and was eventually rescued by a Navy submarine. He returned to his unit and continued flying missions over the Philippines, eventually totaling fifty-eight missions and 126 carrier landings. He mustered out in 1945 after receiving a distinguished flying cross and two gold stars.

BELOW AVERAGE

THEODORE ROOSEVELT   5

Theodore Roosevelt joined the New York National Guard in 1882 as a Second Lieutenant and was later promoted to Captain. In order to serve in the Spanish-American War in Cuba, Roosevelt resigned his position as Assistant Secretary of the Navy in 1898 and was commissioned a Lieutenant Colonel in a volunteer infantry regiment famously called the "Rough Riders." He was officially second in command, but he was the dominant figure in the regiment. He trained with his troops for several months and then led about 500 men in two battles in June and July of 1898—the Battle of Las Guasimas and the Battle of San Juan. He resigned his commission later in 1898 after being promoted to Colonel.

HARRY TRUMAN   5

Harry Truman joined the Missouri National Guard in 1905 during peacetime and served as a reservist until the 1940s. When America entered World War I in 1917, he helped organize a Missouri volunteer artillery regiment and was promoted to First Lieutenant in command of the regiment. He trained for much of 1917, and was sent to the Western Front in France in 1918. He served for about a year in France. For several months he received specialty training in modern artillery. Then, before the armistice in November, he and his regiment joined in several battles (at one point firing poison gas at German troops). He loved the camaraderie of military life, and discovered he was a good leader of men.

JIMMY CARTER   5

Jimmy Carter graduated from the U.S. Naval Academy in 1946 and served his first two years on the U.S.S. Wyoming, an old battleship that was decommissioned in 1948. In 1948, he was accepted to the prestigious submarine service and attended submarine officer training school that summer, graduating third in his class of 52. He was assigned to the U.S.S. Pomfret submarine.

Carter was next assigned to help build nuclear submarines in Connecticut in 1951, first as the engineering officer and later as the executive officer. He worked closely with the renowned submarine commander Captain Hyman Rickover and became known for being very hard-working and leading by example. He resigned from the Navy in 1953 as a full Lieutenant.

FRANKLIN PIERCE   4

Franklin Pierce was a Colonel in the New Hampshire Militia from 1831 to 1847, during which time he commanded a militia unit during the twice-annual muster and drilling of militia troops. He never received any formal military training.

Pierce was commissioned as a Brigadier General in the U.S. Army in 1847. He recruited a regiment of almost 2,500 men and then travelled to Mexico to reinforce General Winfield Scott. He and his men entered into several skirmishes with Mexican troops, but his military accomplishments were minor. He successfully marched his troops 150 miles through Mexico, but early in his first battle—the

Battle of Contreras—he injured himself and had to primarily rely on subordinates to command his troops in subsequent battles. He returned to New Hampshire later in 1847 on a ninety-day leave but chose to remain at home and resigned his commission.

ANDREW JOHNSON   4
Andrew Johnson served as a Colonel in the Tennessee Militia in the 1830s but never saw combat. He served as Military Governor of East Tennessee from 1862 to 1864 during the Civil War. His duties were civilian in nature, but he did coordinate with the Union Army and help recruit Union troops.

CHESTER A. ARTHUR   4
Chester A. Arthur served in the New York Militia from 1861 to 1863 during the first years of the Civil War. Due to his connection to the New York governor, he was appointed Engineer-in-Chief of the New York Militia in 1861 with the rank of Brigadier General. He soon also became acting Assistant Quartermaster General. His responsibilities were to manage the massive quantities of paperwork generated by raising, equipping, housing, and supporting the New York regiments in the Union Army. He negotiated and awarded military contracts and audited military expenditures. He resigned from the New York Militia in 1863 with the rank of Major General. He never fought in a battle or received formal military training.

RONALD REAGAN   3
Ronald Reagan served in the U.S. Army Reserve from 1937 to 1942. In 1942, he was called into active duty. Partially because poor eyesight made him ineligible for combat, he served most of his time in the public relations department of the Army. He ended up touring the country and acting in many pro-American war effort films. He was at the height of his acting career at the time of World War II and was a recognizable public person. He left the Army in 1946 after being promoted to Captain.

GEORGE W. BUSH   3
George W. Bush was commissioned an officer in the Texas Air National Guard in 1968 after graduating from college. He trained for two years

to become a pilot and then flew missions stateside in Convair F-102s (air defense interceptor aircrafts). He was first assigned to Houston and the 147th Fighter Interceptor Group and later to the 187th Tactical Reconnaissance Group of the Alabama Air National Guard. Some have alleged that his attendance during 1973 and 1974 was irregular. He was honorably discharged in November 1974 as a First Lieutenant.

POOR

John Adams   2

John Adams never served as a soldier or commanded troops, but he educated himself by reading military books and performed very effectively as the head of the Second Continental Congress's Board of War from 1776 to 1777. This committee was responsible for managing virtually every part of the Revolutionary War except the fighting (e.g., funding, equipping, recruiting, appointing officers, paying and feeding the soldiers).

Thomas Jefferson   2

Thomas Jefferson never served as a soldier or commanded troops. As Governor of Virginia from 1779 to 1781, he was in command of the Virginia Militia. In that role he failed to meet Virginia's quota of soldiers for the Continental Army; he approved a futile militia expedition to fight Indians which left Virginia vulnerable to British troops who swept in and burned Richmond; and he was forced to flee Monticello on horseback minutes before he would have been captured by British cavalry. His conduct later was investigated by the Virginia General Assembly but he was absolved of any wrongdoing.

Abraham Lincoln   2

Abraham Lincoln served as a Captain in the Illinois Militia in 1832 during the Black Hawk War, but he never saw combat. He mustered out after several months.

William Howard Taft   2

William Howard Taft never served in any military capacity. He did serve as Secretary of War from 1904 to 1908, although he took a largely hands-off approach to the peacetime administration of the War

Department, partially because President Roosevelt was a very hands-on Commander in Chief of the military.

LYNDON JOHNSON   2
Lyndon Johnson enlisted in the U.S. Navy on December 9, 1941, two days after the Japanese bombed Pearl Harbor. He served twelve months in the Navy at the rank of Commander while still serving in Congress. His primary duties were as an inspector and observer of military bases and operations. He was sent on one inspection mission to the South Pacific near Australia, during which time his flight was fired upon for several minutes. Interestingly, he was the only person aboard the flight to be awarded a medal, although he was just an observer, receiving a Silver Star for gallantry from General Douglas MacArthur.

HERBERT HOOVER   2
Herbert Hoover never served in a military capacity. He did, however, live in London and direct the non-military war effort concerning food relief in Belgium and France during World War I. As such, between 1914 and 1917 he frequently negotiated and interacted with many military leaders from Germany, Great Britain, France, and the United States. He also frequently traveled back and forth across military lines.

JAMES K. POLK   1
James K. Polk served as a Colonel in the Tennessee Militia during peacetime in the 1820s and never saw combat.

JAMES MADISON   1
James Madison helped his father procure and distribute arms and supplies to the local militia from 1774 to 1775 as a member of the local Committee of Safety. He was commissioned a Colonel in the Virginia Militia in 1775 and participated in a few drills and marches, but due to his fragile health he never served in the field.

JOHN QUINCY ADAMS   0
John Quincy Adams never served in any military capacity.

MARTIN VAN BUREN   0
Martin Van Buren never served in any military capacity.

JOHN TYLER 0
John Tyler never served in any military capacity.

MILLARD FILLMORE 0
Millard Fillmore never served in any military capacity.

JAMES BUCHANAN 0
James Buchanan never served in any military capacity.

GROVER CLEVELAND 0
Grover Cleveland never served in any military capacity. During the Civil War, he avoided the draft by paying for another man to serve in his place (a completely legal alternative).

WOODROW WILSON 0
Woodrow Wilson never served in any military capacity.

WARREN G. HARDING 0
Warren G. Harding never served in any military capacity.

CALVIN COOLIDGE 0
Calvin Coolidge never served in any military capacity.

BILL CLINTON 0
Bill Clinton never served in any military capacity. He avoided joining an ROTC program while he was a student and also avoided being drafted.

BARACK OBAMA 0
Barack Obama never served in any military capacity.

FOREIGN EXPERIENCE RANKINGS

Rank	Score	President	Historical Ranking
Great	15	John Quincy Adams	Average
		Herbert Hoover	Below Average
		Dwight Eisenhower	Near Great
	14	Richard Nixon	Below Average
	13	John Adams	Above Average
Above Average	12	James Monroe	Above Average
	11	George H.W. Bush	Average
	10	Thomas Jefferson	Near Great
Average	9	Franklin Roosevelt	Great
	8	James Buchanan	Failure
		William H. Taft	Average
	7	John F. Kennedy	Above Average
		Bill Clinton	Average
		Barack Obama	Not Ranked
	6	George Washington	Great
		Theodore Roosevelt	Near Great
Below Average	5	James Madison	Above Average
	4	Jimmy Carter	Below Average
		George W. Bush	Not Ranked
	3	Andrew Jackson	Near Great
		Martin Van Buren	Average
		William H. Harrison	Not Ranked
		Ulysses S. Grant	Below Average
		Harry Truman	Near Great
Poor	2	James K. Polk	Near Great
		Zachary Taylor	Below Average
		James Garfield	Not Ranked
		Woodrow Wilson	Near Great
		Warren G. Harding	Failure
		Calvin Coolidge	Average
	1	Franklin Pierce	Failure
		Rutherford B. Hayes	Average
		Chester A. Arthur	Average
		Lyndon Johnson	Above Average
		Gerald Ford	Below Average
		Ronald Reagan	Near Great
	0	John Tyler	Below Average
		Millard Fillmore	Below Average
		Abraham Lincoln	Great
		Andrew Johnson	Failure
		Grover Cleveland	Above Average
		Benjamin Harrison	Below Average
		William McKinley	Above Average

SEVEN
FOREIGN EXPERIENCE

In foreign affairs we must make up our minds that, whether we wish it or not, we are a great people and must play a great part in the world. It is not open to us to choose whether we will play that great part or not. We have to play it. All we can decide is whether we shall play it well or ill.

— Theodore Roosevelt

We must face the fact that the United States is neither omnipotent nor omniscient; that we are only six percent of the world's population; that we cannot impose our will upon the other ninety-four percent of mankind; that we cannot right every wrong or reverse every adversity; and that therefore there cannot be an American solution to every world problem.

— John F. Kennedy

THE FOURTH RESUME CATEGORY is Foreign Experience. Every president is America's Head of State, meaning he or she is the primary representative of the country at home and abroad. With only a few exceptions or qualifications (such as matters that require congressional funding or Senate consent), the president is the federal official most responsible for foreign relations and foreign policy decisions.

"Foreign policy" is America's formal expression of its national interests and the resulting strategies meant to achieve international goals. For instance, the State Department's official mission is to "create a more secure, democratic, and prosperous world for the benefit of the American people and the international community."

Serving in a foreign relations position or working directly on foreign policy matters provides very valuable foreign experience, but foreign experience does not necessarily mean knowledge of foreign policy. There are multiple ways a candidate can accrue valuable foreign experience without necessarily becoming a foreign policy expert. These include: (i) living, studying, or working abroad; (ii) extensive foreign travel; (iii) learning foreign languages; (iv) interacting frequently with foreigners; and (v) studying or reading about foreign history or foreign cultures.

FOREIGN RESPONSIBILITIES

Every president has certain constitutional, historical, and practical responsibilities related to foreign relations and policy.

Constitutional Responsibilities

Article II, Section 2 of the Constitution provides:

> *[The President] shall have Power, by and with the Advice and Consent of the Senate, to make Treaties, provided two thirds of the Senators present concur; and he shall nominate, and by and with the Advice and Consent of the Senate, shall appoint Ambassadors, other public Ministers and Consuls. . . .*

Under the "Treaties Clause," presidents have the power to negotiate and enter into treaties with foreign countries. But this executive power is limited by the requirement that two-thirds of the Senate concur. The most famous treaties that presidents (often through their secretaries of state, ambassadors, or other foreign commissioners) have negotiated and signed include:

- the Treaty of Paris (1783) which formally ended the Revolutionary War;
- the Louisiana Purchase Treaty (1803) which acquired the Louisiana Territory from France;
- the Adams-Onis Treaty (1819) which included the acquisition of Florida from Spain;
- the Oregon Treaty (1847) which defined the northwest boundary between the United States and Canada;
- the Treaty of Guadalupe Hidalgo (1848) which ended the Mexican-American War;
- the Treaty of Versailles (1919) which formally ended World War I;
- the treaty in 1945 that formed the United Nations;
- the treaty in 1949 that formed the North Atlantic Treaty Organization (NATO); and
- the treaty in 1954 that formed the Southeast Asian Treaty Organization (SEATO).

There are thousands of other treaties which presidents have

negotiated that are related to commerce, human rights, military defense, copyright, labor, and many other topics in which America has an interest.

Related to the Treaties Clause is a president's claimed inherent power to enter into what are called "executive agreements" with foreign nations. Unlike a treaty, an executive agreement does not require congressional approval. Some scholars assert that the Constitution does not permit such agreements because they essentially serve the same function as a treaty and sidestep Senate participation, but such agreements are common and are generally accepted by most politicians and the Supreme Court.

The Appointments Clause found in Article II, Section 2, Clause 2 of the Constitution also vests the president with the power to nominate, and with the advice and consent of the Senate, appoint all American ambassadors, foreign ministers, and consuls. Currently, the United States has sent ambassadors to most of the 191 other nations in the world, with several notable exceptions such as Iran and North Korea.

Historical and Practical Responsibilities

Early presidents set foreign relations precedents that have become long-standing traditions. George Washington immediately assumed the power of the executive branch to negotiate treaties with foreign nations and only asked for Senate approval after the treaty's language had already been finalized. This process easily could have been different by having much greater Senate involvement from the very beginning of treaty negotiations. President Washington also set a precedent by issuing proclamations with respect to foreign policy, the most famous being the Proclamation of Neutrality in 1793 which declared that the United States would not side with either Great Britain or France in any future military conflict (e.g., the Napoleonic Wars). Each of these presidential prerogatives is still followed today.

Some voters may believe that, because there were far fewer sovereign nations in the late eighteenth and nineteenth centuries due to global colonization by the major European powers, American foreign relations were simpler and easier to grasp then than they are today. This is not necessarily true, however. America was by no means a superpower for the first 150 years of its existence, meaning that conducting effective foreign policy may have been even more difficult because it required far more nuance and gentility. Weak nations can rarely be blunt in their foreign policy without risking serious consequences from stronger nations.

Not until the announcement of the Monroe Doctrine in 1823, and even to a certain extent thereafter, was America free from the lingering threat of European nations trying to establish new colonies or dependent territories in the Western Hemisphere. By the early 1900s, America was finally able to play a more significant role on the world stage. And only during and after World War II, with its massive military mobilization and the following economic booms, did America become a world leader and superpower.

The rapid technological advancements in communications and travel that have occurred since the turn of the twentieth century have created a truly global community. There are now almost seven billion people living in the world, and fewer than 5% live in the United States. The United States is one of 192 sovereign countries, only thirty-six of which are considered "industrialized" or "developed." The United States is also the world's only remaining economic and military superpower, a status which essentially forces it to be engaged to some extent in every world conflict and international issue.

With increased global communications, global economics, global military conflicts, and global travel, every president needs to engage with all major foreign issues and develop close working relationships with many foreign leaders. Strict isolationism is no longer a legitimate foreign policy option. Any president who hopes to be a successful national and world leader must be involved in serious foreign policy and manage foreign affairs on a truly global scale.

QUICK FACTS
The following are some quick facts about the presidents' foreign experiences upon taking office.

11   Presidents who never traveled outside of the United States (Madison, Jackson, Tyler, Polk, Fillmore, Lincoln, A. Johnson, Cleveland, B. Harrison, McKinley, and Coolidge).

13   Presidents who have lived outside of the United States for at least one year (J. Adams, Jefferson, Monroe, J.Q. Adams, Buchanan, Grant, Taft, Hoover, Truman, Eisenhower, G.H.W. Bush, Clinton, and Obama).

5   Presidents who served as an ambassador, foreign minister, or foreign commissioner (Adams, Monroe, J.Q. Adams, Van Buren, and Buchanan).

6   Presidents who served as Secretary of State (Jefferson, Madison, Monroe, J.Q. Adams, Van Buren, and Buchanan).

METHODOLOGY

The scoring and ranking methodology for the Foreign Experience resume category is as follows:

1. Any person who knows at least one foreign language (other than Latin or Greek) receives at least one point, with more points added for multiple foreign languages or great fluency.

2. Any person who has traveled outside of the United States receives at least one point, with additional points for: (i) being of a mature age while traveling outside of the United States; (ii) foreign education; (iii) number of countries and continents visited; (iv) total length of foreign travel; and (v) any interaction with foreign leaders.

3. Any person who has served as an ambassador, commissioner, or foreign minister receives one point per year of service.

4. Any person who served as secretary of state receives at least one point for every two years of service (plus one point for every year of service in Executive Experience resume category).

5. Any person who served in another foreign policy-related position (e.g., modern vice presidents, congressional foreign relations committees) will receive additional points depending on the specific position and length of service.

6. No person will be ranked Above Average without extensive foreign travel to multiple countries.

7. No person will be ranked Great without extensive overseas travel and substantial foreign leadership experience over multiple years.

FOREIGN EXPERIENCE SUMMARIES

The following detailed summaries are listed in descending order based on the president's individual score, with earlier presidents appearing first within the same score.

GREAT

JOHN QUINCY ADAMS   15

John Quincy Adams had perhaps the most extensive foreign experience in American political history. He was a youth during the Revolutionary Era and then became a world traveler.

Adams accompanied his father to France in 1778 when he was 11 years old. He returned briefly to America in 1779 and then returned to Europe. He studied and traveled throughout Europe from 1779 through 1785, visiting many countries including France, Spain, Great Britain, Belgium, Holland, Germany, Poland, Russia, Finland, Sweden, and Denmark. He became secretary to the American envoy to Russia in 1781 at 14 years old. In 1783, he became his father's secretary in Great Britain.

In Europe, Adams was exposed to many American and foreign dignitaries, and his social and intellectual maturity advanced rapidly. He soon became comfortable talking on equal terms (and fluently in multiple languages) with some of the world's most influential and knowledgeable people. When he returned to America in 1785 at 17 years old, he was something of an American celebrity who notable politicians (including President Washington and Treasury Secretary Alexander Hamilton) sought out for his opinions on world affairs.

Adams returned to Europe in 1794 at 27 years old. He served first as Minister to The Hague and then as Minister to Prussia from 1794 to 1801. His talent for diplomacy and understanding of European affairs were widely acknowledged. He was recalled in 1801.

Adams once again returned to Europe from 1809 to 1817. He served as Minister to Russia from 1809 to 1814, quickly becoming one of the most respected members of the diplomatic corps. He then traveled in 1814 to Great Britain and then Sweden to be chief American negotiator of the Treaty of Ghent which formally ended the War of 1812. Finally he served as Minister to Great Britain from 1815 to 1817.

He returned to America in 1817 and served as Secretary of State from 1817 to 1824.

Adams was fluent in at least French, Dutch, and German.

HERBERT HOOVER   15

Herbert Hoover had as extensive foreign experience as any American in his generation. From 1897 to 1917 he traveled, worked, and lived all around the world. He was an expert mining engineer by trade and quickly became a talented international business executive.

Hoover's first foreign experience was from 1897 to 1899, living and working to develop mining operations in Australia. He then lived and worked in China from 1899 to 1902. During this five-year stretch, he also traveled throughout Europe and the South Pacific.

For the next five years from 1902 to 1907, Hoover traveled around the world five times, each trip taking several months. He visited dozens of countries in North America, South America, Asia, Europe, Africa, and Australia, establishing and overseeing mining operations.

Hoover lived at least half of each year in London from 1903 to 1917, spending the other months at his home in California or traveling throughout the world. He was by this time an internationally known and respected businessman who interacted with top businessmen and government officials.

During the first half of World War I from 1914 to 1917, Hoover served as the head of the Commission for Relief in Belgium, an international organization responsible for saving millions of starving Belgians during the German occupation. He continued to live in London but traveled unimpeded throughout Europe and frequently across military lines.

DWIGHT EISENHOWER   15

Dwight Eisenhower served many years of his thirty-seven-year military career overseas. He was second in command in the Panama Canal Zone from 1922 to 1925. He was second in command over the Philippine military (an American commonwealth at that time) from 1935 to 1939. He traveled to and studied U.S. Army history in France in 1928. He then served as the top American general and then as Supreme Allied Commander over the entire European Theater from 1942 to 1945, visiting many countries and North Africa. Finally, he returned to Europe from 1951 to 1952 as the first NATO Supreme Allied Commander, visiting eleven European capitals and meeting with the leaders of each country.

Not only did Eisenhower have extensive experience living, working, and fighting in many foreign countries, he also personally interacted with most (if not all) of the world leaders during the 1940s and early 1950s. As Supreme Allied Commander (both during World War II and in NATO), he met frequently with other world leaders and often received great fanfare for his foreign visits. He was one of the leading world figures from 1942 to 1952.

RICHARD NIXON   14
Richard Nixon first traveled outside of the United States as a military officer during World War II, serving in the Pacific Theater from 1943 to 1945.

Nixon then traveled to Great Britain in 1947 as a member of the congressional committee which was considering the Marshall Plan. He met with foreign officials and then joined a subcommittee which visited Greece and Italy.

As Vice President from 1953 to 1961, Nixon was frequently sent by President Eisenhower as a fact-finder and goodwill ambassador to foreign nations all around the world. Most of these trips were between several weeks and several months long. He proved to be a foreign policy wiz. He was always carefully prepared, well-informed, and sensitive to foreign cultures. Over eight years, he visited dozens of countries on six continents, always meeting with top foreign leaders and giving detailed reports and many foreign policy speeches upon his return. He was one of the Eisenhower administration's chief proponents of establishing SEATO as a complement to NATO. During his many travels to Europe, he became a friend and mentee of the French statesman Charles De Gaulle.

Between 1961 and 1968, Nixon continued to be a world traveler similar to when he served as Vice President. He traveled around the world multiple times, visiting dozens of countries and always meeting with foreign leaders and international businessmen. By 1968 he was the Republican Party's most knowledgeable foreign policy expert.

JOHN ADAMS   13

John Adams was born, educated, lived, and worked within the British Empire for over forty years, including during the French and Indian War and the Revolutionary War. Untrained and inexperienced in diplomacy (like every American at that point in history except, perhaps, Benjamin Franklin), he joined Benjamin Franklin in 1778 to 1779 as Commissioner to France, soon becoming fluent in French. He returned to America for several months in late 1779.

Adams returned to France as Minister in early 1780 to negotiate an end to the Revolutionary War with Great Britain. From 1780 to 1782, he was then Minister to the Netherlands, sent to negotiate a considerable loan. From 1782 to 1783, he was a member of the American commission responsible for negotiating the Treaty of Paris which ended the Revolutionary War. Finally from 1783 to 1788, he was Commissioner and later Minister to Great Britain, where he tried to negotiate commercial treaties with Great Britain and other European countries.

Adams served as a Commissioner or Minister in Europe for approximately ten years, visiting multiple European countries and meeting with dozens of Europe's most important leaders. He was fluent in French and Dutch.

ABOVE AVERAGE

JAMES MONROE   12

James Monroe, among the youngest of the Founding generation, lived in the British Empire and was a young adult and soldier during the Revolutionary War. As a soldier and later as a delegate to the Confederation Congress, he became close to the Marquis de Lafayette and other members of the French political delegation, developing a strong affinity for French culture and politics. He also became fluent in French.

Monroe served as Minister to France from 1794 to 1797. This included the transition period for the French Revolution from Robespierre to the Directory and ultimately to Napoleon. Monroe was a successful diplomat who helped release Thomas Paine and Madame Lafayette from French prisons.

Monroe served as Commissioner to France and then as Minister to Great Britain from 1803 to 1807. He was involved in negotiating the $15 million Louisiana Purchase from France in 1803. As Minister to Great Britain, he negotiated a treaty (ultimately rejected by President Jefferson) trying to end the British practice of impressments (seizing American sailors on trade ships and impressing them to serve in the British Navy).

After returning from Europe, Monroe served as Secretary of State from 1811 to 1816.

GEORGE H.W. BUSH   11

George H.W. Bush served as Ambassador to the United Nations from 1971 to 1973. He was praised for his diplomatic abilities which showcased his talent for listening and empathy. The opening of China to the West was the dominant issue during his tenure.

Bush then served as the head of the liaison office in Beijing, China (there was no ambassadorship yet) from 1974 to 1976. He turned down a European ambassadorship for the position in China. Again, his diplomatic abilities received much praise.

Bush took an around-the-world trip in 1978, visiting many countries and meeting with many foreign leaders in preparation for a presidential campaign in 1980. Then, as Vice President from 1981 to 1988, he had significant foreign policy input and responsibilities in the Reagan administration and had much foreign travel.

Bush also served throughout the Pacific Theater during World War II.

THOMAS JEFFERSON   10

Thomas Jefferson, although younger than some of the other Founding Fathers, was born, educated, lived, and worked within the British Empire. This period included the French and Indian War and the Revolutionary War.

During his only trip abroad, Jefferson served as Minister to France from 1784 to 1789, succeeding Benjamin Franklin. He was a thoughtful and hardworking partner with John Adams representing America in Europe. His and Adams's successes were few, resulting in only one $400,000 loan from the Dutch (negotiated primarily by Adams) and obtaining a slight reduction in the whale oil tariff. He also experienced the lead-up to the French Revolution first-hand. Jefferson returned to

America in 1789 with a budding reputation as a respected American statesman and with a strong affection for all things French.

Jefferson also gained foreign experience as Secretary of State from 1790 to 1794 during the French Revolution and the lead-up to the Napoleonic Wars.

Jefferson also knew French, Italian, and Spanish.

AVERAGE

FRANKLIN ROOSEVELT   9

Franklin Roosevelt traveled throughout Europe with his parents eight times (for at least several months each trip) before he was 14 years old. During that time he studied and became fluent in both German and French.

Roosevelt traveled throughout Europe for three months while he was a student at Harvard University, and again toured Europe on an extended honeymoon in 1905, this time for almost four months.

Roosevelt visited Europe again as Assistant Secretary of the Navy in 1918 near the close of World War I. During this time he worked with American military commanders and foreign leaders overseeing the military operations.

JAMES BUCHANAN   8

James Buchanan served as Minister to Russia from 1832 to 1834. He was able to negotiate the first ever reciprocal commercial treaty with Russia. He also toured the European continent, visiting Germany, Belgium, France, Great Britain, and Ireland. He did not know French (the international language of diplomacy at that time), but still proved a competent diplomat.

Buchanan served as Minister to Great Britain from 1853 to 1856. He dealt with several major diplomatic issues including the British seizure of the Bay Islands off the coast of Honduras, Canadian and American fishing rights in the Atlantic Ocean, reciprocal trade with Canada, the attempted purchase of Cuba, and European events surrounding the Crimean War.

Buchanan also served as Secretary of State from 1845 to 1849.

WILLIAM HOWARD TAFT   8

William Howard Taft lived in the Philippines from 1900 to 1904 while serving as President of the Philippine Commission and Governor of the Philippines. During this time he also traveled to Japan, Hong Kong, and Italy to meet with the Pope.

Taft had considerable knowledge and experience in foreign affairs after returning to the United States in 1904 and was occasionally sent by President Roosevelt on foreign trips as a personal envoy. He visited Japan, Cuba, and Panama, and then in 1907 he went on an around-the-world trip, visiting with the leaders of eight more countries.

JOHN F. KENNEDY   7

John F. Kennedy spent four summers in the 1930s (1935, 1937, 1938, and 1939) traveling and studying throughout Europe. Due to his wealth he always traveled in style, and due to his father's high positions in President Roosevelt's administration (which included being Ambassador to Great Britain from 1938 to 1940) he frequently met with top American and foreign officials. His access gave him great exposure to serious foreign policy as a young man. He took another several months in 1941 and traveled throughout South America with his mother and sister.

Kennedy maintained his strong interest in foreign policy and politics as a congressman, writing many articles focused on foreign relations. In 1951, he took two more foreign trips as a congressman. He first traveled throughout Europe for five weeks meeting with foreign leaders and seeing the early effects of the Cold War. He later traveled with his younger brother Robert Kennedy throughout the Middle East and Asia. His travels made him a well-informed member of the Senate Foreign Relations Committee from 1957 to 1960.

BILL CLINTON   7

Bill Clinton lived and studied at Oxford University in Great Britain from 1968 to 1970 on a Rhodes Scholarship. During breaks from studying, he traveled throughout Great Britain and much of Europe, including Wales, Ireland, France, Belgium, Germany, Austria, Poland, Russia, Spain, Czechoslovakia, Norway, and Finland.

Clinton had substantial exposure to foreign policy working as a student clerk on the Senate Foreign Relations Committee headed by Arkansas Senator J. William Fulbright. As an adult, Clinton traveled to multiple foreign countries including Spain, Mexico, and Haiti. He studied German for his foreign language requirement in college.

Barack Obama   7
Barack Obama lived in Jakarta, Indonesia, with his mother from 1967 to 1971. He attended elementary school from first through fourth grade before returning to live with his grandparents in Hawaii. He learned some of the Indonesian language but never became fluent.

Obama visited college friends and family in Asia for three weeks in 1981, traveling to Pakistan and then Indonesia. He visited Indonesia again in 1983. In 1988, he visited Great Britain, France, and Spain for three weeks, and then Kenya for five weeks.

Obama served on the Senate Foreign Relations Committee starting in 2004. In 2005, he traveled to Russia, Ukraine, and Azerbaijan on a fact-finding trip. He also traveled to Africa for two weeks in 2006 (Kenya, Djibouti, Chad, and South Africa) on another fact-finding trip. During the 2008 presidential campaign, he visited and gave speeches in France, Germany, Israel, Jordan, and Great Britain.

George Washington   6
Born in 1732, George Washington lived in and developed his knowledge and beliefs about America's role in the world while it was still part of the British Empire and within the context of the French and Indian War and Revolutionary War. As a military officer, he served with or alongside the British Army and fought against the French and Indians in the 1750s. In the 1770s and 1780s, he fought against the British and received crucial military aid from the French, negotiating directly with French General Rochambeau to successfully plan and win the Battle of Yorktown which effectively won the Revolutionary War.

Washington also had extensive business dealings within the British mercantile system in the 1760s and 1770s. His engagement in international trade gave him personal experience with American economic interests vis-à-vis foreign interests.

Washington never learned a foreign language and only once travelled outside of what became the United States (he accompanied his uncle on a trip to Barbados in 1751).

THEODORE ROOSEVELT 6

Theodore Roosevelt traveled overseas multiple times. As a teenager, he went on two one-year tours with his family. He visited nine European countries from 1869 to 1870. He then visited at least as many European countries from 1872 to 1873, during which time he also visited Northern Africa and the Middle East. Both trips were education-focused. By 1873, he was fluent in both French and German.

Roosevelt then had extended travels through Europe at least twice more during the 1880s. He took a five-month tour in 1881 with his first wife Alice (deceased in 1884). During this trip he climbed the Matterhorn. He then took a four-month tour with his second wife Edith in 1887.

Roosevelt also spent a few months in Cuba in 1898 fighting in the Spanish-American War.

BELOW AVERAGE

JAMES MADISON 5

James Madison lived his youth and early adult life in the British Empire and developed many of his ideas of America's place in the world in that context. He disliked travel, however, and never traveled outside of the United States. He turned down political posts overseas multiple times. Even so, his close relationships with Thomas Jefferson and James Monroe and his other Revolutionary Era experiences gave him a deep animosity towards the British and a deep attachment to the French.

Madison served as Secretary of State from 1801 to 1808 and was a competent diplomat.

JIMMY CARTER 4

Jimmy Carter had several overseas trips as a naval officer. In 1948 he sailed to Hong Kong but had little shore leave, and in 1952, he sailed to the Bahamas but refused to go ashore because the black member of the crew was not invited by the British officers to a reception.

As Governor of Georgia, Carter made multiple trade missions to foreign countries trying to solicit foreign business investment in Georgia. The countries he visited included Mexico, Costa Rica, Brazil, Argentina, Great Britain, Belgium, West Germany, Canada, Japan, and Israel. He also became involved in an international business commission which focused on Western Europe, Japan, and North America. In 1975, he gave a foreign policy speech in Japan near the start of his presidential campaign.

Carter learned Spanish moderately well through studying it in college, practicing it with his wife, and occasionally visiting Latin American countries.

George W. Bush   4
George W. Bush occasionally traveled outside of the United States, particularly to Mexico. As Governor of Texas, he developed good working relationships with Mexican officials (including Mexican president Vicente Fox) while dealing with important border and trade issues.

Bush learned to speak Spanish relatively well, but never became a fluent speaker.

Andrew Jackson   3
Andrew Jackson was a youth during the Revolutionary War, during which he experienced several unpleasant run-ins with British troops. He also lived most of his life on the Tennessee frontier in close proximity to Indian tribes, fighting against Indians and British and French soldiers between 1813 and 1817. He never traveled outside of the United States and never learned a foreign language.

Martin Van Buren   3
Martin Van Buren served as Secretary of State from 1829 to 1831. He traveled to Europe from 1831 to 1832, visiting Great Britain and the Netherlands and socializing with notables in each country. He expected to be Minister to Great Britain, but his nomination was not confirmed by the U.S. Senate.

William Henry Harrison   3
William Henry Harrison was a youth during the Revolutionary War. He served as Minister to Colombia from 1828 to 1829, during which time he once upset Colombian President Simon Bolivar by lecturing him on the problems with dictatorships. Other than fighting in Southern Canada during the War of 1812, this was Harrison's only trip abroad.

ULYSSES S. GRANT   3
Ulysses S. Grant spent two years in Mexico from 1846 to 1848 during the Mexican-American War. Almost a year of that time was during "peacetime," where he grew to love the Mexican people and culture and learned to speak Spanish quite well.

HARRY TRUMAN   3
Harry Truman traveled outside of the United States twice. He served in France from 1918 to 1919 during World War I. Many years later in 1940, he joined others senators on a fact-finding trip to Mexico and several other countries in Central America. He never learned a foreign language.

POOR

JAMES K. POLK   2
James K. Polk never traveled outside of the United States and never learned a foreign language. When he served in the U.S. House of Representatives, he was a member of the Foreign Relations Committee.

ZACHARY TAYLOR   2
Zachary Taylor served in Mexico for about one year from 1846 to 1847 during the Mexican-American War. He never learned a foreign language.

JAMES GARFIELD   2
James Garfield traveled outside of the United States once in 1867 when he and his wife spent seventeen weeks as tourists in Europe, visiting England, Scotland, Belgium, the Netherlands, France, and Italy. He studied German in college and spoke it fairly well.

WOODROW WILSON   2
Woodrow Wilson took several short vacations outside of the United States. He spent a summer hiking in England in 1906 and he spent the winters of 1907 and 1908 in Bermuda. He never learned a foreign language.

WARREN G. HARDING 2

Warren G. Harding traveled outside of the United States several times. He vacationed in Europe in 1907 and 1909 and in Bermuda in 1911. He never took any intellectual interest in foreign culture, however, and never learned a foreign language.

CALVIN COOLIDGE 2

Calvin Coolidge never traveled outside of the United States. He learned French and Italian in college.

FRANKLIN PIERCE 1

Franklin Pierce served for a few months in Mexico in 1847 during the Mexican-American War. He never learned a foreign language.

RUTHERFORD B. HAYES 1

Rutherford B. Hayes never traveled outside of the United States. He spoke German fairly well and also took French lessons.

CHESTER A. ARTHUR 1

Chester A. Arthur never traveled outside of the United States. He studied French in college and spoke and wrote it fairly well.

LYNDON JOHNSON 1

Lyndon Johnson traveled outside of the United States once, participating in an inspection mission to the South Pacific in 1942 during World War II. He never learned a foreign language.

GERALD FORD 1

Gerald Ford spent a little over a year from 1943 to 1944 in the Pacific Theater during World War II. He never learned a foreign language.

RONALD REAGAN 1

Ronald Reagan traveled to Europe at least once while he served as President of the Screen Actors Guild in the 1950s. He never learned a foreign language.

JOHN TYLER 0

John Tyler never traveled outside of the United States and never learned a foreign language.

MILLARD FILLMORE   0
Millard Fillmore never traveled outside of the United States and never learned a foreign language.

ABRAHAM LINCOLN   0
Abraham Lincoln never traveled outside of the United States and never learned a foreign language.

ANDREW JOHNSON   0
Andrew Johnson never traveled outside of the United States and never learned a foreign language.

GROVER CLEVELAND   0
Grover Cleveland never traveled outside of the United States and never learned a foreign language.

BENJAMIN HARRISON   0
Benjamin Harrison never traveled outside of the United States and never learned a foreign language.

WILLIAM MCKINLEY   0
William McKinley never traveled outside of the United States and never learned a foreign language.

Jamin Soderstrom

Rank	Score	President	Historical Ranking
		PRIVATE WORK EXPERIENCE RANKINGS	
Great	10	Abraham Lincoln	Great
		Woodrow Wilson	Near Great
	9	John Adams	Above Average
		Benjamin Harrison	Below Average
		William H. Taft	Average
Above Average	8	Andrew Jackson	Near Great
		Millard Fillmore	Below Average
		Franklin Pierce	Failure
		Grover Cleveland	Above Average
		Herbert Hoover	Below Average
		Ronald Reagan	Near Great
	7	George Washington	Great
		Martin Van Buren	Average
		Chester A. Arthur	Average
		Theodore Roosevelt	Near Great
		Jimmy Carter	Below Average
		George H.W. Bush	Average
		George W. Bush	Not Ranked
Average	6	Thomas Jefferson	Near Great
		John Quincy Adams	Average
		Warren G. Harding	Failure
		Harry Truman	Near Great
		Richard Nixon	Below Average
	5	John Tyler	Below Average
		James Buchanan	Failure
		Andrew Johnson	Failure
		Rutherford B. Hayes	Average
		William McKinley	Above Average
		Barack Obama	Not Ranked
	4	James Monroe	Above Average
		James K. Polk	Near Great
		James Garfield	Not Ranked
		Calvin Coolidge	Average
		Franklin Roosevelt	Great
		Lyndon Johnson	Above Average
		Bill Clinton	Average
Below Average	3	William H. Harrison	Not Ranked
	2	Gerald Ford	Below Average
Poor	1	James Madison	Above Average
		Zachary Taylor	Below Average
		Ulysses S. Grant	Below Average
		Dwight Eisenhower	Near Great
		John F. Kennedy	Above Average

EIGHT
PRIVATE WORK EXPERIENCE

The most important political office is that of the private citizen.
– Louis Brandeis

Experience is not what happens to a man; it is what a man does with what happens to him.
– Aldous Huxley

THE FIFTH RESUME CATEGORY is Private Work Experience. This category covers any work experience outside of the military and most governmental legislative and executive positions.

There are literally thousands of possible private work experiences that a presidential candidate could have prior to becoming president. A short list includes experience as a lawyer, doctor, teacher or professor, business executive, administrative assistant, author, reporter, small business owner, plumber, farmer, truck driver, and judge. The main drawback to having great private work experience is that time spent working in a private position is time not spent in a position focused more exclusively on gaining legislative, executive, military, and foreign experiences.

PRIVATE WORK EXPERIENCE STANDARDS

As previously discussed, the second four resume categories—Private Work Experience, Education/Intellect, Writing Ability, and Public Speaking Ability—are complementary to the "core" presidential responsibilities embodied in the Legislative Experience, Executive Experience, Military Experience, and Foreign Experience resume categories.

Constitutional Standards

No provision in the Constitution places any restrictions on a president's prior private work experiences.

Historical and Practical Standards

Very few presidents have entered full-time government service (including military service) at a young enough age to have avoided working in the "private sector." Most have fallen into a few specific categories that include attorneys and business owners, executives, and managers. Many, but not all, presidents were successful in the private sector before taking office. Some notable exceptions are:

- James Madison, whose entire life revolved around academic study and public service;
- Ulysses S. Grant, who was a complete failure in his work life outside of the military; and
- John F. Kennedy, who wrote several books (with substantial assistance) but who never really worked in a position outside of the military or Congress.

Other presidents were very successful in private practice prior to taking office. They include most notably:

- John Adams, who was a great trial lawyer who successfully defended British soldiers involved in the Boston Massacre in 1770;
- Abraham Lincoln, who was a great trial lawyer who also became a leader of both the Illinois Whig Party and the Illinois Republican Party;
- Benjamin Harrison, who was a brilliant constitutional lawyer;
- Woodrow Wilson, who was a renowned university professor, university president, political science scholar, and author; and
- Herbert Hoover, who was a very talented mining engineer and international businessman.

Some presidents have had private work experiences that have been completely unrelated to presidential responsibilities. A few of the more interesting private work experiences presidents have had include:

- John Quincy Adams, who was a professor of Rhetoric and Oratory at Harvard College;
- Andrew Johnson, who was a tailor;
- Ulysses S. Grant, who was a lumber salesman and rent collector;
- James Garfield, who was a revival era preacher;

- Grover Cleveland, who was a sheriff in the City of Buffalo, New York, and who personally pulled the lever to hang criminals several times;
- Theodore Roosevelt, who was a cattle rancher in the Badlands;
- Warren G. Harding, who was a small town newspaper reporter and publisher;
- Harry Truman, who was the owner of a haberdashery;
- Gerald Ford, who was a boxing and football coach and a male clothing model; and
- Barack Obama, who was a community organizer.

Many of a president's decisions should be informed by his or her private work experience prior to taking office. As an attorney, a president should have learned how to analyze and interpret complicated federal laws. As a business executive, a president should have learned how to delegate responsibilities while remaining ultimately responsible for every decision made by a subordinate. As a small business owner, a president should have learned what the effects of government regulations, tax rates, and financing could have on local economies and consumers. And as a former teacher or professor, a president should have learned how to effectively communicate complicated concepts in simple ways to less-experienced listeners.

Ultimately, some private work experiences will better prepare a candidate to become a successful president than other private work experiences. Working as a waiter, plumber, retail clerk, or car salesperson are respectable private work experiences, but they rarely hone the skills in legal analysis, leadership, mass communications, and negotiation that presidents regularly need. This is why attorneys, business leaders, and teachers tend to excel in high-level government roles and the presidency.

QUICK FACTS
The following are some quick facts about the presidents' private work experiences before taking office.

27   Presidents who were attorneys (J. Adams, Jefferson, Madison, Monroe, J.Q. Adams, Jackson, Van Buren, Tyler, Polk, Fillmore, Pierce, Buchanan, Lincoln, Hayes, Garfield, Arthur, Cleveland, B. Harrison, McKinley, Taft, Wilson, Coolidge, F. Roosevelt, Nixon, Ford, Clinton, and Obama).

8   Presidents who were business owners or executives (excluding farmers) (Jackson, A. Johnson, Harding, Hoover, Truman, Carter, G.H.W. Bush, and G.W. Bush).

11   Presidents who owned working farms or ranches (Washington, J. Adams, Jefferson, Madison, Jackson, W.H. Harrison, Tyler, Taylor, T. Roosevelt, Truman, and Carter).

2   Presidents who were judges (Jackson and Taft).

0   Presidents who were doctors.

METHODOLOGY
The scoring and ranking methodology for the Private Work Experience resume category is as follows:

1.   Some jobs will not be considered for scoring purposes (e.g., jobs performed only as a youth, jobs performed for only a very short period).

2.   Any person who held a non-government job (includes jobs such as city attorney, sheriff, and judge) receives at least one point.

3.   A person will generally receive one point for every three years of private work experience. A person will receive partial credit for years spent divided between private work and governmental work (21 years as a private attorney = 7 points; 21 years as a private attorney practicing only intermittently = 3 or 4 points).

4.   No person will be ranked Above Average without significant private work experience in a role somewhat related to one of the "core" presidential responsibilities (24 years as a business executive or lawyer = 8 points; 24 years as a farmer or plumber = maximum of 6 points regardless of excellence).

5.   No person will be ranked Great, regardless of length of private work experience, unless he or she demonstrated true excellence in his or her chosen field (e.g., renowned author on political subjects, great trial attorney, executive of a large company, acknowledged political party leader).

PRIVATE WORK EXPERIENCE SUMMARIES

The following detailed summaries are listed in descending order based on the president's individual score, with earlier presidents appearing first within the same score.

GREAT

ABRAHAM LINCOLN   10

Abraham Lincoln established a private law practice in Illinois in 1837 after self-studying law for three years. From 1837 to 1860, he became a renowned trial attorney whose argumentative and persuasive talents helped him win thousands of jury trials. Just as impressive were his appellate advocacy skills, which he used when he appeared in approximately 175 cases before the Illinois Supreme Court.

Lincoln was also a leader in the Illinois Whig Party beginning in 1834. He remained a Whig leader even after he stopped serving in the state and federal legislatures. Lincoln left the splintering Whig Party in 1854, and became one of the first leaders in the new Illinois Republican Party. He was the Republican nominee for the U.S. Senate in 1854, committing his delegates to a rival candidate after reaching an electoral stalemate in the state legislature. He was the Republican nominee for the U.S. Senate again in 1858, losing narrowly to Stephen A. Douglas.

WOODROW WILSON   10

Woodrow Wilson was admitted to the Georgia bar in 1882 with the highest exam score of all test takers. He started a small private law practice in Atlanta, but he had few cases to work on and chose to pursue an academic career in 1883.

Wilson became a college professor in 1885 when he was almost finished with the doctoral program at Johns Hopkins University. He taught political science, government, and history, with his specialty being public law and public administration. He taught at Bryn Mawr College from 1885 to 1888, at Wesleyan College from 1888 to 1890, and at Princeton University from 1890 to 1910. He also taught part-time at Johns Hopkins University from 1887 to 1890, and was a frequent lecturer at other colleges and universities across the country. He was an excellent teacher and was frequently selected as the student body's favorite professor.

Wilson served as President of Princeton University from 1902 to 1910. As a university administrator, he was effective, bold, and visionary. He was the person most responsible for turning Princeton into an academic powerhouse in the twentieth century.

Wilson was also a professional author. Throughout his academic career, he published a number of books and hundreds of articles, essays, and speeches.

JOHN ADAMS   9

John Adams taught school in Worcester, Massachusetts, from 1755 to 1758 while he self-studied law at night. He was admitted to the Massachusetts bar in 1759 and started taking cases immediately.

Adams rode the Massachusetts judicial circuit between 1759 and 1777, gaining widespread recognition and respect for his legal brilliance and oral advocacy talents. He quickly became Boston's busiest attorney. For example, in 1772 alone he tried more than 200 cases. His most famous case was his successful defense in 1770 of the British soldiers accused of murder in what is known as the Boston Massacre.

In addition to his legal work, Adams inherited over forty acres of farmland in 1761. He steadily bought and farmed several dozen more acres over his lifetime.

BENJAMIN HARRISON   9

Benjamin Harrison moved to Indianapolis and established a private law practice in 1854. He practiced from 1854 to 1888 and became the preeminent attorney in Indiana. He was a diligent worker with a quick, brilliant analytical mind who matched his mental abilities with equally great speaking abilities.

At various times during his legal career in Indiana, Harrison served as the legal clerk for the federal district court, the Indianapolis city attorney, and the reporter for the Indiana Supreme Court (an elected position which published each of the court's decisions). Over the years he was very busy and successful, arguing at trial two now-famous cases: the *Ex Parte Milligan* case and the Whiskey Ring case.

WILLIAM HOWARD TAFT   9

William Howard Taft practiced law in Cincinnati from 1880 to 1887. His positions included assistant prosecuting attorney from 1881 to 1883 and Collector of Internal Revenue in 1883, in addition to private practice.

Taft finally found his calling as a judge on the Ohio Superior Court. He served on the bench from 1887 to 1890. He loved judicial work and was good at it. He hoped someday to be appointed to the U.S. Supreme Court.

Taft reluctantly gave up his seat on the bench to serve as the U.S. Solicitor General (the federal government's advocate before the Supreme Court) from 1890 to 1892. He did not enjoy it and was not great at making oral arguments before the Supreme Court (though he won 16 of 18 cases).

Taft returned to the bench from 1892 to 1900, this time as an appellate judge on the federal court of appeals based in Cincinnati. He was widely respected and became known for his thorough and analytical legal opinions.

ABOVE AVERAGE

ANDREW JACKSON   8

Andrew Jackson's youth and young adult life was filled mainly with horse racing, gambling, drinking, and cock fighting. When he finally needed a career, he apprenticed in a Tennessee frontier lawyer's office from 1785 to 1787, and then practiced as a lawyer from 1787 to 1798. He knew little law, but was bold, combative, and fairly successful in trying cases which usually concerned fistfights, land disputes, and livestock theft. In addition to his private practice, he became the government prosecutor for Middle Tennessee and judge advocate for the local militia. Jackson then served as a judge on the Superior Court of Tennessee from 1798 to 1804. He heard mainly simple cases and his decisions were described as untechnical, unlearned, ungrammatical, and generally right.

Beginning in 1798 and continuing through 1828, Jackson was also a farmer and merchant, farming several hundred acres of land with the help of more than twenty slaves, and operating a general store, a tavern, a boatyard, a horse racing track, and horse stables. He also speculated in risky land deals. His business was modest and he was often deeply in debt and near financial disaster, but by the 1820s he finally started turning a comfortable profit.

MILLARD FILLMORE   8

Millard Fillmore was born on the western New York frontier and spent much of his early life working on his parents' farm and at a local cloth-dressing mill. Then after receiving a rudimentary legal education as a clerk for a local judge, he established the only private law practice in the small town of East Aurora, New York, in 1823. He practiced there from 1823 to 1830 before moving to Buffalo. He joined a successful law partnership in Buffalo in 1830, and then established a new law firm in 1833 where he was the senior partner. By 1848, his firm had become the preeminent Buffalo law firm.

Fillmore was one of the New York leaders of the short-lived Anti-Mason Party from 1831 to 1834. He then helped found the Whig Party in 1834. While he was a Whig leader in New York, he remained a marginal figure in the national Whig Party.

FRANKLIN PIERCE   8

Franklin Pierce established a private law practice in New Hampshire in 1827 with the help of his father who was then serving as the state's governor. He became a very successful trial lawyer between 1827 and 1852, but sometimes practiced only intermittently between periods of public service. He was able to focus most of his energies on his trial practice during the decade from 1842 to 1852. His oral advocacy skills became famous in New Hampshire.

In addition to his law practice, Pierce was a leader in the New Hampshire Democratic Party beginning in 1829. His father was a famous New Hampshire war hero and politician, and Pierce followed in his footsteps. He was the chairman of the New Hampshire Democratic Committee from 1842 to 1845, and afterwards remained the most influential Democrat in the state.

GROVER CLEVELAND   8

Grover Cleveland was forced to quit school as a teenager in the early 1850s to help support his family. He worked for a time on the boats and barges passing through the Erie Canal, and then for a year as a teacher at the Institute for the Blind in New York City.

Cleveland joined a private law practice in 1860, and became a successful and well-respected Buffalo attorney from 1860 to 1882. He was a very good trial attorney who was known for his prodigious work ethic and scrupulous honesty.

Cleveland had several short stints outside of private law practice. From 1862 to 1865, he was Buffalo's assistant district attorney. Then from 1871 to 1873, he was Buffalo's elected sheriff. He distinguished himself in both positions. He refused to delegate important official responsibilities, to the point that several times he even sprang the trap himself for public hangings. He became a beloved and respected local attorney and official, even as a Democrat in a heavily Republican county.

HERBERT HOOVER   8

Herbert Hoover was a talented mining engineer who became a famous international businessman. From 1895 to 1914, he traveled and lived throughout the world, establishing and overseeing mining operations and business dealings on six continents. He frequently negotiated and interacted with top American and foreign officials and other top businessmen.

Hoover's management style was pure technocrat, focusing on efficiency, standardization, entrepreneurship, and innovation. He was an individualist who believed the market, the private sector, and simple hard work could improve people's lives, and that the government could assist in focusing resources and in times of crisis.

RONALD REAGAN   8

Ronald Reagan was a radio broadcaster in Iowa from 1932 to 1937. He was a sports announcer who covered the Chicago area teams and the Big Ten conference. More often than not he had to dramatically describe (i.e., make up) details of games he never watched in person.

Reagan moved to California in 1937 and soon became a successful Hollywood actor. For the next five years he starred or co-starred in dozens of popular movies. Between 1937 and 1957 he appeared in over fifty films. After he left the Army in 1946 he tried to reclaim success in Hollywood, but his career was winding down. He dabbled with becoming a Las Vegas nightclub host, but moved to television instead.

Reagan was the host of the *General Electric Theater* television program from 1954 to 1962, giving weekly pitches for General Electric products and sometimes acting on the program. During those eight years he was also a vice president for General Electric, touring many of its facilities each year giving speeches.

In the 1940s and 1950s, Reagan served on the board of directors of the Screen Actors Guild (1941, 1946-1952, 1959), serving as chairman for several years and testifying before the House Un-American Activities Committee in 1947 during the "Red Scare" over communism.

GEORGE WASHINGTON 7

George Washington married Martha Dandridge Custis in 1759 and became one of Virginia's wealthiest landowners. He was an obsessive manager of his personal business and economic interests. Under his watchful eye, his Mount Vernon estate doubled in size between 1759 and 1775, and his overall property holdings eventually included close to 20,000 acres of land. Over 200 slaves worked his properties.

In the 1760s, Washington changed his primary cash crop from tobacco to wheat and built a flour mill. He also built boats that he used for commercial fishing (herring) and to ship his goods to local markets and markets in the Caribbean and Europe. His properties and business interests never brought in more than a marginal profit, but compared to many of his contemporaries in the Virginia planter community he was an assiduous and able businessman and remained wealthy his entire life.

MARTIN VAN BUREN 7

Martin Van Buren was admitted to the New York bar in 1803 and soon started a private law practice in the Hudson River Valley near Albany. He practiced from 1803 to 1812 and became successful, making lots of money and gaining a good professional reputation. He mostly represented small clients against large land and business interests. He practiced only intermittently after 1812 due to his various public service positions.

Van Buren's other profession was politics. He was a sharp student of politics ever since he was a teenager listening to political talk in his father's tavern. He travelled to New York City in 1801 and became an acolyte of the charismatic and scandalous Aaron Burr. He befriended and socialized with politicians and was constantly active in New York politics and elections until he became a professional politician himself in 1812.

Over time Van Buren became a political visionary, creating state and national party structures and processes that were not dependent on individual politicians' personalities. He was a brilliant political organizer, forming local committees, political networks, party caucuses, and nominating conventions that are still in use today. Between 1826 and 1828, he was the primary creator of the political party now known as the Democratic Party (Andrew Jackson was its figurehead).

Van Buren was the person most responsible for America's enduring political party processes and structures (e.g., party discipline, statewide committees, communication networks, platforms, and message control).

CHESTER A. ARTHUR   7

Chester A. Arthur taught at, and eventually became the principal of, a local Vermont school from 1849 to 1853.

Arthur then practiced law in New York City from 1854 to 1871. He was moderately successful, but was never considered an outstanding lawyer. He dealt mostly with transactional legal work (e.g., contract negotiation and business deals), and only rarely performed any trial work. In 1869, he was appointed counsel to the New York City Tax Commission due to his connections to Senator Roscoe Conkling, but he resigned in 1870. After being suspended as Collector of the New York Customhouse in 1877, he returned to private law practice and remained a moderately successful attorney from 1877 to 1880.

Starting in the 1850s, Arthur was a New York Republican Party loyalist who held several different state and local positions. He was sometimes a party leader (e.g., member of the New York Republican Central Committee), but it was generally understood that he held these positions only with the consent of his political mentor and patron, the powerful Senator Conkling.

THEODORE ROOSEVELT   7

Theodore Roosevelt was a widely published and highly respected professional author from 1880 to 1900. During that time he wrote a dozen books and published hundreds of essays and articles.

Roosevelt was also a professional rancher in the Badlands (now part of North Dakota) from 1884 to 1886. He wrote extensively about his big game hunting and other experiences during these years, but ultimately his ranch was not a financial success.

JIMMY CARTER   7

Jimmy Carter took over the family peanut farming business in Plains, Georgia, in 1953 after his father died. By 1956 the business was becoming more successful. He implemented modern technology into the peanut farming operations, which included a shelling plant, a drying system, additional storage capacity, and a state-of-the-art cotton gin. He was a fairly wealthy man by 1964 when his interests became divided between his small business ownership and state and national politics.

Between 1953 and 1976, Carter was also a very involved civic leader in Plains, and was increasingly involved in the state Lions Club activities. He used his various leadership positions as stepping stones to higher office in the 1960s and 1970s. Most of his activities between 1966 and 1970 were focused on a statewide campaign for the Georgia governorship, and most of his time in 1975 and 1976 was focused on a national campaign for the presidency.

GEORGE H.W. BUSH   7

George H.W. Bush grew up in a prominent, wealthy family (his father was a member of the U.S. Senate), but followed a family tradition and moved to Midland, Texas, in 1949 to make it on his own instead of taking a job on Wall Street. He took a job with an oil field supply company—Dresser Industries—which was owned by a family friend. In 1950, he raised several hundred thousand dollars and formed his own oil company, Bush-Overbey Oil Development Company. His company later joined with other partners and became Zapata Petroleum in 1953. Bush bought the entire company in the late 1950s, making his first million dollars, and then moved to Houston. He was the top executive at Zapata until he became a full-time politician in 1967, and maintained ownership thereafter.

Bush was active in Republican politics and became chairman of the Harris County Republican Party from 1963 to 1967. Several years later, he served as chairman of the Republican National Committee from 1973 to 1974.

GEORGE W. BUSH   7

George W. Bush moved to Midland, Texas, in 1975 after graduating from Harvard Business School and began working in the oil industry. He soon started a petroleum and energy company called Arbusto Energy in 1977, and worked as its top executive. In 1982, the company's name changed to Bush Exploration. In 1984, the company merged with Spectrum 7 Energy Corporation, and Bush became the chairman and CEO of Spectrum 7. Spectrum 7 was bought by Harken Energy in 1986, and Bush became a member of the Harken board of directors.

Bush worked on his father's presidential campaign full-time from 1987 to 1988. His formal roles were as a political adviser, media liaison, and speechwriter.

Bush returned to Texas after the 1988 election and headed a group of investors that bought the struggling Texas Rangers baseball team. Bush became the managing partner and helped turn the team into a profitable enterprise. He managed operations until 1994 when he decided to run for the Texas governorship.

Bush also had significant access to and interaction with his father when his father was Vice President and President between 1981 and 1993, acting at times as both an informal and formal political adviser.

AVERAGE

THOMAS JEFFERSON   6

Thomas Jefferson was admitted to the Virginia bar in 1767 and practiced from 1767 to 1769. He gained a reputation for being a good researcher but never distinguished himself in trials. He gave up his legal practice in 1769.

Jefferson was born wealthy and doubled his properties in 1772 when he married Martha Ales Skelton. His properties included nearly

11,000 acres spread throughout Virginia and worked by over 200 slaves. Farming was never profitable for him, however, and he was perpetually deeply in debt. Unlike George Washington, he never focused great time or energy on managing his properties like a businessman, preferring his inventive and scholarly activities. He was never able to fully acknowledge his overwhelming debt and lost much of what he owned to creditors upon his death.

For a decade beginning in the early 1790s, Jefferson became the acknowledged (though behind-the-scenes) leader of the nascent political movement that ultimately became the Democratic Republican Party. He collaborated with James Madison and James Monroe (both younger, talented Virginian politicians) to lead the opposition to the Federalist Party and President Washington's administration.

JOHN QUINCY ADAMS   6

John Quincy Adams begrudgingly studied law at his parents' insistence, and then practiced law in Massachusetts from 1790 to 1794 and from 1801 to 1809 (intermittently). His practice was modest, and he never loved being an attorney.

More in line with his particular interests, Adams became the Boylston Professor of Rhetoric and Oratory at Harvard College from 1805 to 1809. He loved being a scholar. His formal lectures were rigorously prepared and well-received by the students and other community members who often attended. In 1809 he published, at his students' request, a two-volume book which included the thirty-six lectures he was unable to deliver because he returned to Europe as Minister to Russia.

WARREN G. HARDING   6

Warren G. Harding worked several jobs between 1882 and 1884, including as a schoolteacher and an insurance agent. In 1884, he finally found his calling as a local newspaper man.

Harding started working as a local reporter for the Marion *Star* newspaper in 1884. At that time, Marion, Ohio, had several thousand residents and the *Star* had several hundred weekly subscriptions. He soon joined with a friend and bought the newspaper, making himself a reporter, editor, and owner/publisher. From 1884 to 1894, he was a hands-on reporter and businessman. He became more hands-off in his business management and reporting starting around 1894, leaving most of the daily reporting, editing, and business work to others. He continued to write occasional editorials and make some business decisions, but after 1894 he operated more as a passive business owner. Over the years, the *Star* grew to several thousand daily subscriptions. He still owned the *Star* in 1920.

HARRY TRUMAN   6

Harry Truman worked several jobs between 1901 and 1906, including as a mailroom clerk at a local newspaper, a timekeeper for road construction crews, and a teller at two different Kansas City banks. Then, from 1906 to 1917, family finances forced Truman to return to his small hometown and work on and manage the family farm. The 1910s were the golden age of farming in America, so it was both a financially stable and back-breaking occupation.

After returning from France in 1919, Truman moved to Kansas City and partnered with an army buddy to establish a small haberdashery selling hats, ties, shirts, belts, etc. Truman was a popular small businessman, but business suffered and the haberdashery failed in 1922.

RICHARD NIXON   6

Richard Nixon grew up working in his father's general store in Yorba Linda, California, waking up before dawn most mornings to go buy fresh produce at the local farmers' markets before going to school. He then returned to work after school.

Nixon passed the California bar exam in 1937 and became an associate at Wingert & Bewley, a private law firm in Whittier. From 1937 to 1942, he became one of the area's most skilled trial lawyers. He became a full partner at the firm in 1939, and later opened a new branch in the nearby town of La Habra. He stopped practicing during World War II and while he served in political office.

After losing the 1960 election, Nixon returned to Los Angeles and joined the law firm Adams, Duque & Hezeltine. After losing the California gubernatorial election in 1962, he moved to New York City and became the named partner at an established law firm that handled the business for Warner-Lambert, a large pharmaceutical company. He was a very hard worker and a very good lawyer, and due to his constant foreign travel and foreign relationships, the firm's international business boomed. He proved to be an excellent rainmaker, attracting a significant amount of domestic and international legal business to his firm.

JOHN TYLER   5
John Tyler established a private law practice in Virginia in 1809 and quickly became successful due to his speaking talent and persuasive jury arguments. His law practice suffered over the thirty years he was an attorney, however, due to his many public service positions.

Tyler also owned a 631-acre farm in Virginia on which approximately two dozen slaves worked. The farm was never particularly profitable, and due to his other duties as an attorney and a politician, his wife Letitia was generally responsible for overseeing the management of the farming operations.

JAMES BUCHANAN   5
James Buchanan established a private law practice in Lancaster, Pennsylvania, in 1812. He had a rough time at first, but after a few years he became more confident and more successful. He was always a thorough researcher and competent advocate, but was never a great trial lawyer. He practiced law intermittently from 1812 to 1856, balancing his private practice with his numerous public service positions.

ANDREW JOHNSON   5
Andrew Johnson was a completely self-made man. After apprenticing for several years for a North Carolina tailor, he moved to Tennessee and found employment as a journeyman tailor in 1824. He developed a reputation for making handsome clothes, and he eventually established a successful tailor business. By 1841, he had become moderately wealthy and had taken his business revenue and invested in some real estate and a small farm for his parents. He was eventually able to acquire eight or nine slaves.

RUTHERFORD B. HAYES   5
Rutherford B. Hayes established a private law practice in Sandusky, Ohio, in 1845. His practice remained small and unimpressive until he used a relative's influence to partner with one of the most respected attorneys in the community.

Hayes moved to Cincinnati in 1850 and soon became a well-known and well-respected attorney. From 1850 to 1861, he was known as a lawyer's lawyer—other attorneys turned to him for help on a case and for careful research. He also stood out as a sober lawyer in a legal community where many of his colleagues drank alcohol to help themselves prepare for arguing before judges and juries. From 1859 to 1861, Hayes also served as the Cincinnati city attorney.

WILLIAM MCKINLEY   5

William McKinley taught at a small Ohio school from 1860 to 1861. Then, after serving in the Civil War and studying law for two years, he was admitted to the Ohio bar and joined a private law practice in Canton, Ohio. He practiced law from 1867 to 1891, but only intermittently during the fourteen years he served in Congress.

As a lawyer, McKinley was a hard worker, diligent in his preparation and methodical in his performance in court. His friends believed he could have been one of the leading lawyers in the state had he focused entirely on the law and not devoted a substantial amount of time to public service.

BARACK OBAMA   5

Barack Obama worked as a researcher and report writer for the financial services division of Business International Corporation in New York City from 1983 to 1985. He then worked as a community organizer at New York Public Interest Research Group for several months in 1985 helping mobilize students in New York City to become politically involved on different issues. He later moved to Chicago and continued his community organizing work as director of the Developing Communities Project from 1985 to 1988.

After law school, Obama moved back to Chicago and worked in multiple positions. He started writing a book which became his memoir *Dreams From My Father* (1995). He became an associate attorney at the civil rights law firm Davis, Miner, Barnhill & Galland in Chicago from 1993 to 1996, and then he became "of counsel" at the firm from 1996 to 2004. His focus was primarily writing memos, motions, and briefs. He also taught a constitutional law seminar as a lecturer from 1992 to 1996, and then as a senior lecturer from 1996 to 2004 (both part-time positions). He was well-liked in the classroom but never published any formal legal scholarship.

From 1991 to 2004, Obama's professional attention was constantly divided between law firm work, teaching, book writing, and state politics, making his work at each of his positions part-time.

JAMES MONROE   4

James Monroe grew up as a relatively poor Virginia farmer who inherited 800 acres when his parents died when he was a teenager.

After studying law under then-Governor Thomas Jefferson and being admitted to the Virginia bar in 1782, Monroe established a private law practice in 1784 and was also appointed the city attorney in Fredericksburg. While he served in the U.S. Senate, he was also admitted to the Supreme Court bar in 1791. Due to his frequent public service, he practiced law only intermittently from 1786 to 1811.

JAMES K. POLK   4

James K. Polk established a private law practice in Tennessee in 1820. He was a good attorney, but he practiced only intermittently from 1820 to 1844 due to his numerous public service positions.

JAMES GARFIELD   4

James Garfield worked on a canal ship, as a school teacher, and as a carpenter prior to 1851. Discovering his great speaking abilities, he became a renowned Revival Era preacher in the Disciples of Christ congregations in Ohio from 1853 to 1954 and again from 1856 to 1859. He preached only occasionally (as opposed to multiple times every week) after 1859.

Garfield became a professor at and president of the Eclectic School from 1857 to 1861. He was a diligent worker, teaching up to six classes each day in addition to other administrative duties. He started the school's movement away from offering a purely classical education by incorporating more history, science, government, modern languages (as opposed to Latin and Greek), and physical education into the curriculum.

After spending several years casually self-studying the law, Garfield became a practicing attorney in 1865. His first case happened to be handling the appeal in the famous *Ex Parte Milligan* case before the U.S.

Supreme Court. He argued occasional cases throughout the 1860s and 1870s but never became a full-time practicing attorney.

CALVIN COOLIDGE   4

Calvin Coolidge was admitted to the Massachusetts bar in 1897 and established a small private law practice in Northampton, Massachusetts. He practiced law from 1897 to 1916, but only intermittently during his many periods of public service. He proved to be a good local attorney, respected for his diligence, integrity, and straightforwardness. He also served as the Northampton city solicitor from 1900 to 1902, as counsel and vice president of a small local bank beginning in 1899, and as clerk of courts beginning in 1903.

Coolidge was also active in local Republican politics beginning in 1896. He eventually became a local party leader, serving as chairman of the Republican City Committee beginning in 1904.

FRANKLIN ROOSEVELT   4

Franklin Roosevelt was an unsalaried apprentice at Carter, Ledyard, & Milburn, a prestigious Wall Street law firm, from 1907 to 1910. He was well-liked and a reasonably good worker, but had no love for the practice of law. He worked primarily on small cases and joined the firm's admiralty practice. He left in 1910 to run for state office.

After losing the election for the vice presidency in 1920, Roosevelt became a vice president at Fidelity & Deposit Company of Maryland, a national surety bonding company. From 1921 to 1928, he was a liaison with Wall Street working primarily on client development.

In August 1921, Roosevelt was struck with Poliomyelitis, a debilitating disease that left his legs paralyzed. He spent the next twelve months recuperating. He returned to work part-time from 1922 to 1928. He split his time between working at Fidelity, working as the named partner at a New York City law firm which he founded, and recuperating at his home in Warm Springs, Georgia, or on a yacht off the coast of Florida. During this time he remained very involved in state and national politics, serving as the campaign chairman for Democratic presidential nominee Al Smith in 1924.

LYNDON JOHNSON   4

Lyndon Johnson worked in multiple jobs from 1924 to 1927 after graduating from high school, including picking grapes, washing dishes, fixing cars, and working on road crews. During and after college, he taught school for two years, first from 1928 to 1929 in the rural Texas town of Cotulla, and then from 1930 to 1931 in Houston. In 1930, he also successfully managed a local candidate's campaign for the Texas Senate.

Johnson and his wife purchased the only radio station covering Austin, Texas, in 1943. They soon turned it into a very profitable enterprise and became multi-millionaires. He used his money and political connections to make many more successful investments, and by 1960 he had become one of the richest members of Congress.

BILL CLINTON   4

Bill Clinton worked on multiple political campaigns before becoming a professional politician himself, including for Arkansas politician Frank Holt in 1966, for Arkansas Senator J. William Fulbright in 1968, for Connecticut politician Joe Duffey in 1970, for Senator George McGovern's presidential campaign in 1972 in Texas, and for Jimmy Carter's presidential campaign in 1976 in Arkansas.

Clinton started teaching legal classes for law enforcement personnel part-time in 1971 while still a student at Yale Law School. After graduation, he became a full-time law professor at University of Arkansas Law School from 1973 to 1976. He was a good classroom teacher but was fairly disorganized and had little interest in legal scholarship. He taught a number of classes including agency and partnership, trade regulation, antitrust, and constitutional law. He also taught criminal justice and law enforcement classes part-time at the Little Rock campus.

Clinton served as "of counsel" at the Little Rock law firm Wright, Lindsey & Jennings from 1981 to 1983 between terms as Governor of Arkansas.

BELOW AVERAGE

WILLIAM HENRY HARRISON   **3**

William Henry Harrison's father was a wealthy Virginia land owner and signer of the Declaration of Independence. Harrison, however, never received a large inheritance and was forced to quit college and join the military. In between his various public offices, he often faced financial distress. Beginning around 1800 he owned farmland in Indiana and Ohio and was sometimes able to make a decent living as a farmer and public official. He also entered into occasional business dealings and speculative land transactions, none of which was financially successful. Needing money to help support his family and the families of two of his sons, he served as clerk of court in Cincinnati from 1834 to 1840.

GERALD FORD   **2**

Gerald Ford was a boxing coach and assistant football coach at Yale University from 1935 to 1938. After law school graduation in 1941, he went to New York City for a few months to be a clothing model. In 1942, he moved back to Grand Rapids, Michigan, to begin a legal career. He soon joined the U.S. Navy.

After World War II, Ford returned to Grand Rapids and started working at a well-regarded local law firm. He practiced law from 1946 to 1948. On the side he became active in the local Republican Party and gained notice for work as an advocate for war veterans.

POOR

JAMES MADISON   **1**

James Madison never had a private career outside of his constant study of government and public affairs. He considered becoming an attorney, but only studied law intermittently to augment his political knowledge. After devoting his life to study and government, he returned to his father's Montpellier plantation in Virginia in 1797 and became the family patriarch and farmer. He generally oversaw the management of 10,000 acres and over 100 slaves.

ZACHARY TAYLOR 1

Zachary Taylor never had a career outside of the military. He did, however, start acquiring farm land beginning in 1810 and by the 1840s had accumulated over 10,000 acres worked by slaves. He never worked the land himself, however, and was a completely hands-off manager of his properties. He also made stock investments which earned him a net worth of over $1 million (modernly) by 1848.

ULYSSES S. GRANT 1

Ulysses S. Grant spent seven years outside of the military. From 1854 to 1861, he tried a number of common occupations including farming, real estate sales and rent collection, lumber sales, and other small business ventures. He failed at each of them. For most of those years he stared poverty in the face. From 1860 to 1861, he ended up working for his younger brothers as a low-level clerk in his father's business.

DWIGHT EISENHOWER 1

Dwight Eisenhower served as President of Columbia University in New York City from 1948 to 1950. He disliked having to work in academia with professors, however, who he believed preferred discussion over decision-making. He resigned in 1950 to head NATO.

JOHN F. KENNEDY 1

John F. Kennedy was interested in becoming a foreign news correspondent if politics did not work out. In 1945, he spent a month covering the United Nations convention in San Francisco for the Hearst newspapers. He also liked to write and published two books (with significant help) which became bestsellers. He never had a career outside of politics or the military.

EDUCATION/INTELLECT RANKINGS			
Rank	**Score**	**President**	**Historical Ranking**
Great	10	John Adams	Above Average
		Thomas Jefferson	Near Great
		James Madison	Above Average
		John Quincy Adams	Average
		Abraham Lincoln	Great
		Theodore Roosevelt	Near Great
	9	Benjamin Harrison	Below Average
		Woodrow Wilson	Near Great
		Bill Clinton	Average
Above Average	8	James K. Polk	Near Great
		Rutherford B. Hayes	Average
		William H. Taft	Average
		Dwight Eisenhower	Near Great
		Richard Nixon	Below Average
		Barack Obama	Not Ranked
	7	George Washington	Great
		John Tyler	Below Average
		Franklin Pierce	Failure
		James Buchanan	Failure
		Calvin Coolidge	Average
		Franklin Roosevelt	Great
		John F. Kennedy	Above Average
		Gerald Ford	Below Average
		Jimmy Carter	Below Average
		George W. Bush	Not Ranked
Average	6	James Monroe	Above Average
		George H.W. Bush	Average
	5	Ulysses S. Grant	Below Average
		James Garfield	Not Ranked
		Chester A. Arthur	Average
		Herbert Hoover	Below Average
		Harry Truman	Near Great
		Lyndon Johnson	Above Average
		Ronald Reagan	Near Great
	4	Martin Van Buren	Average
		William H. Harrison	Not Ranked
		Grover Cleveland	Above Average
		William McKinley	Above Average
Below Average	3	Millard Fillmore	Below Average
		Warren G. Harding	Failure
	2	Andrew Jackson	Near Great
		Andrew Johnson	Failure
Poor	1	Zachary Taylor	Below Average

NINE
EDUCATION/INTELLECT

The principal goal of education is to create men who are capable of doing new things, not simply of repeating what other generations have done.

— Jean Piaget

He was so learned that he could name a horse in nine languages; so ignorant that he bought a cow to ride on.

— Benjamin Franklin

It is the mark of an educated mind to be able to entertain a thought without accepting it.

— Aristotle

THE SIXTH RESUME CATEGORY is Education/Intellect. This category is focused on several things: the quality of a candidate's formal and informal education; the breadth of a candidate's personal reading; and a candidate's overall intelligence and intellectual capacity.

Most American voters prefer for the president to have an exceptional mind and a great education. But many voters would at the same time refuse to vote for "the smartest person in the room" if it would risk sacrificing another equally qualified presidential candidate's good judgment and other valuable experiences. A few voters may even prefer (or at least be more comfortable with) a candidate who is plainspoken, simple, and more "average" rather than a candidate who is intellectually sophisticated and more "elitist."

There have been many highly intelligent men and women in American history. Happily, a surprising number have risen in the political ranks to the presidency. At the same time, there have also been a surprising number of men and women with average or below average intellects who have risen to political power and even to the presidency.

EDUCATION/INTELLECT STANDARDS

Constitutional Standards

There are no provisions in the Constitution which establish educational or intellectual requirements for presidents. Such requirements would have been anathema to the core American principles of self-reliance, individual merit, and democratic selection. Moreover, there were comparatively few schools in the eighteenth century, so such a requirement would not have made practical sense.

Historical and Practical Standards

George Washington was less formally educated than many of his famous contemporaries. He had the formal equivalent of a grade school education while many of the Founding Fathers had college educations and were well-educated and brilliant men (e.g., John Adams, Thomas Jefferson, Alexander Hamilton, and James Madison). Even Benjamin Franklin, who himself had little formal education, was a naturally brilliant man. But even among all of these men, Washington stood out as the unanimous choice for becoming the first American president.

One thing many people fail to remember (or have never learned) is that Washington received an excellent informal education in government, political theory, and policy. He had the best personal "tutors" any man could have asked for on the many issues facing America. Throughout the 1770s and 1780s, he had extensive correspondence with all of the important Founding Fathers, and he developed close personal relationships with several of them. Most importantly, James Madison and Alexander Hamilton constantly discussed with and instructed him on every issue he would face as a leader in the new American government. Additionally, in 1787 he presided daily over the most interesting and important political debates in American history, hearing the best possible arguments on every side of every issue. This informal education did not make him an exceptionally intelligent man, but he was certainly better informed on the most important political issues of the era than he is often given credit for.

There has been a wide range in the educations and intellects of the forty-three presidents. A number have been undeniably brilliant. Several may have been true geniuses. And the most celebrated presidential intellects were possessed by men with very different types of education and intelligence. For example, James Madison was intensely studious and had a refined intellect. Abraham Lincoln had incredible natural mental abilities and great originality in framing and solving problems. Theodore Roosevelt had a powerful intellect and an almost incomprehensible ability to absorb information without ever forgetting what he read. And Bill Clinton was a top performer at several of the world's top universities and possessed one of the finest minds of his generation.

The least impressive presidential educations and intellects have less diverse stories. Most had little (if any) formal education, did not improve themselves through constant reading, and were not intellectually curious. Each of the uneducated or undereducated presidents was successful in other areas of life, but none could be considered as well-educated or intelligent as his contemporaries.

The modern American political system—and American life in general—is certainly far more complex than it was in 1790, 1860, or even 1945. But that does not necessarily mean that modern American leaders will be (or need to be) better educated and more naturally intelligent than their predecessors in order to succeed as president. The ubiquity of formal education in modern America has not changed the fact that there will be very intelligent and well-educated politicians in every generation, just as there will be less intelligent and poorly educated politicians. A brilliant man in 1789 would have been a brilliant man in 2012, and vice versa.

A superb education and dazzling intellect will never become a proper substitute for lack of experience or poor judgment. And great experience and judgment cannot ensure that a president will be mentally capable of understanding all of the issues he or she will be forced to deal with. No level of experience, ability, or intelligence will ever guarantee that a president will make good decisions.

QUICK FACTS
The following are some quick facts about the presidents' educations and intellects upon taking office.

2   Presidents with one year or less of formal education (Lincoln and A. Johnson).

33   Presidents with a college education.

10   Presidents without a college education (Washington, Jackson, Van Buren, W.H. Harrison, Taylor, Fillmore, Lincoln, A. Johnson, Cleveland, and Truman).

9   Presidents with advanced degrees (Hayes, Taft, Wilson, F. Roosevelt, Nixon, Ford, Clinton, G.W. Bush, and Obama). All of these presidents had law degrees except for Wilson who had a Ph.D. and George W. Bush who had an M.B.A.

METHODOLOGY

A person's education and intellect is difficult to examine, especially in an historical context. One historian's description as "brilliant" may be another historian's description as "smart" or "above average intelligence." Other difficulties arise in comparing the educations and intellects of modern presidents with those who lived when less than 1% of the nation's population attended college. However, after careful analysis of historians' descriptions of the presidents' educations and intellects, factoring in the historical changes in the American education system, the scoring and ranking methodology for the Education/ Intellect resume category is as follows:

1. Every person's starting point is a baseline score of Average as compared with other American politicians living during the same time period.

2. If a person was less formally educated or was otherwise described as less intelligent than his or her contemporaries, the score is reduced to Below Average or Poor, depending upon the specific intellectual or educational deficiencies.

3. If a person was more formally educated or was otherwise described as more intelligent than his or her contemporaries, the score is increased to Above Average. Most often, particular diligence and accomplishment in college, graduate school, or other professional training will give a candidate an Above Average score.

4. Only if a person's education and/or intellect is consistently described as "brilliant" or "exceptional" compared with his or her contemporaries, or if his or her scholastic success was truly remarkable, will a person receive a Great score.

5. Modernly, a standard college education will give a person an Average score. Exceptional success in college and/or an

advanced professional education (e.g., law school, business school) will give a person an Above Average score. Only the combination of a great formal education and exceptional intelligence will give a person a Great score.

6. Personal reading may raise a person's score, depending on the breadth of reading and the value of the topics chosen (e.g., history, government, classical literature).

EDUCATION/INTELLECT SUMMARIES

The following detailed summaries are listed in descending order based on the president's individual score, with earlier presidents appearing first within the same score.

GREAT

JOHN ADAMS   10

John Adams was one of the most brilliant men of the Founding generation. As a youth, he was taught both at home and in local schools by tutors. He then received a classical education at Harvard College from 1751 to 1755. He worked extremely hard and performed well in his class of twenty-seven students. After graduation, he studied law at night under an accomplished local attorney from 1755 to 1758, and was admitted to the bar in 1759.

Adams was one of the most voracious readers in an era of well-read people. The breadth of his reading let him speak authoritatively on practically any subject, from history to military to science to poetry to government. His great mind and his extensive learning made him well-known and well-respected as a man who could "see large subjects largely."

THOMAS JEFFERSON   10

Thomas Jefferson was unqualifiedly brilliant. As a youth, he boarded with a local schoolmaster to learn Latin and Greek before entering the College of William and Mary in 1760. From 1760 to 1762, he received a superb classical education and developed a scholastic reputation of being an obsessive student, spending up to fifteen hours with his books and three hours practicing his violin. From 1762 to 1767, he studied law under the renowned Virginia attorney George Wythe, maintaining the same studious discipline.

Beginning as a young man and continuing his entire life, Jefferson was a voracious reader, usually taking extensive notes on his reading. Along with his extensive reading, he studied mathematics, horticulture, architecture, and science, and attempted agricultural and mechanical inventions. Serious scholarship, even more than politics, was his life's true passion. Not a particularly profound or original political thinker, he was a virtuoso political rhetorician and visionary.

JAMES MADISON   10

James Madison was the most intense scholar and most studious member of the Founding Fathers. Even at a young age he was a brilliant student of politics, government, and public affairs. His career as a serious student started in 1762 when he began seven years of tutoring by two classically-trained teachers. After his excellent private schooling, he entered the College of New Jersey at Princeton (now Princeton University) in 1769. He compressed four years of work into two years and graduated in 1771, but remained on campus and studied under the highly respected university president Dr. John Witherspoon for much of 1772. At times he studied so intensely that he put his health at risk.

Madison studied law intermittently from 1784 to 1786, but never intended to practice law as a career. In 1786 and 1787, he prepared himself ceaselessly for the Constitutional Convention in 1787. His matchless preparation, scholarly discipline, and intellectual polish led him to become a top advisor to and collaborator with many other great men in the founding generation, including George Washington, Thomas Jefferson, and Alexander Hamilton. For much of his life he was the best informed man in any room.

JOHN QUINCY ADAMS   10

John Quincy Adams, like his father, was one of the most brilliant and well-educated men of his generation. As a child he was tutored by his exceptional parents before he began his extensive European travels. In Paris he studied at excellent boarding schools from 1777 to 1779, and in Holland as a young teenager, he was tutored and attended lectures at the internationally renowned Leyden University from 1779 to 1781. A very diligent student, he made great progress in the classics, sciences, philosophy, and languages. At 17 years old he was already intellectually sophisticated due to his education and extensive travels.

Upon returning from Europe, Adams was tutored for several months before entering Harvard College in 1786 and graduating in 1787. He distinguished himself in many areas of study and graduated second in his class of fifty-one. Somewhat begrudgingly and at his parents insistence, he studied law intermittently from 1788 to 1790 under Theophilus Parsons (future Chief Justice of the Massachusetts Supreme Court), and was admitted to the Massachusetts bar in 1790.

Outside of his formal education, Adams was a voracious reader his entire life, reading many hours each day. He could read in many languages, and he read all types of publications—literature, history, poetry, up to forty newspapers each week, etc. His knowledge of foreign languages was so thorough that he developed a passion for translating foreign works into English, and he was great at it (his 1800 translation of *Oberon* from German into English is still considered one of the best translations of any work by an American author).

ABRAHAM LINCOLN   10
Abraham Lincoln had less than one year of formal education in his life, yet was so naturally gifted and so diligent in self study that he became one of the most intellectually impressive men of his era.

As a youth, Lincoln received several months of rudimentary schooling in rural Kentucky, but he never had the opportunity to be formally tutored or to attend a preparatory school or college. He was taught how to read when he was young, and he devoured every book and newspaper he could lay his hands for the rest of his life. Based on whatever books were available to him, he taught himself English grammar, geometry, trigonometry, and surveying, among other subjects.

Lincoln self-studied law from 1834 to 1837. He studied at night after working as a store keeper and postmaster during the day. His extraordinary diligence helped him be admitted to the Illinois bar in 1837 and become an excellent attorney.

While not as broadly read or formally educated as many more socially and financially advantaged peers of his generation (e.g., William H. Seward, Salmon P. Chase), Lincoln proved himself to be even more intellectually brilliant. He had strong concentration abilities, a phenomenal memory, acute reasoning faculties, and great interpretive penetration. While always a humble person, he also possessed the comfortable self-confidence of a man who had never met his intellectual equal.

THEODORE ROOSEVELT   10

Theodore Roosevelt was exceptionally intelligent and likely a true genius. His photographic memory was legendary (quoting long passages verbatim after having read them only once twenty years prior), and his breadth of reading was perhaps unparalleled. He was a speed reader who could finish three full-sized books in a day if given the time (he read an average of 500 books on a wide variety of topics each year), and he remembered everything that he read.

Roosevelt received his early education at home from his family and private tutors, as well as from his father's extensive library. As a teenager he spent two full years on educational tours of Europe with his family (from 1869 to 1870 and from 1872 to 1873). He was later tutored by the eminent teacher Arthur Hamilton Cutler in preparation for Harvard College.

Roosevelt attended Harvard College from 1876 to 1880, graduating magna cum laude. While at Harvard, he started writing his first best-selling book—*The Naval War of 1812*—while also being very socially active and the runner-up in the school boxing championships. While not the best student at the school, his amazing mental abilities were noticed.

Roosevelt attended Columbia Law School in New York City from 1880 to 1882, but his attendance became sporadic after the first year as it was increasingly evident that he was not interested in becoming a practicing attorney. He never finished his courses in order to graduate. While he received a strong foundation in a legal education, his professional interests had moved to writing and politics.

BENJAMIN HARRISON   9

Benjamin Harrison grew up in Indiana and received his early education in the library at the farm of his grandfather, William Henry Harrison. He loved to read and proved to be a very intelligent boy. He attended Farmers' College near Cincinnati for his college preparatory studies from

1847 to 1850, studying under Robert Hamilton Bishop, a distinguished professor of history and politics.

Harrison then attended Miami University of Ohio from 1850 to 1852. He was a talented and diligent student, graduating third in his class. While in college, he demonstrated a great talent for public speaking, both in giving prepared speeches and in extemporaneous debating.

Harrison then studied law as a clerk under the renowned Ohio attorney Bellamy Storer from 1852 to 1854. He continued to be a very determined student with a brilliant mind. He became one of the top constitutional lawyers of his generation.

WOODROW WILSON   9

Woodrow Wilson grew up and received his early education in Georgia schools and from his Presbyterian preacher father. He attended Davidson College in North Carolina from 1873 to 1874, and joined the literary society where he demonstrated great skill at debate. He left Davison in 1874 and attended the College of New Jersey at Princeton (changed to Princeton University in 1896) from 1875 to 1879. At Princeton, he experienced an intellectual awakening. He graduated in the top quarter of his class in 1879.

Wilson studied law from 1879 to 1882. He took classes at the University of Virginia Law School until late 1880, and then he spent the remaining year-and-a-half self-studying back home in Georgia. He took the Georgia bar in 1882 and passed with the top exam score. In 1883, he chose to pursue an academic career instead of a legal career.

Wilson was a doctoral candidate at Johns Hopkins University in Maryland from 1883 to 1886. By this time he was an excellent student and an aspiring intellectual. As a student, he wrote and published what would remain his finest book, *Congressional Government*. He started teaching at Bryn Mawr College in 1885 before he received his Ph.D. in 1886.

One of Wilson's intellectual drawbacks was that he was a very slow reader, so he was never particularly well-read outside of his areas of expertise.

BILL CLINTON   9

Bill Clinton grew up in Hot Springs, Arkansas, and attended the local schools. He was one of the golden boys of the city, excelling in academics and in band (which was more popular than sports in Hot Springs). He was a star saxophone player and band major at Hot Springs High School, a Boys State and Boys Nation participant, and a student government leader. He graduated fourth out of a class of 363 in 1964.

Clinton attended Georgetown University's School of Foreign Service from 1964 to 1968. He quickly became a recognizable campus politician, serving as freshman and sophomore class president. He became a "crammer" who could absorb large amounts of information quickly and perform well on exams without extensive studying. He was a low A student and graduated with honors in 1968.

Clinton was awarded a Rhodes Scholarship (one of thirty-two chosen nationally) and attended classes at Oxford University in Great Britain from 1968 to 1970. Unlike American universities, the program at Oxford was based on individual tutorials, lectures, and essay assignments. His focus was primarily politics and philosophy. He ultimately did not receive a degree while at Oxford (not too unusual), but was considered a very sharp student with a strong analytical mind.

Clinton then attended Yale Law School from 1970 to 1973. At that time, Yale Law School was both prestigious and experimental, using a new pass/fail grading system that gave students more freedom to pursue legal and non-legal interests during their three years. He was a very good student, but was not considered outstanding due mostly to the fact that he was constantly off campus or working on political campaigns outside of the state.

Throughout his life, Clinton was also an avid reader on a wide variety of subjects.

ABOVE AVERAGE

JAMES K. POLK   8

James K. Polk attended a good college preparatory academy from 1813 to 1816 and distinguished himself as an excellent student. He entered the University of North Carolina in 1816 as a sophomore, graduating with honors in 1818. In college, he began to excel at debate and public speaking and was twice chosen as president of the school's debating society.

Polk served as an apprentice under the celebrated Tennessee attorney Felix Grundy from 1818 to 1820. He continued his diligent studying habits by immersing himself in the office's law books. Throughout his life, Polk was considered to be intelligent, scholarly, and a policy wonk.

RUTHERFORD B. HAYES   8

Rutherford B. Hayes had a sheltered childhood, with his mother and sister tutoring him in reading and writing during his early years. As a teenager they finally sent him to a boys' academy in Norwalk, Ohio, where he was a diligent student and excelled in Latin and Greek.

Hayes attended Kenyon College in Gambier, Ohio, from 1838 to 1842, receiving a standard classical education. He was a natural peacemaker who tried to calm the conflicts in the student body between pro-slavery and anti-slavery factions. He gradually became a serious scholar, graduating first in his class and delivering the valedictory address at graduation.

Hayes attended Harvard Law School from 1843 to 1845. He continued to be a diligent student, studying under Supreme Court Justice Joseph Story and Professor Simon Greenleaf, two of the nation's greatest legal minds. He was a diligent student and an intelligent adult, but never distinguished himself intellectually like some of the other men of his era.

WILLIAM HOWARD TAFT   8

William Howard Taft was very intelligent and a strong student, but was never considered a truly brilliant man. School did not come easy for him, but he succeeded through perseverance. He graduated second in his class from Woodward High School in Cincinnati in 1874.

Taft then attended Yale University from 1874 to 1878, following in the footsteps of his even more intelligent brother. He was not a competitive person and was a natural procrastinator, but he continued to excel scholastically. He graduated second in his class in 1878.

Taft chose to attend Cincinnati Law School in his beloved home town from 1878 to 1880. He was considered one of the most intelligent students in the school.

Taft ultimately became one of the nation's most respected politicians and judges, but was never thought to have an exceptional intellect.

DWIGHT EISENHOWER   8

Dwight Eisenhower was raised and educated in the small town of Abilene, Kansas. He was a good athlete and an above average but not great student.

After high school, Eisenhower attended West Point Military Academy from 1911 to 1915. At that point in time, the educational focus of West Point was still military and civil engineering, with most instructors being recent West Point graduates themselves. He excelled in English, but was content to be average in most other subjects. He graduated in the top half of his class in 1915 and was commissioned a Second Lieutenant.

As an officer, Eisenhower excelled in every educational opportunity the military offered. He had what could be considered an informal graduate school on military affairs when he worked closely with the brilliant General Fox Conner from 1922 to 1925 in Panama, reading extensively on military history, strategy, and tactics. He then attended the Army's grueling Command and General Staff School for a year, competing against 275 of the best officers in the Army and graduating first in his class in 1926. He also studied military history at the Army War College from 1927 to 1928, and traveled to France to further study the U.S. Army's battle history in France in World War I.

Eisenhower was praised throughout his career for his great intelligence and his ability to master details without losing sight of the big picture.

RICHARD NIXON   8

Richard Nixon was an outstanding student attending Yorba Linda and Whittier, California schools as a youth. He was a prodigiously hard worker, forcing himself to persevere and succeed even when he did not enjoy or have a natural inclination for a subject. In addition to his studies he became an accomplished pianist and played the violin. Throughout his formal education, he also was a successful student politician, holding student government positions in elementary school, high school, college, and law school.

Nixon attended Whittier Union High School. He was a champion public speaker, although he was not a natural orator. He ended up graduating third in his class of 207 in 1930. Due to family finances, he could not attend Harvard or Yale and instead attended Whittier College from 1930 to 1934. In college, he was a dedicated but average football player, a champion debater, a very good theater actor, and a student body leader. He graduated second in his class of eighty-five in 1934.

Nixon received an academic scholarship and attended Duke University Law School from 1934 to 1937. He spent many hours in the law library and once again performed well, graduating third in his class of forty-four.

As an adult, Nixon was known for being very intelligent and having a great memory. He was never a naturally brilliant person with easy-going self-confidence (he often envied such traits in others), but he made up for it in hard work and dogged determination.

BARACK OBAMA   8

Barack Obama's early education was split between schools in Hawaii and Indonesia. He attended an Indonesian elementary school for the first through fourth grades before returning to Hawaii in 1971. He attended the prestigious and private Punahou High School from 1975 to 1979, graduating with a B average. He was not a hard worker in high school, focusing mainly on basketball and having fun.

Obama attended Occidental College near Los Angeles from 1979 to 1981. He started working a little harder in school and became a bit more politically active. His favorite classes were creative writing courses, and he considered becoming a professional writer. He transferred to Columbia University in New York City in 1981, which he attended from 1981 to 1983. He became a more serious student at Columbia, and focused on political science.

Obama attended Harvard Law School from 1988 to 1991. He was by then a hard worker and excelled in class, ultimately graduating magna cum laude. As a student research assistant, he worked on several projects with the renowned legal scholar Lawrence Tribe. He also became a member of the Harvard Law Review, and served as President (i.e., editor-in-chief) during his third year. He received significant press attention as he was the first minority race student to hold that position.

Particularly in law school and afterwards, Obama impressed people with his intelligence, his ability to synthesize complicated information, and his feeling for nuance.

GEORGE WASHINGTON   7

George Washington's formal schooling was the modern equivalent of a grade school education. He was never exposed to a classical curriculum and he never attended a college. Most of his education was from hands-on military, business, and political experiences, rather than books. But unlike his formal education, his informal education was impressive.

Washington's informal education was through extensive interactions and correspondence with some of the most brilliant Americans in history. This group includes George Mason, Benjamin Franklin, John Adams, Thomas Jefferson, James Madison, John Jay, and Alexander Hamilton. Starting in the 1760s, he frequently corresponded and interacted with these men and others who helped him develop a more expansive political vocabulary and a better theoretical understanding of politics and government.

With respect to his understanding of the foundations of the Constitution and American government, Washington was extensively tutored throughout the 1780s by Madison and Hamilton, among others. This included many in-depth discussions immediately prior to the Constitutional Convention in 1787. He presided over all of the Convention debates, and in doing so gained a comprehensive understanding of the issues facing the early federal government.

JOHN TYLER   7

John Tyler attended a local Virginia school as a youth before attending a college preparatory academy from 1802 to 1804. He then entered the College of William and Mary in 1804, graduating in 1807 with a good (but not excellent) classical education.

Tyler then studied law from 1807 to 1809, first under his father (a well-respected Virginia judge who later served as Governor of Virginia), and then under Edmund Randolph (President Washington's first Attorney General and second Secretary of State). He excelled in his legal studies and quickly set up a successful private law practice in 1809 upon his admission to the Virginia bar.

Along with being intelligent and a capable student, Tyler read fairly extensively. Throughout his career he was always considered intelligent and well-educated.

FRANKLIN PIERCE   7

Franklin Pierce attended a college preparatory academy as a youth and then had a private tutor for one year in preparation for a classical college education. He then attended Bowdoin College in Maine from 1820 to 1824. He excelled in Latin, struggled in mathematics, and was generally an average student. He did, however, show an early inclination for leadership.

Pierce studied law as a clerk for several local New Hampshire judges from 1824 to 1829. He proved to be a diligent student and a talented advocate. As an adult and professional attorney and politician, Pierce was always considered intelligent and well-educated.

JAMES BUCHANAN   7

James Buchanan received a college preparatory education at a local academy in Lancaster, Pennsylvania. He then attended Dickinson College from 1807 to 1809 and was a strong student. After his first year he was expelled for rowdy behavior and in- and out-of-classroom "conceit" in the face of the faculty, but his businessman father complained and he was readmitted to complete his degree. He ended up graduating in 1809 near the top of his class of nineteen students.

Buchanan studied law as a clerk to one of the region's top attorneys from 1810 to 1812. He continued to be a diligent student, reading day and night and organizing what he learned logically in his mind. He was an intelligent man, but was never as intelligent as some of his colleagues in law and politics. Regardless, he maintained the intellectual vanity and "conceit" he developed as a youth for his entire life.

CALVIN COOLIDGE   7

Calvin Coolidge received his early education in rural Vermont and later attended the college preparatory school Black River Academy in Vermont from 1887 to 1890. He was a good but never a great student. He then attended Amherst College in Massachusetts from 1891 to 1895. He was an average student his first several years, but steadily improved and ended up graduating cum laude. He particularly liked philosophy, Latin, the modern languages of French and Italian, and political science.

After college, Coolidge studied law as a clerk in a Northampton, Massachusetts, law office from 1895 to 1897. He continued to be a diligent but strong student. As an adult, he was considered intelligent and well-educated. He was an avid reader, preferring philosophy, history, political science, and literature.

FRANKLIN ROOSEVELT   7

Franklin Roosevelt had a series of fine private tutors as a youth. He also studied during his frequent travels throughout Europe, becoming fluent in both German and French. As an only child, he spent most of his time around adults and became very comfortable in sophisticated company.

Roosevelt attended the Groton School in Massachusetts from 1896 to 1900. At that time, Groton was the most exclusive and prestigious college preparatory school in the nation. He received a good education but was only an average student.

Roosevelt then attended Harvard University from 1900 to 1903. He again was only an average student. Much of his time was concentrated on his activities with the Harvard *Crimson* student newspaper. He gained a spot on the editorial board, and became President (i.e., editor-in-chief) of the *Crimson* in his third year. Due to his Groton studies, he was able to graduate in only three years, but stayed on campus another year (supposedly to take a graduate degree, which he never actually pursued) in order to manage the newspaper.

Roosevelt then attended Columbia Law School in New York City from 1904 to 1907. He started his law school career as a poor student, failing multiple classes due to his general disinterest in preparing for or attending classes. He never developed at passion for the law, but he ultimately graduated near the middle of his class.

The brilliant Supreme Court Justice Oliver Wendell Holmes, Jr. once commented that Roosevelt had "a second-class intellect but a first-class temperament." This is generally accurate. Roosevelt was certainly intelligent—intuitively so—and well-educated, but his intelligence was not exceptional.

JOHN F. KENNEDY   7

John F. Kennedy attended several of America's most prestigious schools as a youth, including Riverdale County Day School, the Canterbury School, and Choate Hall. He was a popular student but was generally in the middle of his class.

Kennedy attended several months of classes at Princeton University in 1935, but recurring health problems forced him to leave school. He then attended Harvard University from 1936 to 1940. He again was an average student who did not take school very seriously outside of the government classes in which he took a deep interest. He also served on the Harvard *Crimson* student newspaper's business board and occasionally wrote articles. In the fall of 1940, he took several graduate classes at Stanford University, but stopped after one semester.

Kennedy was a clever, creative, and intelligent individualist, but was never a great student or a brilliant man. Due to his broad international experiences and personal reading, he was generally very well informed about the subjects in which he took a specific interest.

GERALD FORD   7

Gerald Ford was raised in Grand Rapids, Michigan, and attended good public schools. He was a good but not a great student. In high school, he became a star football player, playing center on offense, linebacker on defense, and winning the state championship his senior year.

Ford received a football scholarship to play at and attend University of Michigan from 1931 to 1935. He played little his first several years, but finally became the starting center in the 1934 season. After the college all-star game, he received offers to play for the Green Bay Packers and Detroit Lions, but he chose instead to become a football and boxing coach and to pursue graduate school at Yale University. He graduated from college in 1935 with a B average and a degree in economics and political science.

Ford attended Yale Law School from 1938 to 1941. He was considered a respectable student and a hard worker, but without any trace of brilliance. He graduated in 1941 in the top half of his class.

JIMMY CARTER   7

Jimmy Carter was raised in the small town of Plains, Georgia, and attended the local public schools. He was an intelligent boy and a strong student. He joined the debate team in high school and worked hard to get good enough grades to attend the U.S. Naval Academy. He graduated near the top of his high school class in 1941.

Carter attended Georgia Southwestern College from 1941 to 1942, then Georgia Tech from 1942 to 1943, and finally the U.S. Naval Academy in Annapolis from 1943 to 1946. The Naval Academy's academic program was accelerated to three years to prepare the graduates to enter World War II. He graduated in 1946 with a solid but not outstanding academic record.

Carter took several additional educational courses during his service as a naval officer. He performed well in the submarine officer training school, and then took two graduate-level courses in reactor technology and nuclear physics for one semester at Union College while working as an engineering officer in Connecticut. He later took several college agriculture classes as a peanut farmer and business owner. As an adult, he was known for being intelligent and having the ability to absorb and recall large amounts of complex information.

GEORGE W. BUSH   7

George W. Bush received his early education in Midland, Texas, before moving to Houston and attending the prestigious Kinkaid School. He then followed in his father's footsteps and attended Phillips Academy in Andover, Massachusetts, graduating as an average student.

In 1964, Bush became the fifth generation of Bushes to attend Yale University. He was again a popular student, becoming a cheerleader and president of his Delta Kappa Epsilon fraternity, and he graduated near the middle of his class in 1968.

Bush attended Harvard Business School from 1973 to 1975 after serving several years in the Texas Air National Guard. He received his master's degree in business administration (M.B.A.) in 1975.

Bush is considered by those who know him well as an intelligent and well-educated person. As is frequently the case, his below average speaking ability (particularly in extemporaneous settings) causes some people to discount his overall intelligence.

AVERAGE

JAMES MONROE   6

James Monroe's parents taught him to read, write, and calculate using whatever materials were available to them in rural Virginia. He was enrolled in the local school and carried his books and a musket five miles each way to school for about three months each year from 1769 to 1774.

Monroe attended the College of William and Mary from 1774 to 1776, receiving a good classical education. His studies were interrupted during his service in the Revolutionary War, but he returned to Virginia to study law from 1800 to 1801 as an apprentice under his close friend Thomas Jefferson. His lifelong relationship with Jefferson, who was like an older brother to him, helped him expand and improve his education due to his easy access to Jefferson's extensive library.

GEORGE H.W. BUSH   6

George H.W. Bush grew up a privileged youth and had a fine early education. He attended the prestigious Phillips Academy in Andover, Massachusetts, from 1937 to 1941, receiving a superb college preparatory education. He was a fine athlete and also became an editor on the student newspaper and president of his senior class.

After serving in World War II, Bush attended Yale University from 1946 to 1949. He was the fourth generation of the Bush family to attend Yale. He was a natural leader and became captain of the school baseball team. He was also a strong student. As an adult, he was known as an intelligent man but never particularly philosophical or a conceptual thinker.

ULYSSES S. GRANT   5

Ulysses S. Grant's early formal education was unremarkable. His father enrolled him in West Point Military Academy to receive a free college education and military training (at that time West Point primarily schooled its cadets in military and civil engineering). He was intelligent and excelled at mathematics, but he was only an average student who was generally uninterested in school.

Grant had several great abilities. He was a fantastic artist, a talent which came in particularly handy with military maps and landscapes.

He was also one of the best equestrians in West Point and military history. Even as a youth he was a local "celebrity" as a horseman.

Grant was intelligent and had good judgment, particularly with respect to "big picture" questions.

JAMES GARFIELD   5

James Garfield received a rudimentary early education in rural Ohio schools. As a teenager, he attended two local academies (high school equivalents) from 1848 to 1849 and performed quite well.

After several years working in various low-level jobs, Garfield returned to school, enrolling in the Western Reserve Eclectic School in Ohio (now Hiram College) in 1851. It was founded by the Disciples of Christ in 1850. He soon became the school's prize student, exhausting the school's intellectual offerings by 1853. He started teaching several classes in 1854 before he graduated. He then attended Williams College in Massachusetts from 1854 to 1856. He was only an average student, but excelled in debating and was popular with the students and faculty.

CHESTER A. ARTHUR   5

Chester A. Arthur received his early education from his well-educated preacher father in Vermont. He then attended a college preparatory academy in Union Village, Vermont, prior to receiving a respectable classical education at Union College in Schenectady, New York, from 1845 to 1848. Following graduation in 1948, he studied law briefly at a newly-opened law school in New York before returning home to self-study law from 1848 to 1853 while teaching at a local Vermont school. As an adult, he was considered to have average intelligence.

HERBERT HOOVER   5

Herbert Hoover received his early education in rural Iowa. After his parents died and he became an orphan, he moved to Oregon and attended high school, although he never graduated.

Hoover joined the inaugural class at Stanford University and studied mainly geology from 1891 to 1895. He was a good student when he was interested in the subject (especially mathematics and geology). Much of his focus as a student, however, was entrepreneurial. He started a profitable laundry business and became the class treasurer. In the end, his education at Stanford was simply a stepping stone for him to dive into the mining industry and become an entrepreneurial businessman.

HARRY TRUMAN 5

Harry Truman attended local Independence, Missouri, schools as a youth. He was an average student throughout high school, performing well in Latin and mathematics. He also loved playing the piano and became an accomplished pianist. He was financially unable to go to college, and his terrible vision helped keep him out of West Point Military Academy, so high school marked the end of his formal education. He was, however, an avid reader (a true book worm) and was very receptive to everything he read. He was a man of average intelligence, but who maximized his natural gifts with great common sense and judgment.

LYNDON JOHNSON 5

Lyndon Johnson received his early education in rural Texas schools. He was a mediocre student and graduated from high school in 1924. He learned to read from a very young age, but never loved reading for its own sake.

After working in several labor-intensive jobs, Johnson attended Southwest Texas State Teachers College in San Marcos from 1927 to 1930. During this time he was known for his endless energy, his enthusiasm, and his overwhelming personality. He took menial jobs like assistant to the college president's secretary and soon turned them into positions of influence. He became the president's right hand man, a gate keeper and advisor who would accompany him on trips to the state capital. He also joined the debate team, was active in campus politics, was editor of the campus newspaper, and graduated as an honors student.

As an adult, Johnson was completely absorbed by politics and legislation. He would read many of the local and national newspapers, and the daily legislative materials including the congressional record, committee reports, and pending bills. He read little that could not give him information which he could use to his political advantage, however.

RONALD REAGAN   5

Ronald Reagan was raised and received his early education in Dixon, Illinois. He was an active and popular student in high school, serving as student body president, writing for the yearbook, and starring in school plays.

Reagan attended Eureka College in Illinois from 1928 to 1932. He was again active in the drama club, the school newspaper, the yearbook, and the student government. Due largely to general disinterest in classes, he was only an average student, graduating with a C average in economics. He had average intelligence, and was a thoughtful adult who read a lot (e.g., newspapers, magazines, political theorists, western novels).

MARTIN VAN BUREN   4

Martin Van Buren grew up poor in the village of Kinderhook in upstate New York. His parents were unable to afford to provide him with a formal education, so he attended a local one-room schoolhouse until 1796 when he was 13 years old. He then became an apprentice for a local attorney from 1797 to 1803 and in exchange for keeping the office clean and other duties he received a rudimentary legal education.

As an attorney he tried to make up for his relatively poor education and lack of reading by purchasing a small law library and reading at night. However, throughout his professional and political life he remained insecure in the face of his better educated rivals due to his lack of a formal education and lack of extensive reading.

WILLIAM HENRY HARRISON   4

William Henry Harrison received his early education at local schools in Virginia. From 1787 to 1790, he attended Hampden Sidney College, then Southampton College, and finally for a few weeks University of Pennsylvania's medical school. At those colleges he received a basic classical education and studied some medicine. He also became interested in the military and read several military books before quitting school for financial reasons and joining the military in 1791.

GROVER CLEVELAND   4

Grover Cleveland's early education was in rural New York schools. He learned the basics—reading, writing, and arithmetic—but was forced to start working as a teenager to help support his family and was never able to attend college. He was interested in education, however, and loved to read history.

Cleveland moved to Buffalo, New York in 1855, and studied law as a clerk in a local attorney's office. After several years of working and studying, he was admitted to the New York bar in 1859. Cleveland was never known for having a great intellect, but he was known for being extremely diligent and hardworking, studying a question or an issue as long as it took him to grasp it completely.

WILLIAM McKINLEY   4
William McKinley's early education came first in a one-room schoolhouse in rural New York and later in a college preparatory academy in Ohio. He was a determined student of about average intelligence who succeeded because of simple perseverance and hard work. Intuition, not natural brilliance, was his strength.

McKinley attended Allegheny College in Meadville, Pennsylvania, from 1859 to 1860, but was unable to complete his courses and graduate due to a combination of illness and lack of finances. After the Civil War, he studied law as a clerk in the office of a notable Ohio attorney from 1865 to 1866, and then attended the Albany Law School in New York from 1866 to 1867. His diligence helped him prepare enough to return to Ohio without graduating and become an attorney.

BELOW AVERAGE

WARREN G. HARDING   3
Warren G. Harding received a rudimentary early education in rural Ohio, learning to read and write, and learning basic arithmetic and history. He attended Iberia College (later Ohio Central College) from 1880 to 1882. Iberia was not a strong educational institution, and Harding received only a basic formal education. He did learn a bit about journalism, however, a subject that interested him greatly. He was never considered particularly intelligent and he frequently admitted that complicated political issues were beyond his personal understanding and capacity.

MILLARD FILLMORE   3

Millard Fillmore attended rural New York schools as a youth and received only minimal formal education. He learned basic reading, writing, and arithmetic, but little else. As a teenager, he tried to read every book available to him.

Fillmore studied law intermittently from 1819 to 1822 as a clerk to a local judge who provided him with only a rudimentary legal education. When was admitted to the New York bar and started his own law practice in 1823, he started buying and reading as many books as he could find to improve his limited education. As an adult, he was considered a moderately intelligent man but never particularly well-educated or well-read.

ANDREW JACKSON   2

Andrew Jackson learned the fundamentals of how to read, write, and make basic calculations as a youth in several rural schools, but his interest in education soon waned. He never learned proper grammar or spelling, leading to accusations of illiteracy in his later campaigns for public office. Jackson had the last formal training in his life from 1785 to 1787, apprenticing in a frontier lawyer's office in Tennessee and emerging with little actual knowledge of the law.

Jackson had virtually no formal education and did not read often (though he did read the few books he owned and in the 1820s subscribed to a number of newspapers). Ultimately, he was self-reliant and confident in his own judgments, never deferring to others in matters where he felt his own common sense was sufficient.

ANDREW JOHNSON   2

Andrew Johnson never attended a single day of school in his entire life and was always self-conscious about his lack of formal education. As a tailor's apprentice, he was taught how to read, however, and spent much of his time reading books, especially ones on politics and oratory. As a member of Congress, he spent many hours in the Library of Congress trying to improve himself. Ultimately, he never became well-read and was never considered particularly intelligent.

POOR

ZACHARY TAYLOR 1

Zachary Taylor had only minimal formal education. He attended a local Louisville, Kentucky, school as a youth, but never learned proper grammar or spelling. He learned enough basic arithmetic to make some investments later in life. Throughout his life, he never showed any inclination to learn about public affairs or the larger world. He read very little and was considered by many to be uneducated and ignorant. Even his friends and supporters considered him simple and straightforward but not especially intelligent.

WRITING ABILITY RANKINGS			
Rank	**Score**	**President**	**Historical Ranking**
Great	10	John Adams	Above Average
		Thomas Jefferson	Near Great
		James Madison	Above Average
		John Quincy Adams	Average
		Abraham Lincoln	Great
		Theodore Roosevelt	Near Great
	9	Woodrow Wilson	Near Great
Above Average	8	William Howard Taft	Average
	7	John F. Kennedy	Above Average
		Richard Nixon	Below Average
		Bill Clinton	Average
		Barack Obama	Not Ranked
Average	6	George Washington	Great
		James Monroe	Above Average
		James K. Polk	Near Great
		James Garfield	Not Ranked
		Herbert Hoover	Below Average
		Franklin Roosevelt	Great
		Ronald Reagan	Near Great
	5	John Tyler	Below Average
		Ulysses S. Grant	Below Average
		Rutherford B. Hayes	Average
		Benjamin Harrison	Below Average
		Calvin Coolidge	Average
		Dwight Eisenhower	Near Great
		Jimmy Carter	Below Average
		George W. Bush	Not Ranked
	4	William H. Harrison	Not Ranked
		Franklin Pierce	Failure
		James Buchanan	Failure
		Chester A. Arthur	Average
		Grover Cleveland	Above Average
		William McKinley	Above Average
		Gerald Ford	Below Average
		George H.W. Bush	Average
Below Average	3	Martin Van Buren	Average
		Millard Fillmore	Below Average
		Warren G. Harding	Failure
		Harry Truman	Near Great
		Lyndon Johnson	Above Average
	2	Andrew Jackson	Near Great
Poor	1	Zachary Taylor	Below Average
		Andrew Johnson	Failure

TEN
WRITING ABILITY

A pen is certainly an excellent instrument to fix a man's attention and to inflame his ambition.

— John Adams

If you would not be forgotten as soon as you are dead, either write things worth reading or do things worth writing.

— Benjamin Franklin

THE SEVENTH RESUME CATEGORY is Writing Ability. Some of the greatest political statements in American history were not spoken, they were written. And most of the great political statements that were spoken were first carefully written (and revised and re-written) before they were eventually spoken. A president's writing ability is an important skill that is far too often overlooked and underappreciated.

With the rise of professional speechwriters in the twentieth century, many presidents and other top government officials rarely sit down and write first, fifth, or final drafts of any document anymore. But before a candidate has reached a position where speechwriters or ghostwriters are frequently engaged, his or her ability to write exactly what he or she thinks and believes remains on full display. Even after a president hires speechwriters, he or she still must be involved in the idea generation and the overall editing process of every important speech or paper. After all, the ability to carefully edit and improve a speech or paper is nearly as important as the ability to write a great speech or paper in the first place.

Voters should be wary of those presidential candidates who are unable to write for themselves, because that may signify an inability to think and speak for themselves. Presidential writing need not always be elegant or eloquent (professional wordsmiths can help with that), but it should at least accurately portray the thoughts and beliefs of the president rather than some unelected aide. A president who cannot meaningfully participate in the construction of a speech or other written document cannot lead. He or she becomes a follower or actor.

WRITING RESPONSIBILITIES
Every president has certain writing responsibilities, some of which can be classified as constitutional responsibilities, while others can be classified as historical and practical responsibilities.

Constitutional Responsibilities
Two provisions in the Constitution expect the president to write.

Article I, Section 7, Clause 2 provides that if a president does not approve of a bill that passes through both houses of Congress, the president "shall return it with his Objections to that House in which it shall have originated." Pursuant to Clause 2, a president must write down the reasons why he or she objects to or disagrees with a bill that has passed the House of Representatives and the Senate. Some objections are simply political while others may be constitutional.

Beginning with James Monroe, many presidents have also issued "signing statements" when they sign a bill into law. Signing statements, which can be very controversial, are official pronouncements made simultaneously with the signing of a bill and are typically used to advance or explain the president's interpretation of or disagreement with certain parts of the bill.

Article II, Section 3 provides:

[The President] shall from time to time give to the Congress Information of the State of the Union, and recommend to their Consideration such Measures as he shall judge necessary and expedient.

George Washington and John Adams delivered each of their "State of the Union" Addresses as an annual speech to a joint session of Congress. But beginning with Thomas Jefferson (a poor public speaker), for 112 years the State of the Union Address was an annual written report hand delivered to Congress to be distributed and read by a congressional clerk. In 1913, Woodrow Wilson revived the oral tradition and delivered the State of the Union Address as a speech to both Houses of Congress.

Several written State of the Union Addresses have been memorable.

In 1790, George Washington set the precedent that the State of the Union Address be an *annual* message. In 1823, James Monroe made an important foreign policy pronouncement which became the Monroe Doctrine. In 1862, in the midst of the Civil War, Abraham Lincoln announced his intention to end slavery and one month later he issued the Emancipation Proclamation.

But the constitutional language "Information of the State of the Union" is not restricted simply to an annual address. George Washington delivered his *Farewell Address* in 1796 as an open letter to Congress and to the American people. It was a defense of his administration's record, an expression of support for the continuing government, and a reflection on emerging national and international issues. He also used it to decline a third term, setting the two-term precedent that was finally constitutionalized in 1951 with the ratification of the Twenty-Second Amendment.

Historical and Practical Responsibilities

A president's writing ability is very important to his or her ability to communicate effectively with the American people, Congress, and foreign nations. For over a century of American government, there was no radio, television, Internet, or other mass communications media. If a president wanted to communicate with a broad audience, he either traveled to speak directly to the audience or wrote something that could be published and widely distributed on his behalf. Writing was the most common method of personal and mass communication.

But even in the modern age of mass communications, writing ability remains important. Unless a president is a superb extemporaneous speaker (and few truly are), every important speech must be carefully prepared before it is delivered.

Well-known presidential speechwriters—who include Ted Sorensen, William Safire, Pat Buchanan, Ben Stein, Peggy Noonan, David Frum, and John Favreau—all say that while they may have written the exact words spoken by the president, the content, meaning, and vision of every important presidential speech or message was always the president's own.

Quick Facts

The following are some quick facts about the presidents' writing abilities upon taking office.

18   Presidents who wrote and published at least one full-length book (J. Adams, Jefferson, Madison, Monroe, J.Q. Adams, T. Roosevelt, Wilson, Coolidge, Hoover, Eisenhower, Kennedy, Nixon, Ford, Carter, G.H.W. Bush, Clinton, G.W. Bush, and Obama).

4   Presidents who were to a certain extent professional writers (T. Roosevelt, Wilson, Kennedy, and Obama).

Methodology

The scoring and ranking methodology for the Writing Ability resume category is as follows:

1. Every person's starting point is a baseline score of Average as compared with other American politicians living during the same era.
2. If a person was poorly educated and particularly weak in spelling, grammar, and other literary devices, the score is reduced to Below Average or Poor, depending upon the specific writing deficiencies.
3. If a person was fairly well-educated but was neither considered a particularly good writer nor a particularly poor writer, the score will remain in the Average ranking. Occasional publications may help increase the score one or more points to Above Average.
4. If a person was both a strong writer and he or she frequently published articles, essays, other documents, or more than one well-reviewed book, the score is increased to Above Average.
5. Only if a person was considered an excellent writer and he or she prolifically published articles, essays, other documents, or numerous books, will the person receive a Great score.
6. The extent and quality of a person's letter writing and formal speechwriting may help to increase the score one or more points.

WRITING ABILITY SUMMARIES
The following detailed summaries are listed in descending order based on the president's individual score, with earlier presidents appearing first within the same score.

GREAT

JOHN ADAMS   10
John Adams was a great and prolific writer, particularly with respect to history, politics, and government. His writing is slightly less elegant than some other great writers, but his power of expression and insightful analysis makes up for any lack of beauty in his prose.

Adams wrote his first extended political essay called *A Dissertation on the Canon and the Feudal Law* which was published in 1765 and was well-received. Also in 1765, he drafted the *Braintree Instructions*, instructions by the local government to the colonial Massachusetts legislature which were ultimately (and unprecedentedly) adopted by forty-two town governments.

While a delegate at the Second Constitutional Convention in 1776, Adams drafted the first set of rules and regulations for the new American Navy, and wrote what became an influential pamphlet called *Thoughts on Government.* He also served on the committee of five that drafted the *Declaration of Independence* (Thomas Jefferson was the primary author).

Adams was the primary drafter of the Massachusetts Constitution, which he wrote in 1779 and which was adopted in 1780. What he wrote—which includes a *Declaration of Rights*—is still in use today and is the longest-functioning written constitution in the world. While in England in 1787, he wrote *A Defence of the Constitutions of Government of the United States of America.* And while serving as Vice President in 1790, he published a series of historical and political essays titled *Discourses on Davila* which was later published as a book.

Apart from his formal published writings, Adams was an impressive and prolific correspondent for much of his life. Many days he would spend hours writing letters to his friends, colleagues, or Congress generally, often providing his analysis of important world events. His most frequent correspondence partner was his impressive wife Abigail. He also kept a diary that is fascinating reading. The diary shows that he was a great student and observer of human nature, with such interesting and often humorous insights about people that he could have been a successful novelist.

THOMAS JEFFERSON   10

Thomas Jefferson's writing style settled in the early 1770s into a clear, unpretentious, elegant form. His writings were prolific and beautiful, beginning in 1774 with his *A Summary View of the Rights of British America.*

Jefferson crafted what he wrote with near-poetic felicity, with memorable phrasings, and with eloquence few could match. Writing was his specialization in the Second Continental Congress which was dominated by great orators and debaters. Utilizing his "masterly pen," he was frequently responsible for drafting committee reports which included the *Declaration of the Causes and Necessity for Taking Up Arms* in 1775 and the *Declaration of Independence* in 1776. Best known for the *Declaration of Independence*, his words in the second paragraph beginning "We hold these truths to be self-evident . . ." are the most visionary statement of the American dream ever written.

For the next two decades, Jefferson wrote frequently. He drew up three drafts of a new Virginia Constitution in 1776. He wrote Virginia's *Act for Establishing Religious Freedom* in 1779, *Notes on the State of Virginia* in 1781, and the *Ordinance of 1784* in 1784. While in France, he published numerous articles and essays in Paris's *Encyclopedie Methodique*, and wrote a draft of what became the French *Charter of Rights* in 1789. As Secretary of State in 1793, he drafted the *Report on American Trade Policy* which heavily favored France over Great Britain. And in response to the Alien and Sedition Acts, he drafted the *Kentucky Resolutions* in 1798 which condemned the Acts.

In addition to his public writings, Jefferson was a prodigious personal correspondent with many of the era's most notable people, including most conspicuously his frequent letters exchanged with James Madison, a close friend and political ally.

JAMES MADISON   10

James Madison wrote thoughtfully and prolifically on matters of government and public affairs. As an influential state and federal legislator, he frequently drafted important legislation including initial drafts of the constitutional amendments which became the *Bill of Rights* in 1791. In 1787, he wrote *Vices of the Political System of the United States* which analyzed the American form of government under the Articles of Confederation. His *Notes on the Constitutional Convention* are also the most comprehensive and authoritative record of those historic debates and proceedings.

In 1787 and 1788, Madison contributed twenty-nine of the eighty-five political essays contained in *The Federalist*, which is still the authoritative commentary on the Constitution and history's best work of American political theory. In the 1790s, he often drafted President Washington's formal papers and addresses as well as the congressional responses. He drafted the *Virginia Resolutions* in 1798 in opposition to the Alien and Sedition Acts, and then drafted the *1800 Report* in 1800 on the same topic. As Secretary of State, he drafted *An Examination of the British Doctrine, Which Subjects to Capture a Neutral Trade, Not Open in Time of Peace* in 1805, arguing America's case against Great Britain's seizure of American trade ships during the Napoleonic Wars.

As a writer, Madison was deliberate, analytical, and persuasive, but his writing never reached the eloquence or elegance of his friend Thomas Jefferson.

John Quincy Adams 10

John Quincy Adams was a great and prolific writer. He wrote multiple books, foreign language translations, many official reports, thousands of very long and detailed letters, well-respected formal lectures, poems, hymns, and America's most impressive and important personal diary.

Adams's career as a published writer began in 1791 with a series of eleven essays called *Letters of Publicola*, a gracefully written and well-received political response to the radical Thomas Paine who was publically advocating overthrowing the new American government. From 1791 forward, he was a prolific essayist in the nation's newspapers, writing on numerous topics and often (as was common) under pen names such as "Menander," "Marcellus," "Columbus," and "Barneveld." He also wrote many essays for wide American consumption describing his many travels and events in Europe.

As a Senator in 1804, Adams wrote a five-part series of essays addressed to the citizens of Massachusetts which he called *Serious Reflections*. In 1809, he published *Lectures on Rhetoric and Oratory*, a collection of thirty-six lectures which he prepared but was unable to deliver to his students at Harvard. In 1821, he completed a tome-like *Report of the Secretary of State Upon Weights and Measures* which is considered one of the finest scholarly evaluations of the subject ever written. In 1822, he published a book-sized pamphlet entitled *The Duplicate Letters—Documents Relating to Transactions at the Negotiations of Ghent.* Other of his formal writings included translations of foreign literature, most notably *Oberon* from German to English in 1800.

Adams exchanged thousands of letters with many of the era's most influential people, often detailing at great length and with great insight his thoughts and understandings of important public events. Almost unique in American history is his personal diary. Begun in 1779 and written in daily almost without exception (now published in fifty-one volumes encompassing over 14,000 pages), his diary is the most comprehensive personal account of public and personal affairs ever written by an American (particularly one of such brilliance who held so many important positions).

ABRAHAM LINCOLN   10

Abraham Lincoln had extraordinary writing ability and he was one of America's master craftsmen of the English language. He wrote extensively on political and legal subjects for much of his adult life and was widely published, contributing many political essays to Illinois newspapers. He often wrote out and polished his most important speeches and later had them published for broader consumption. As an attorney, Lincoln also drafted hundreds of legal briefs which he researched and argued before Illinois appellate courts.

As a writer, Lincoln knew the value of revision. He would often edit a draft many times (even a short document) before settling on a final version. He was a very economical writer, using simple words and short sentences, but he would still labor intensely over the precise phrasing or word choice in order to express his exact meaning. He was also an amateur poet, which can be seen in his more memorable (even beautiful) phrasings. Lincoln, like Thomas Jefferson, had the gift of writing both eloquently and elegantly.

Lincoln's habit of reading aloud likely helped him master the sound and rhythms of language and helped him develop a great sense of style in his writings. The clarity and power of his literary expressions helped create a more modern political prose for a more modern America.

THEODORE ROOSEVELT   10

Theodore Roosevelt was a prolific and widely admired professional author beginning in 1880 when he was still a student at Harvard College. He was an expert in multiple fields, including naval history, big game hunting, and ornithology (the study of birds). His writing style was never elegant, but it was exquisitely descriptive, simple, and clear.

Roosevelt published fifteen books and hundreds of articles and essays between 1880 and 1900. His books include: *The Naval War of 1812* (1880); *Hunting Trips of a Ranchman* (1885); *The Life of Thomas Hart Benton* (1887); *Ranch Life and the Hunting Trail* (1887); *Essays in Practical Politics* (1887); *The Winning of the West* (four volumes, 1889 (2), 1894, 1896); *The History of New York* (1891); *The Wilderness Hunter* (1893); *Hero Tales from American History* (1895; a collaboration with Henry Cabot Lodge); *American Ideals* (1897); *The Rough Riders* (1899); and *Oliver Cromwell* (1899). Particularly *The Naval War*, *The Winning of the West*, and *The Wilderness Hunter* were critically acclaimed and continue to be authoritative works in their areas.

His hundreds of essays and articles on topics ranging from international politics to copyrights to bird watching were also of very high quality and widely read. By 1900, his published works already filled fifteen volumes.

WOODROW WILSON   9

Woodrow Wilson was a superb writer and a prolific published author. He began writing for the Princeton University student paper in 1875. As a professional writer and scholar, he focused on his authorship and public lectures at least as much as he did his classroom teaching. His writings were always polished and articulate. His process was typically to compose long passages in his mind and then transfer them onto paper fully formed.

Wilson wrote multiple books throughout his career. His first book, *Congressional Government* (1884), was his best and most highly acclaimed. Other books included *The State* (1889), contributions to *History of Political Economy in the United States* (a textbook that was ultimately never published), *A History of the American People* (1907), and *Constitutional*

Government (1908). He also wrote hundreds of published articles and essays beginning in the early 1880s. Some of his best known articles are *Cabinet Government* (1879), *Stray Thoughts from the South* (1881), *Government by Debate* (1884), and *Mere Literature* (1896).

ABOVE AVERAGE

WILLIAM HOWARD TAFT   8
William Howard Taft was a very good and prolific writer, but he was never a brilliant writer. His great education gave him command of the English language, which he showed particularly as a judge in hundreds of written legal opinions, and as Governor of the Philippines in his meticulous drafting of legal codes. His writing process was to thoroughly analyze an issue from all sides, taking painstaking care to use precise language to express the exact meaning he intended.

JOHN F. KENNEDY   7
John F. Kennedy was a strong writer with a good grasp of language and political rhetoric. As a college student he occasionally wrote articles for the student newspaper, the Harvard *Crimson*. He wrote his senior thesis (with the help of a personal research assistant) on the lead-up to World War II. It received better than average marks, and after helpful editing by Arthur Krock, a well-known columnist for the *New York Times*, was turned into a bestselling book titled *Why England Slept* (1940). For a month in 1945, he covered the United Nations convention in San Francisco for the Hearst newspapers and filed several dozen short columns.

Throughout the 1940s and 1950s, Kennedy published hundreds of articles which were focused on politics and foreign relations and which typically showed astute analysis. He started receiving more assistance in writing from his political aides in the 1950s (particularly from the great writer Ted Sorenson), but always maintained editorial control over everything he published.

Kennedy's best known work was the book *Profiles in Courage* (1956) which ended up winning a Pulitzer Prize. It was well-written, but is generally thought of as being written by committee with Kennedy being the primary author.

RICHARD NIXON   7

Richard Nixon was a very good writer who was widely published. He started writing and publishing frequent opinion pieces and other articles in 1947, and continued to write extensively on many subjects—particularly on foreign affairs—for over two decades. In 1963, his obligatory essay for the New York bar exam was singled out as the best essay the grader had seen in three decades.

After losing the 1960 presidential election, Nixon wrote a book titled *Six Crises* in 1961. It dealt with six events in his political life: the Alger Hiss case, the campaign fund controversy in 1952, Eisenhower's heart attack in 1955, one of his trips to South America, his kitchen debate with Soviet leader Nikita Khrushchev, and the 1960 presidential election. He did most of the writing himself, some of which was very good, and the book received good reviews and became a bestseller.

More than most major politicians since Franklin Roosevelt, Nixon devoted extensive personal time and effort in drafting and editing his speeches. In the mid-1960s, he hired two talented aides as speechwriters—William Safire and Patrick Buchanan—but always maintained complete control over his speeches, ensuring they were his own work.

BILL CLINTON   7

Bill Clinton was a strong writer with good command of the English language, and was fairly widely published. His writing skills, honed particularly in frequent essay writing assignments as a Rhodes Scholar, showcased his sharp analysis and an ability to synthesize complicated material in a clear presentation. He was at his best when writing longer, more thorough pieces in which he could set forth multiple lines of arguments and evaluate each in turn.

As a law school professor, Clinton never researched and wrote any serious academic articles for publication. As a politician, he wrote occasional political articles and opinion pieces, some of which appeared in national publications. He wrote and published the book *Putting People First: How We Can All Change America* in 1992.

BARACK OBAMA   7

Barack Obama was a strong writer who was fairly widely published. As a college student, he published occasional articles or poems in student publications and took several writing courses. In his early jobs he researched and wrote reports on financial issues and wrote reports on his community organizing activities. At law school, he read and edited dozens of scholarly articles as President of the Harvard Law Review.

After graduating from law school, Obama started working on a book which became the memoir *Dreams From My Father* (1995). His initial drafts were overly long, incomplete, and indulgently written, but he was receptive to editing which improved the book substantially. The book sold 9,000 copies at first, but upon its re-release in 2004 it became a bestseller.

As a state politician, Obama wrote an occasional column for the Hyde Park Herald between 1996 and 2004, publishing more than 40 opinion pieces. Immediately after becoming a U.S. Senator, he signed a $2 million deal to write three books. The first book was *The Audacity of Hope* (2006), which explained his views on certain political issues. It was generally well-written and a bestseller, but it was not great literature.

AVERAGE

GEORGE WASHINGTON   6

George Washington's lack of formal education initially hampered his writing ability, but over several decades his writing steadily improved. His knowledge and useful vocabulary were greatly expanded through his frequent correspondence and collaboration with many of the era's great writers and thinkers.

When compiled for posterity, his wartime correspondence alone totaled well over 10,000 pages. His personal correspondence was also extensive and concerned most of the great issues and ideas of the day. His prose was muscular and awkward at first, but improved greatly and was best displayed in his last Circular Letter to the States, written in June 1783, which used classical cadences and was at times eloquent.

His use of "pen men" to help draft his official correspondence and occasional speeches—men such as Alexander Hamilton and later James Madison, both great writers—helped him clearly express his thoughts and steadily improve his own writing and editing skills. Ultimately, even when the actual drafting of a written work was done by an aide or collaborator, it was always his own ideas which prevailed throughout.

JAMES MONROE 6

James Monroe, like many notable politicians in the Founding era, occasionally published political essays in newspapers under pseudonyms. For example, in 1791, he published three essays under the name "Aratus" in support of the French Revolution. In 1797, he compiled and published many of his personal and public documents written when he was Minister to France, titling them *A View of the Conduct of the Executive, in the Foreign Affairs of the United States, connected with the mission to the French Republic, during the years 1794, 5, and 6.*

Like most of his political contemporaries, Monroe also had extensive correspondence with many notable political figures of the era, particularly his close friends Thomas Jefferson and James Madison.

JAMES K. POLK 6

James K. Polk was a capable writer, but was never prolifically published. He learned to write out well-formed arguments as a college student by writing weekly essays on topics which he and his classmates would then debate. Like most of his political contemporaries, he exchanged many letters with friends and colleagues including many between himself and his longtime friend and mentor Andrew Jackson. In 1839, during his gubernatorial campaign, he wrote and published a lengthy *Address to the People of Tennessee.* It was well-written, but was criticized for being too focused on national issues while he was running for state office.

JAMES GARFIELD 6

James Garfield was a clear and precise writer. He developed a writing style similar to his speaking style, often using elegant literary flourishes and lofty rhetoric. Although he was an accomplished extemporaneous speaker and orator, he also wrote out many of his speeches and memorized them. As a writer, he was slow and painstaking. Like most of his political contemporaries, he wrote many letters to friends and colleagues, and occasionally published his letters or other papers. His *Review of the Credit Mobilier,* a defense of his alleged role in the famous scandal of the Grant administration, was both well-written and well-received.

HERBERT HOOVER   6

Herbert Hoover was a respectable and somewhat prolific writer, although his prose sometimes suffered due to his frequent unwillingness to accept editing. Beginning as early as 1896, he became a widely-published author of mining- and engineering-focused articles. He eventually broadened his writing topics to include business and management. He wrote a mining textbook called *Principles of Mining* (1909), which became standard classroom material for at least a generation. Ultimately, he was a strong technical writer, but less accomplished at subjects outside his areas of expertise.

FRANKLIN ROOSEVELT   6

Franklin Roosevelt was a strong writer with great instinct for language and political rhetoric, but he was never prolifically published. As a college student, he was on the editorial board of the Harvard *Crimson* student newspaper, becoming its president (i.e., editor-in-chief) in his third year. In that position, he was responsible for overseeing the newspaper's operations as well as selecting its content. This experience helped him develop a good feel for language.

As a politician, Roosevelt carefully prepared written texts of his speeches—especially the important speeches—crafting and re-crafting them until they expressed his exact meaning and the tone he wished to convey. He was a master at explaining complex subjects using simple, straightforward language. Every speech or public remark was painstakingly crafted to achieve perfect clarity without becoming overly formal. He relished having the ability to say large things using simple words. He wrote almost all of his speeches between 1910 and 1932, but started turning increasingly to aides for assistance in speechwriting during the late 1920s and early 1930s. The voice, vision, and word choice ultimately remained Roosevelt's own, however.

RONALD REAGAN   6

Ronald Reagan was a strong writer who was widely published. As host of *General Electric Theater* for eight years from 1954 to 1962, he wrote and delivered hundreds of on-air pitches for General Electric. During that same time, he served as a General Electric vice president and wrote and delivered hundreds of speeches at over 100 General Electric plants. His recurring themes were individual freedoms and anti-communism.

After serving as Governor of California, Reagan started writing a political column which appeared regularly in hundreds of newspapers around the country in 1975. He also recorded these political essays and aired them on several hundred radio stations. His many letters, political essays, and speech transcripts all reveal an intelligent man with a very good grasp of persuasive language and clear, concise storytelling.

JOHN TYLER 5

John Tyler wrote well but was never prolifically published. He usually wrote out his speeches before delivering them, and many of his speeches were very good. His public reports and addresses were generally clear, well argued, and persuasive. Like most of his political contemporaries, he wrote many letters to friends and colleagues.

ULYSSES S. GRANT 5

Ulysses S. Grant was a good writer with strong command of the English language. He wrote thousands of orders as a military officer, each one sparkling with precision and clarity. His military orders could not be misunderstood. They were concise and business-like, crisply stated and exact in meaning. He never published writings or papers or any political essays, but his military records read very well.

RUTHERFORD B. HAYES 5

Rutherford B. Hayes was a respectable writer but was not widely published. His strong educational background taught him to write well, but he was never particularly original. He wrote out many of his speeches, but none of them ever stood out as being particularly good. Like most of his political contemporaries, most of his writing was letters to friends and colleagues.

BENJAMIN HARRISON 5

Benjamin Harrison was a strong writer but was not widely published. He wrote precise and well-reasoned analytical essays in college, focusing mostly on government and politics. His habit was to write out his arguments but then deliver them extemporaneously without relying on a text.

CALVIN COOLIDGE   5

Calvin Coolidge was a respectable writer but was not widely published. He was known for his brevity, writing much as he spoke: concise, straightforward, and with good command of the English language. He was not a particularly profound or original writer, however. He wrote an essay as a college senior titled *The Principles Fought for in the American Revolution* (1895), which won a national essay contest, and he published *Have Faith in Massachusetts* (1919) which was a collection of his political speeches.

DWIGHT EISENHOWER   5

Dwight Eisenhower was a strong writer but not widely published. English and composition were always his best subjects in school. He excelled at being able to write quickly and precisely. His reports as a military officer were always well written, though not great literature. In 1948, he wrote his memoirs, *Crusade in Europe*, which was critically acclaimed at the time and remains one of the better American military memoirs.

JIMMY CARTER   5

Jimmy Carter was a good writer but was never widely published. He worked painstakingly on every speech he delivered, even those written by aides, making sure that everything he said reflected his exact opinion and his personal style of speaking. As a writer he had a clear and straightforward style, but he tended to shy away from strong policy statements, preferring to speak to guiding principles rather than specific, substantive ideas or goals. While campaigning for the presidency, Carter wrote and published multiple opinion articles and an autobiography titled *Why Not The Best* (1975).

GEORGE W. BUSH   5

George W. Bush was a capable writer but was never widely published. He was not himself a wordsmith, but was a strong and involved editor of his political speeches and papers as governor. He had a clear and conversational writing style. He occasionally published opinion editorials and other articles. While campaigning for the presidency, he wrote an autobiography titled *A Charge to Keep* (1999).

WILLIAM HENRY HARRISON   4

William Henry Harrison was a respectable writer but was not widely published. Most of his writings were letters exchanged with friends or for official business. When he served as a legislator, he occasionally submitted bills which he personally drafted (usually on military or militia matters). In 1810, he wrote two long letters that were later published under the title *Thoughts on the Subject of the Discipline of the Militia of the United States.* In 1819, he published his own version of the events under his command during the War of 1812.

FRANKLIN PIERCE   4

Franklin Pierce was a respectable writer but was not widely published. Like most of his political contemporaries, he wrote many letters to friends and colleagues. In 1845, he wrote at least one editorial for a New Hampshire newspaper promoting Democratic Party causes.

JAMES BUCHANAN   4

James Buchanan was a respectable writer but was not widely published. His reports written as a legislator, foreign minister, and cabinet secretary were usually thoroughly researched and meticulous. He purposely avoided strong political rhetoric and attempted to appear as a statesman above the normal political fray. Like most of his political contemporaries, most of his writings were letters to friends and colleagues.

CHESTER A. ARTHUR   4

Chester A. Arthur was a respectable writer but he was never widely published. In college he was editor of the school newspaper. He published one letter in 1877 in which he defended himself against charges of corruption. It was smartly written but otherwise unremarkable. His first ever public statement on public issues came in 1880 after he was nominated for the vice presidency. Like most of his political contemporaries, he wrote many letters to friends and colleagues.

GROVER CLEVELAND   4

Grover Cleveland was a respectable writer but was not widely published. He wrote precisely and concisely, but he was not original or profound. Until he became mayor in 1882 and governor in 1883, it appears that he had no occasion to publish any writings on public matters. As mayor and governor, he took painstaking care in drafting all of his public speeches and other papers, editing and re-editing everything he wrote. His personal letters, however, show he had the ability to write more quickly and just as clearly in his personal or private correspondence.

WILLIAM MCKINLEY 4

William McKinley was a respectable writer but was not widely published. He preferred face-to-face meetings with friends and colleagues rather than sending letters, and started using the telephone as soon as it became widely used. He wrote all of his own speeches, often taking a long time to put his exact thoughts down on paper. His personal and official writings were never great literature, but they were simple, concise, and easily understood.

GERALD FORD 4

Gerald Ford was a respectable writer, but was never widely published. As a congressional leader he would occasionally write and publish articles concerning the Republican point of view on legislative matters. He co-authored a book titled *Portrait of the Assassin* (1965), which was based on his service on the Warren Commission. The book tried to put to rest the conspiracy theories about the Kennedy assassination.

GEORGE H.W. BUSH 4

George H.W. Bush was a respectable writer but was never prolifically published. He served on the editorial board of the student newspaper at Phillips Academy. He sometimes resisted efforts by speechwriters to insert more flowery language in place of his less elegant natural style. He co-wrote an autobiography leading up to the 1988 presidential election titled *Looking Forward: An Autobiography* (1988).

BELOW AVERAGE

MARTIN VAN BUREN 3

Martin Van Buren never became a good writer largely due to his relative lack of a formal education. He never drafted any notable pieces of legislation, essays, or other political documents. He did help draft President Andrew Jackson's famous Maysville Road veto in 1830 which restricted the federal government's involvement in internal (i.e., state and local) improvements. Like most of his political contemporaries, he wrote many letters to friends and colleagues.

MILLARD FILLMORE   3
Millard Fillmore was an adequate but unremarkable writer. Like most of his political contemporaries, he wrote many letters to friends and political colleagues. Other than a series of four letters railing against Mason candidates published in 1832 in a Buffalo newspaper, it appears that he never published any of his writings.

WARREN G. HARDING   3
Warren G. Harding was a prolific local newspaper writer and editorialist, but he was not particularly articulate, eloquent, or profound. He knew Marion, Ohio, and the surrounding communities like the back of his hand and became a popular, local political voice, but not much more. His ardently-Republican editorials tended to be simple partisan bloviating. Outside of his local news stories and editorials, he was not widely published.

HARRY TRUMAN   3
Harry Truman was an adequate writer. Ever since high school, he struggled with spelling and to a certain extent with grammar. Because he was not an accomplished public speaker, he rarely wrote out long speeches. He wrote like he spoke—simple and straightforward. Truman remained part of a bygone era, disliking the telephone and preferring to send personal letters to friends and family.

LYNDON JOHNSON   3
Lyndon Johnson was an adequate writer but was never widely published. He disliked speechmaking and thus would rarely write out public speeches (or if he did, he would often stray from the script on the campaign trail). In college he served as an editor of the student newspaper.

ANDREW JACKSON   2
Andrew Jackson was often criticized by his better educated opponents for his poor grammar and spelling, and was charged with being illiterate in the 1824 and 1828 presidential campaigns. He is not known to have

written anything except for letters that he exchanged with friends and colleagues, poor drafts of legislation, and military orders.

POOR

ZACHARY TAYLOR 1

Zachary Taylor was never a good writer. He never learned proper grammar or spelling, and his handwriting was nearly illegible. He never published any writings. Like most of his contemporaries, he wrote letters, but his letters were usually unclear, convoluted, illogical, and overly long. During the last few months of the 1848 presidential campaign, his supporters convinced him to stop writing letters because they were hurting his candidacy.

ANDREW JOHNSON 1

Andrew Johnson's lack of a formal education greatly affected his writing abilities. He never was taught proper grammar and his spelling was terrible. His wife tried to help improve his writing, but his style always remained repetitious, dull, convoluted, and trite. Like many of his political contemporaries, he wrote letters to friends and colleagues but he rarely published anything or wrote out his speeches.

| \multicolumn{4}{c}{PUBLIC SPEAKING ABILITY RANKINGS} |
Rank	Score	President	Historical Ranking
Great	10	John Adams	Above Average
		Abraham Lincoln	Great
	9	James Garfield	Not Ranked
		Benjamin Harrison	Below Average
		Theodore Roosevelt	Near Great
		Woodrow Wilson	Near Great
		Franklin Roosevelt	Great
		Ronald Reagan	Near Great
Above Average	8	John Quincy Adams	Average
		James K. Polk	Near Great
		Franklin Pierce	Failure
		John F. Kennedy	Above Average
		Richard Nixon	Below Average
		Bill Clinton	Average
	7	John Tyler	Below Average
		Barack Obama	Not Ranked
Average	6	James Madison	Above Average
		Jimmy Carter	Below Average
	5	Grover Cleveland	Above Average
		William McKinley	Above Average
		George H.W. Bush	Average
	4	James Monroe	Above Average
		James Buchanan	Failure
		Andrew Johnson	Failure
		Warren G. Harding	Failure
		Calvin Coolidge	Average
Below Average	3	Andrew Jackson	Near Great
		Martin Van Buren	Average
		Rutherford B. Hayes	Average
		William Howard Taft	Average
		Herbert Hoover	Below Average
		Harry Truman	Near Great
		Dwight Eisenhower	Near Great
		Lyndon Johnson	Above Average
		Gerald Ford	Below Average
		George W. Bush	Not Ranked
	2	William H. Harrison	Not Ranked
		Millard Fillmore	Below Average
Poor	1	George Washington	Great
		Thomas Jefferson	Near Great
		Zachary Taylor	Below Average
		Ulysses S. Grant	Below Average
		Chester A. Arthur	Average

ELEVEN
PUBLIC SPEAKING ABILITY

Speech is power: speech is to persuade, to convert, to compel.
— Ralph Waldo Emerson

The time comes upon every public man when it is best for him to keep his lips closed.

— Abraham Lincoln

THE EIGHTH RESUME CATEGORY is Public Speaking Ability. Historically, a person's public speaking ability was often his or her best ticket to fame, fortune, and political office. The American oratorical tradition in the eighteenth and nineteenth centuries was what radio, television, and movies were in the twentieth and twenty-first centuries: a combination of community discussion and public entertainment.

Public trials were often popular venues for citizens craving good drama and excellent debate, which is one reason why so many talented trial lawyers turned to public service. Outside of court, public speeches and debates were also popular community events. In both instances, the speakers could carry-on for several hours at a time, using grand rhetorical flourishes and lengthy quotations (by memory) from familiar sources such as the Bible, Cicero, and classical literature. In Congress, some famous orators would deliver speeches that lasted all day or several days, always to attentive congressmen and a packed public gallery.

The format for each of the seven Lincoln-Douglas debates in 1858 serves as a great example of the historic public speaking tradition. The first speaker was allotted sixty minutes for an opening argument, the second speaker was then allotted ninety minutes for a response, and the first speaker was finally allotted thirty minutes for a rebuttal. Obviously, sound bites had yet to be invented. The two great orators (Stephen A. Douglas was a good match for Abraham Lincoln) used polished oratory to keep the thousands of audience members' attention, forensic skill in analyzing their opponent's arguments, and timely humor to help score points against their opponent. They openly challenged each other to answer questions, and occasionally had impromptu comments or questions shouted from the crowd.

During the 1830s, 1840s, and 1850s, Abraham Lincoln's reputation grew. This was largely due to his public speaking talents, both as a trial lawyer and a speechmaker. But after the famous 1858 debates, his reputation as a fine public speaker was national. Certainly, Lincoln had other great experiences, abilities, and skills which helped him succeed in politics, but it was his public speaking abilities (and great speechwriting abilities) which placed him forefront on the national stage.

But other politicians have not been penalized by voters for their comparatively weak public speaking abilities. The best example is Thomas Jefferson, a notoriously poor public speaker. Jefferson avoided public speaking at all costs. He refused to debate. He never rose in support of a measure in the legislature. He hated to have attention focused upon him in any but the most intimate gatherings among close friends. He had a beautiful singing voice, but in public speaking he was exceedingly nervous and his voice was weak to the point of being almost inaudible. Yet his other experiences and abilities more than compensated for his public speaking deficiency.

In most candidates' public and private careers, there are many different types of public speaking opportunities.

- **Set Speeches.** Set speeches are carefully prepared and typically focus on specific topics. They tend to be fairly long (from twenty minutes to several hours). They are typically directed at a particular audience and delivered from a prepared text (either read directly from the paper or teleprompter or memorized and delivered verbatim).
- **Stump Speeches.** Stump speeches are typically prepared once and delivered over and over again, with minor variations, to new audiences throughout a campaign. They are intended to rally supporters and attract voters to the candidate (or to whichever other candidate or cause the speaker is supporting).
- **Debates.** A debate is simply a moderated discussion where two or more people compete in a deliberate exchange of arguments and ideas in order to persuade the audience to adopt his or her points of view. Debates can take many formats, but always

pit multiple opponents against each other. Most debaters carefully prepare by predicting what questions may be asked (by a moderator, an opponent, or an audience member), and script possible answers into several minute "mini" speeches. Many participants practice in mock debates prior to the real debate.

- **Questions & Answers.** The most common version of a candidate question and answer session is the town hall meeting. These sessions can be similar to a debate, but they can also be simply informational, where there is no opposing viewpoint and the speaker is simply asked to provide his or her response without further challenge.
- **Interviews.** Interviews are typically conducted by members of the print, radio, television, or Internet media, with immediate or subsequent broadcast or publication. An interview can be similar to a debate (challenging and combative) or similar to a Q&A session (neutral or favorable).
- **Informal Remarks.** Informal remarks often occur at occasions where a speaker is asked to deliver an impromptu address to an audience. Such remarks are typically short and extemporaneous, though many skilled speakers will give "impromptu" remarks using previously prepared or standard material.

Some descriptive terms that are useful to keep in mind while evaluating a candidate's public speaking ability include:

- *Logos* (reasoned discourse), *Pathos* (emotional appeal through passion or storytelling), and *Ethos* (character or moral competence), the three classic persuasive appeals;
- *Delivery*: use of the voice and gestures, including phrasing, pace, and emphasis;
- *Eloquent*: forceful and fluent expression; vividly and movingly expressive;
- *Fluent*: capable of using language easily and effortlessly;
- *Extemporaneous*: delivered without the aid of notes or text, impromptu; typically requiring command of a wide body of knowledge;
- *Articulate*: expressing oneself readily, clearly, or effectively;
- *Inarticulate*: incapable of giving coherent, clear, or effective expression to one's ideas or feelings;

- *Glib*: showing little forethought or preparation; lacking depth and substance; marked by ease and fluency in speaking; and
- *Demagogue*: a leader who makes use of prejudices and false claims to gain power (see also *provocateur, firebrand, instigator*).

PUBLIC SPEAKING RESPONSIBILITIES

Every president has public speaking responsibilities that can be classified as constitutional responsibilities, or historical and practical responsibilities.

Constitutional Responsibilities

Only one provision in the Constitution expects that a president will speak publicly.

Article II, Section 3 provides:

[The President] shall from time to time give to the Congress Information of the State of the Union, and recommend to their Consideration such Measures as he shall judge necessary and expedient.

George Washington began the tradition of delivering the "State of the Union" Address as an annual speech to a joint session of Congress. But many presidents, beginning with Thomas Jefferson and ending with William Howard Taft, wrote instead of spoke the annual State of the Union Address. It is therefore clear that the Constitution does not require but it only permits that the State of the Union Address be a public speech.

Most State of the Union Addresses have not been especially memorable (Inaugural Addresses are generally more famous), but a few are worth noting. In 1941, Franklin Roosevelt delivered what is now called the *Four Freedoms Speech*: freedom of speech and expression, freedom of religion, freedom from want, and freedom from fear. In 1965, Lyndon Johnson unveiled more of his Great Society legislative proposals which created expansive social programs. In 1975, Gerald Ford announced that the state of the Union was "not good," and gave a sobering national assessment. And in 2002, George W. Bush coined the phrase "Axis of Evil" and began laying the groundwork for future military actions.

Historical and Practical Responsibilities

There are dramatic variations in the frequency, length, and content of presidents' public speaking occasions. Historically, a president's public speaking responsibilities depended largely on his or her own inclinations and the demands of the public and the media. George Washington was not an effuse man, partially due to his painful wooden teeth and his taciturn temperament. Before and during his service as President, he spoke publicly only when the situation demanded it. Thomas Jefferson was even less comfortable with public speaking and completely avoided it. The only two public speeches he delivered as President were his First and Second Inaugural Addresses, each of which he read nervously and almost inaudibly directly from his written text. John Adams, on the other hand, was a great public speaker and was always willing to speak publicly on any occasion.

Some presidents have relished every opportunity to give speeches, hold press conferences, join in debates, give interviews, stump in campaigns, and speak publicly in many other forums. These presidents include Abraham Lincoln, James Garfield, Benjamin Harrison, Theodore Roosevelt, Woodrow Wilson, Franklin Roosevelt, John F. Kennedy, Richard Nixon, Ronald Reagan, Bill Clinton, and Barack Obama.

Other presidents have largely shied away from the public podium (the "Bully Pulpit" as Theodore Roosevelt called it) and have only given public speeches or remarks when the circumstances demanded a formal presidential statement. These presidents include George Washington, Thomas Jefferson, Zachary Taylor, Ulysses S. Grant, Chester A. Arthur, William Howard Taft, Calvin Coolidge, Dwight Eisenhower, Lyndon Johnson, and George W. Bush.

There has always been great tension between presidents becoming over-exposed by speaking publicly too often and presidents neglecting their informal role of Communicator in Chief by speaking too infrequently. The proper balance must always depend on the president's talents and best judgment.

Particularly in the modern era with the ubiquity of radio, television, and the Internet, and with a 24-hour news cycle, presidents are expected to be able to effectively communicate their goals and vision to the American voters and to the world. Any failure to effectively communicate with the media and the public can severely restrict a president's ability to accomplish his or her goals, and can lead to lackluster supporters and reinvigorated opponents.

Like it or not, the most useful and effective method of political communication in America has always been the public speech. In 1789, Congress stopped and listened with dignified respect whenever the president spoke. It still does so in 2011, albeit sometimes with less dignity and respect. A well-drafted and expertly delivered presidential speech still has great power of persuasion and the potential to redound to history. A tightly-formed argument in debate can still cause an opponent to stumble and help a president win over an audience. And an articulate or appropriately emotional answer to a press question can still help a president connect personally with the American voters.

As president (or as a candidate), less talented public speakers may be wise to limit their public speaking engagements to momentous occasions where there is time for careful preparation and practice. More talented public speakers may choose to speak publicly on more frequent occasions, but must be careful not to become over-exposed and permit their public speechmaking to suffer from a decline in influence and gravitas (James Garfield is a great example of a fine public speaker who spoke far too often).

Simply put, presidents should stick to whatever are their strengths: powerful set speeches; impromptu debates with the press or political opponents; or silence combined with carefully written statements and public announcements delivered by subordinates. The simple availability of radio microphones, television cameras, Internet video sites, and an available audience should never force a president to speak publicly.

QUICK FACTS

The following are some quick facts about the presidents' public speaking abilities upon taking office.

17   Presidents who were notable and prolific public speakers for at least two decades (J. Adams, J.Q. Adams, Tyler, Polk, Pierce, Lincoln, A. Johnson, Garfield, B. Harrison, McKinley, T. Roosevelt, Harding, F. Roosevelt, Kennedy, Nixon, Reagan, and Clinton).

9   Presidents who competed in major debates (Lincoln, Kennedy, Nixon, Carter, Reagan, G.H.W. Bush, Clinton, G.W. Bush, and Obama).

5   Presidents who rarely gave any public speeches or remarks (Washington, Jefferson, Taylor, Grant, and Arthur).

METHODOLOGY

The scoring and ranking methodology for the Public Speaking Ability resume category is as follows:

1. A Poor public speaker is one who never or only rarely spoke publicly, and who was not very good at it.
2. A Below Average public speaker is one who spoke occasionally or frequently in the prior decade, but who was still not considered an accomplished public speaker.
3. An Average public speaker is one who spoke frequently over the prior decade and was known for usually being articulate and fluent but not necessarily eloquent.
4. An Above Average public speaker is one who spoke frequently over the last two or more decades and was known for always being articulate and fluent and usually being eloquent. He or she will also generally be a skilled extemporaneous speaker.
5. A Great public speaker is one who spoke frequently over the last two or more decades and was known for always being articulate, fluent, and eloquent. He or she will also be a skilled extemporaneous speaker and an excellent debater.
6. A public speaker can earn one or two points for: (i) having delivered multiple widely-acclaimed speeches prior to being elected; (ii) having an especially long or distinguished public speaking career; and (iii) excelling in a particular speech setting (e.g., debates, stump speeches, major addresses, extemporaneous speaking).

PUBLIC SPEAKING ABILITY SUMMARIES

The following detailed summaries are listed in descending order based on the president's individual score, with earlier presidents appearing first within the same score.

GREAT

JOHN ADAMS   10

John Adams loved to talk and he was truly great at it. At Harvard College, he joined the debate and discussion club where it was noted that he had "some faculty" for public speaking. He had a clear and sonorous voice and strong elocution, so he was always easily heard and understood by his listeners.

Adams became renowned for his public speaking talents as a trial attorney. As was typical of the era, his speeches could last several hours, but he almost always spoke extemporaneously. He was both a great orator and a great debater, speaking with polish, eloquence, passion, persuasion, and force. He was also very quick on his feet and witty, often adding humor to his delivery.

As a delegate to the Second Continental Congress, no person spoke more often or to greater effect than Adams. His most famous speech was in the Continental Congress on July 1, 1776, where he spoke powerfully and without notes in favor of declaring independence from Great Britain. He was widely acknowledged to be the Founding generation's best advocate for independence.

ABRAHAM LINCOLN   10

Abraham Lincoln's political fame and talent sprouted largely from his impressive public speaking abilities. As a trial attorney from the 1830s to 1860, he gained professional fame and financial success due to his ability to persuade juries and judges.

Lincoln also became a nationally known public figure due largely to his great oratory. He was comfortable speaking both extemporaneously and from carefully prepared (and often memorized) texts. Several of his speeches over three decades of public speechmaking stand out for their high quality, including his *Lyceum Address* (1838), *Temperance Address* (1842), *Eulogy of Henry Clay* (1852), *Peoria Speech* (1854), *House Divided Speech* (1854), and *Cooper Union Address* (1860).

In addition to speechmaking, Lincoln was a great debater. In combination with his *House Divided Speech* and *Cooper Union Address*, his seven famous debates with Stephen A. Douglas gave him the political credibility to become a top contender for the presidency.

Lincoln was unmatched as a storyteller. This ability made him the center of attention in every group in which he found himself, both large and small. He used his natural charm, brilliant intellect, and abundant humor, in combination with perfect timing, to always keep his audience's attention.

JAMES GARFIELD   9
James Garfield gained local, then state-wide, and finally national fame due to his great public speaking ability. Beginning in college, he was an excellent debater. He was also a prominent local preacher during the revival era. When he served in the Ohio Senate for two years, however, he developed the bothersome habit of speaking on every matter no matter how small or insignificant.

In Congress for seventeen years, Garfield maintained his habit of speaking very frequently. He soon discovered that it bothered many of his colleagues and hurt his effectiveness, but throughout his entire career he struggled with limiting the occasions on which he spoke. He ardently wished he had the self-restraint to speak less.

Garfield was an impressive orator with the ability both to deliver fine prepared speeches and to speak extemporaneously and at length. While he was always fluent and often eloquent, some of his speeches bordered on being glib and did not always contain the depth and substance of other famous orators (e.g., Henry Clay, Daniel Webster, and Abraham Lincoln). Regardless, he was generally acknowledged to be the best Republican stump speaker of the era, and was known for his ability to inspire an audience and persuade a listener.

BENJAMIN HARRISON   9
Benjamin Harrison was a personally cold man with few friends, but who had the great ability to win a debate with skillful argument and move an audience with beautiful oratory and impassioned eloquence. Beginning in the 1850s, his speaking abilities were sought after in Indiana and later around the nation to publically proclaim Republican causes.

Harrison began his public speaking career at Miami University of Ohio, where he excelled at debate and at delivering both prepared and extemporaneous speeches. After studying law under a renowned Ohio attorney, he became a fine trial lawyer who employed both penetrating legal arguments and strong emotional persuasion.

During the 1880s, Harrison traveled widely around the country to speak on behalf of Republican candidates and Republican causes, giving thousands of speeches. He could give several speeches in one day, each one impassioned, original, and delivered without substantial preparation. In the 1888 presidential campaign, Harrison developed the first "front porch campaign," where he gave approximately 100 speeches to hundreds of thousands of people who traveled to his home in Indiana to hear him speak.

THEODORE ROOSEVELT   9

Theodore Roosevelt was a great talker and grew to be an excellent public speaker. He was never a polished orator, but he ultimately gave more public speeches and addressed more audiences than any person of his era.

Early in his public career, Roosevelt could at times be an awkward speaker, though his speeches still made national headlines. He spoke in choppy, aggressive sentences and with a passion and phraseology that was both inspiring and amusing. As a New York State Assemblyman, he refused to be ignored and would at times call out to the Speaker for forty minutes straight until he was acknowledged and given the floor to speak.

Over two decades, Roosevelt steadily became an accomplished public speaker. He could speak extemporaneously or from prepared texts, and was a master in using powerful yet simple language. He had special gifts for political and moral rhetoric as well as humorous invective (the president "has no more backbone than a chocolate éclair"). His energy and personality, as much as the words he used, moved audiences. He could deliver an expert lecture at Harvard on naval history just as effectively as he could deliver a dozen different and memorable speeches a day on the campaign trail. As the vice presidential nominee during the 1900 campaign, he followed the famous orator and Democratic nominee William Jennings Bryan around the country, giving in just a few months over 670 speeches to over three million listeners and proving he could hold his own with the best orators in the country.

WOODROW WILSON   9

Woodrow Wilson was an excellent public speaker. He excelled at debate while he was still a college student, and was a skilled extemporaneous speaker for the rest of his life. Throughout his twenty-five-year career as a professor, lecturer, and university president, he rarely spoke from a prepared text. He preferred to speak from skeletal notes or without notes for all but the most formal occasions. His great communication skills and teaching abilities helped him be voted the most popular professor at Princeton University six years running in the 1890s.

Wilson studied and spoke about the American political system for several decades, but never campaigned for political office until 1910. He was always articulate and often eloquent, but at the beginning of his political career he was overly stiff and formal in his stump speeches. Soon, however, he became more comfortable and developed into a hard-hitting, passionate campaigner who could hold his own with any rival.

FRANKLIN ROOSEVELT   9

Franklin Roosevelt was one of the great orators of the twentieth century. His feel for great political rhetoric and the pace and cadence of great oratory, combined with his great ability to paint vivid pictures using simple words and memorable phrasings, helped him become a master public speaker during the 1910s, 1920s, and early 1930s.

Roosevelt began his public speaking career in 1910 as a candidate for the New York Senate. His early speeches were often awkward, but his natural political ability and his intuitive connection with an audience soon made him a great speechmaker. He gave many public speeches as Assistant Secretary of the Navy and as a popular member of the Democratic Party. In 1920 as the Democratic candidate for the vice presidency, Roosevelt conducted the most extensive national political campaign to date, delivering over one thousand speeches and many other impromptu public remarks to audiences across the country.

Throughout the 1920s, Roosevelt continued to give many speeches as a Democratic Party leader despite his disability caused by polio in 1921. His immeasurable self-confidence helped him cultivate a comfortable and natural speaking style and a way of personally connecting with the audience. As Governor of New York from 1929 to 1932, he started a giving weekly "fireside chats" over the radio, speaking directly to the citizens of New York and communicating how he was running the state government and what he was doing about the widening Depression. He increasingly turned to populist rhetoric and rallying average citizens to his side as the Depression worsened.

Several of Roosevelt's speeches in 1932 leading up to the presidential election were great examples of political rhetoric and expert delivery. In the same speech he could be a hard-hitting politician railing against the Republican Party's failures and a soothing voice of compassion and reason carefully explaining his vision for America's future. His most famous speeches in 1932 include the *Forgotten Man Speech*, the *New Deal Speech*, and the *Four Horsemen of the Republican Apocalypse Speech*.

RONALD REAGAN   9

Ronald Reagan was a spellbinding orator who, with more than forty years practice as a professional actor and public speaker, was one of the most persuasive politicians of his generation. Similar to Franklin Roosevelt, his delivery was natural, comfortable, and compelling, and his understanding and use of modern mass media was near perfect. He was a familiar face and reassuring voice for most Americans, having appeared on television thousands of times as an actor and later as a spokesperson for General Electric.

Reagan started acting in college and became a radio broadcaster and professional actor in the 1930s. Success in his chosen professions relied upon his ability to develop an emotional connection with the audience using his voice and non-verbal communication. These skills were easily transferrable to the political arena in the 1960s. Perhaps more than any politician since the invention of television, he was at home in front of a microphone and a television camera.

Several of Reagan's speeches and public speaking appearances stand out as particularly important and successful. He delivered a powerful address in 1964 on behalf of the Barry Goldwater presidential campaign titled *A Time For Choosing* which became a hugely successful national political debut. Then, in the 1980 presidential election, he won his television debates against President Carter, appearing more relaxed, witty, and confident than his opponent.

Overall, Reagan was a great orator, particularly when he used a prepared text. He occasionally struggled in extemporaneous speaking and in competitive debates where he could at times be caught slightly unprepared, but these were fairly rare occasions.

ABOVE AVERAGE

JOHN QUINCY ADAMS   8

Although not as impressive a public speaker as his father (particularly in debating and extemporaneous speaking), John Quincy Adams became renowned in his own right for his public speaking abilities. He was not as quick or clever a speaker as some of his contemporaries, but he spoke with unmatched knowledge and a skillful formal delivery.

Adams's public speaking career began in 1787 when he gave two public orations connected with his graduation from Harvard. In 1788, he accepted Harvard College's chapter of Phi Beta Kappa's invitation to deliver its annual address, and for many years he gave similar public speeches and addresses on request from various public groups and societies. As a professor of rhetoric and oratory at Harvard College, his lectures were each carefully prepared and expertly delivered to large audiences.

Adams's most notable speech was delivered during an Independence Day celebration in Washington in 1821 when he was serving as Secretary of State. His topic was foreign affairs and he proclaimed that the European practice of colonization would eventually end. His oration stated that America should be prepared to recognize independent nations in South and Central America and that foreign powers were no longer welcome to encroach upon the Western Hemisphere. This foreign policy statement was a precursor to President Monroe's annual message to Congress in 1823 announcing what is now known as the Monroe Doctrine.

JAMES K. POLK   8

James K. Polk excelled in public speaking beginning when he was a college student. For two years he served as president of the school's debating society, competing in weekly debates with his fellow students. He excelled in extemporaneous speaking and debating, honing his ability to think quickly and form strong and logical arguments. During his sixteen years of service in the Tennessee House of Representatives and the U.S. House of Representatives, and later as Governor of Tennessee, he became known as one of the Democratic Party's best stump speakers. Although he was an excellent debater and extemporaneous speaker, he never became a truly great orator.

FRANKLIN PIERCE 8

Franklin Pierce was famous in New Hampshire for his public speaking ability. As a very successful trial lawyer, he made his living making arguments and giving speeches trying to persuade juries. As a legislator, he spoke publically on matters he cared deeply about, but he always followed his own advice—never speak too often on questions of minimal importance in order to retain influence on questions of great importance.

Pierce spoke with great energy and passion. He was known for rousing stump speeches and articulate legislative arguments. He had a pleasant, modulated voice and an intuitive sense that helped him gauge the audience. His natural charisma could keep an audience's attention rapt for hours. Never an exceptional orator, he was always a fluent speaker and often an eloquent one.

JOHN F. KENNEDY 8

John F. Kennedy was a below average public speaker at the start of his political career who became a very good public speaker by 1960. His first public speaking opportunities occurred in 1945 during his first congressional campaign. His early speeches were often awkward and poorly crafted. He was not a natural public speaker, but he worked hard to turn his natural easy-going personality and charisma into a polished speaking style which connected with the audience. Throughout the 1950s, he steadily improved as a speechmaker, giving hundreds of speeches and public appearances in 1956 while aspiring to become the Democratic nominee for the vice presidency.

Kennedy came into his own as a public speaker during the 1960 presidential campaign. He was finally comfortable on stage, and had by then developed a good speaking cadence and the ability to connect with and inspire an audience. He also was very good at using self-deprecating humor to mute his lofty political ambitions. Late in the campaign, he participated in the first ever presidential debates against the Republican presidential nominee Richard Nixon. The four debates were broadcast over radio and television to eighty million viewers. It was generally believed that the debates with Nixon, himself a skilled debater, ended in a draw (a result that favored Kennedy because he had lower expectations going into the debates).

Kennedy's best speech prior to the 1960 election was probably his speech in Houston to a group of Protestant ministers where he stated: "I am not the Catholic candidate for president; I am the Democratic Party's candidate for president who happens also to be a Catholic."

RICHARD NIXON   8
Richard Nixon was a very good public speaker from a young age, although he was never a natural orator. Throughout his life he envied those people who had a graceful, charming, elegant speaking manner seemingly without effort. His practice was to carefully prepare the full text of a speech, memorize it, and then try to deliver it verbatim with as natural a delivery as possible.

In high school, Nixon was a good public speaker who won a speech contest sponsored by the *Los Angeles Times*. Later in college, he became a champion debater, touring California and competing with other university students and developing argumentative and forensic skills that he used later as a hard-hitting politician. As a trial lawyer he excelled at cross-examinations.

Beginning in the late 1930s, Nixon accepted hundreds of speaking engagements each year in venues large and small. He was active in Republican politics in Southern California and started making a name for himself as a party speechmaker while he was still in his twenties. Once he became a congressman, he became known as one of the best Republican campaign speakers and was frequently sought after to campaign for other candidates. As Vice President during the 1950s, he was one of the most prolific public speakers in the country, giving hundreds of speeches each year.

Nixon had two famous public speaking moments prior to 1968 that stand out. The first was his *Checkers Speech* in 1952 which focused on a controversy surrounding a campaign fund. It was watched on television by sixty million viewers and was universally recognized to be a great performance which clinched for him the vice presidency. The second was his four debates in 1960 with John F. Kennedy. Nixon was considered the stronger debater, but Kennedy ultimately won the battle of appearances. Both candidates were articulate and knowledgeable about a full range of domestic and international issues.

BILL CLINTON   8

Bill Clinton was a comfortable and accomplished public speaker starting in his high school days. He had a great ability to connect with an audience, utilizing his active listening skills and showing empathy and earnestness. As a top high school student, he was frequently speaking to local civic organizations about his experiences, and as a student politician he gave frequent speeches. Throughout his educational career, he continued to develop a comfortable, confident speaking style, and was a fine storyteller.

As a professor, Clinton had an easy classroom manner, lecturing and leading discussions without notes. As governor, he gave thousands of speeches and started addressing national audiences more frequently as he became a more visible Democratic leader as chairman of the national governors association. He also started relying on polling to help craft effective public speeches and messages.

Clinton was a talented extemporaneous speechmaker, being able to deliver extended and expertly-crafted speeches from bullet point notes or no notes at all. As a featured speaker at the 1988 Democratic nominating convention, he had a poor primetime performance due in large part to an overly long prepared text (thirty-two minutes, much of which was insisted on by presidential candidate Michael Dukakis's staff). In 1991, he gave a keynote address at a meeting of the Democratic Leadership Council which was hailed as one of the best political speeches of the year. In the 1992 presidential debates against President Bush and Ross Perot, Clinton performed very well, especially in the less formal town hall debate format.

JOHN TYLER   7

John Tyler was a very good but never a great public speaker. At his college graduation, he gave what was called one of the best commencement speeches in the school's history. Once he established his private law practice, his easy manner and persuasiveness helped him become a successful trial lawyer. At grander occasions such as on the floor of Congress where he spoke often, he was known as a fine orator who could sometimes be eloquent but who was never considered brilliant. He was known for speaking clearly and fluently, using logical and well-reasoned arguments and with good command of the English language.

BARACK OBAMA 7

Barack Obama steadily improved his public speaking abilities to become an accomplished orator by 2008. He rarely gave any speeches before becoming a state senator in 1996. As a community organizer, he was very comfortable conversing with individuals and small groups, and as a law school professor he was good at facilitating classroom discussions, but neither of these roles translated directly into political speechmaking. In the Illinois Senate, he started out as a flat, long-winded speaker who was professorial and stiff, and on the campaign trail he was earnest but somewhat awkward and condescending. He was not a great debater, often losing the audience in long and academic answers.

Obama started becoming a better public speaker in the early 2000s, working hard to become more conversational and inspiring. His national political debut came in a primetime nominating speech at the 2004 Democratic convention. He substantially shortened his original speech draft, worked with a speech coach, and practiced on a teleprompter (his first time using the device). When he hit his stride several minutes into the speech, it electrified the audience and immediately made him a rising star in the Democratic Party.

During the 2008 presidential campaign, Obama was thought to have lost the debates with Democratic presidential candidate Hillary Clinton, but to have won the debates with Republican nominee John McCain. He became most comfortable—and most rhetorically inspiring—delivering set speeches using a prepared text and a teleprompter. He was never as comfortable or fluent as an extemporaneous speaker. Probably his best campaign speech was delivered on March 18, 2008, when he addressed the issue of race and the controversy surrounding his former pastor Reverend Jeremiah Wright.

AVERAGE

JAMES MADISON   6

James Madison had a weak, soft voice and a shy reserve that made him reluctant to speak unless he was among friends or he felt that he was in complete command of the issues on which he spoke. In an era of great speechmakers, he was an analytical and dispassionate debater whose arguments were powerful while his tones were quiet and his passion was muted. At the Constitutional Convention in 1787 and at the Virginia ratifying convention in 1788, when his unmatched understanding of the issues were critical to success, he carried the debates for his side, speaking logically and effectively. He often had to compete with opponents such as Patrick Henry who possessed more lung power and rhetorical flamboyance but less expertise.

JIMMY CARTER   6

Jimmy Carter was a respectable public speaker but was never a great orator or debater. He participated on his high school debate team, which helped him overcome his natural shyness and learn to articulate himself assertively. He was a fairly awkward public speaker early in his career. By the 1970s, he could be dynamic when talking to smaller audiences, but he still lost something when he addressed large audiences and especially when speaking directly from a prepared text. Inspiring oratory was never his strong suit. He gave a nominating speech at the 1972 Democratic convention which ended up being delayed until well after primetime and which went largely unnoticed.

Carter debated President Ford three times in 1976. He was generally thought to have performed fairly well each time, but gained his biggest advantage when Ford made a fateful gaffe about there being no Soviet domination of Eastern Europe. Most of his presidential campaign speeches were politely, but not enthusiastically, received.

GROVER CLEVELAND   5

Grover Cleveland was a capable public speaker, known particularly for always speaking without a prepared text or notes even in the most important occasions (his practice was to write out a speech and then memorize it). His voice was strong, clear, and a higher pitch than many expected from such a large man (over six feet tall and over 300 pounds).

Cleveland participated in a debating society as a youth and became known for being a good trial lawyer. He was never known for great oratory, and only occasionally spoke eloquently, but he always spoke clearly and briefly, using simple, straightforward language.

WILLIAM MCKINLEY   5
William McKinley was a good and effective public speaker, although he was never a great orator or a great debater. His voice was clear and ringing, and his manner was methodical and unembellished. In stump speeches on the campaign trail, he could sometimes be spirited and passionate in favor of Republican candidates and causes.

Beginning in the 1870s, McKinley travelled extensively around Ohio and, later, around the country giving campaign speeches that were generally well-received by the audiences. He typically spoke directly from a prepared text or memorized the speech and delivered it without notes. He was never a strong extemporaneous speaker.

GEORGE H.W. BUSH   5
George H.W. Bush was a capable public speaker, but was never a great orator or debater. He lacked the public charisma and expressive rhetoric of truly great speakers. He gave thousands of public speeches over three decades beginning in the 1960s, but partially due to his non-self-referential manner, he occasionally spoke awkwardly and with a garbled syntax (mixing up the arrangement of words and phrases within sentences). He spoke fairly well in prepared speeches, but his speeches often lacked passion and inspiration. He had a somewhat nasal voice and an unusual speaking rhythm.

JAMES MONROE   4
James Monroe was a quiet boy and early in his political career he hesitated entering the public debate or giving speeches. Serving in the Confederation Congress in the 1780s, however, he became more comfortable speaking in public and improved his debating skills. Never a distinguished public speaker, he used his modest speaking ability as effectively as possible.

Monroe spoke in 1788 in opposition to the federal Constitution during the Virginia ratification convention. He was described by Patrick Henry (one of American history's great orators) as a slow, steady, and deliberate speaker. He debated James Madison for a seat in Congress in 1789. As Governor of Virginia from 1799 to 1802, he gave speeches to spur the legislature into action, and started the "State of the State" speech tradition.

JAMES BUCHANAN   4
James Buchanan was a respectable public speaker but never a great one. He was a methodical debater with a tendency to be long-winded and thorough to the point of boring the audience. Both as an attorney and as a politician, he would use piles of data and carefully explain all sides of an argument before finally turning to the crux of the issue.

Buchanan disliked stump speaking and rarely gave rousing political speeches, preferring analytical argument to other forms of persuasion. He failed as a story-teller and struggled to compete against more witty or passionate speakers, but he could be formidable in a serious debate.

ANDREW JOHNSON   4
Andrew Johnson's first experience speaking in public came in 1829 when he participated in a public debate in the town square. He found he had some talent in public speaking, and he enjoyed it so much that he joined a local debating club. As a politician, he became known for fiery, partisan speeches that were often filled with sharp ad hominem attacks and demagoguery. He rarely wrote out a speech in advance, preferring to speak extemporaneously.

Johnson was always a fluent speaker, but he was rarely eloquent. Mostly his speeches were repetitious, convoluted, and trite, starting in a low voice and rising with bombast and passion.

Johnson spoke often in the legislature and as Governor of Tennessee, and made several speaking tours to promote both his positions and his personal ambitions. Famously, on March 4, 1865, Johnson was sworn in as Vice President and gave a drunken harangue as his inaugural speech, only a few minutes before President Lincoln gave his historic Second Inaugural Address.

WARREN G. HARDING   4

Warren G. Harding was a smooth small-town orator from rural Ohio. As a local businessman and later a local politician, he made a name for himself as a speaker who could always be counted on for a patriotic and unapologetically Republican speech. His voice was soothing and his stage presence was like that of a seasoned actor. For several decades, he traveled the rural Ohio speaking circuit giving a set speech highlighting his favorite "great" men: Alexander Hamilton, Caesar, and Napoleon.

Harding was very proud of his speaking abilities and was surprised and hurt in 1915 when he discovered that, on the national scene as a Senator, he was simply a glib and unspectacular public speaker. He stopped speaking as much as he used to, and he became slightly embarrassed to speak publicly in the U.S. Senate or on complex national or international issues.

CALVIN COOLIDGE   4

Calvin Coolidge was never an outgoing or loquacious person, tending to be shy, quiet, and somewhat awkward in public settings. He was, however, considered a fairly able public speaker. He was also known for his wit and was selected as the student who delivered the college graduation address that was meant to be humorous.

As a politician, Coolidge spoke quite often both in campaigns and as a sitting official, typically in a deliberate manner from prepared texts. He developed a style that was concise, simple, and focused on broad principles rather than political agendas or political opponents. Many considered him to be rather stiff and awkward on the stump, and thought his Vermont twang not particularly sophisticated, but he was never a bad public speaker.

BELOW AVERAGE

ANDREW JACKSON   3

Andrew Jackson was not an eloquent speaker or debater, but he was an entertaining enough performer to hold an audience. He usually spoke slowly and forcefully, but spoke much more quickly when excited. Never polished or elegant, his speeches were always bold and candid. He was also famous for being fluent in profanity.

MARTIN VAN BUREN   3

Martin Van Buren was never a great orator or public speaker, but as an attorney he became an adequate debater. With careful practice and presentation he could be both analytical and persuasive. He delivered perhaps the worst maiden speech in U.S. Senate history in 1821, when he lost his way, had a break down, and was forced to sit down in the middle of his speech. He later was able to finish his speech, but he never completely overcame his subsequent timidity in public speaking.

RUTHERFORD B. HAYES   3

Rutherford B. Hayes began his public speaking career with impressive self-assurance and ability. As a youth and a student, he often recited famous speeches for audiences—his favorite was Daniel Webster's historic "Second Reply to Hayne." He also made a good impression when he delivered the valedictory address for Kenyon College in 1842, speaking with a strong, clear voice.

Hayes never became a respected orator as an adult. He was a good attorney, but not known for great jury arguments. As a congressman, he never entered into debates and gave very few speeches. And as Governor of Ohio, he gave a number of speeches, but none were notable.

WILLIAM HOWARD TAFT   3

William Howard Taft greatly disliked public speaking. He was a competent speaker but was very long-winded and never compelling. As Solicitor General, he argued eighteen cases before the U.S. Supreme Court, winning most of them but disliking the experience. As a politician, he avoided giving public speeches (hardly campaigning at all in the 1908 election), and those that he did give were flat, dry, uninspiring, and read directly from the text.

HERBERT HOOVER   3

Herbert Hoover was an average public speaker who often suffered from poor grammar. He was best and most comfortable giving lectures about the technical subjects (mining, engineering, business management) on which he was an acknowledged expert. Many of his speeches as a politician were dull and lacked passion, and were delivered in a flat, monotone voice.

HARRY TRUMAN   3

Harry Truman was never a good public speaker. He avoided giving speeches when possible. He was the quintessential plainspoken country boy who, as a candidate from western Missouri, typically spoke to plainspoken country folk. He generally spoke rapidly with a flat, high-pitched voice. When he spoke in the Senate (which was quite rare), he would use a prepared text packed full of statistics and read it quickly and verbatim. However, when pressed to speak in a campaign, he could overcome his usual reticence and passionately defend himself and his record.

DWIGHT EISENHOWER   3

Dwight Eisenhower was never an accomplished public speaker. He had no occasion to give public speeches or remarks until 1942 when he became the top American general in Europe. He was generally a good performer in press conferences, but he never aspired to be a good speechmaker. He tried to minimize the public speechmaking after World War II, and gave only minimal preparation to all but the most important addresses. He preferred to be seen as the plainspoken country boy and the simple soldier doing his duty, and his speaking style complemented that image. It often frustrated him when people deprecated a person's intelligence by confusing public speaking ability with intelligence or wisdom.

LYNDON JOHNSON   3

Lyndon Johnson disliked public speaking and never became an accomplished speechmaker. His specialty was one-on-one or small group persuasion behind closed doors, something at which he was truly excellent. Large audiences always made him nervous, partially because he was unable to translate his overwhelmingly persuasive personality into an effective mass appeal.

Johnson grew up as a "mumbler," and never truly outgrew this tendency. He joined the high school and college debate teams, and sometimes performed well, but he never enjoyed speechmaking or public debates on controversial issues. In Congress, he preferred to avoid debates and avoid making public statements during the legislative process. Instead, he would attempt to find consensus throughout all stages of the process so that speeches and debates were largely unnecessary once a bill was actually ready to be voted upon. On the campaign trail, he would keep his speeches as short as possible, wanting to save lots of time to meet and greet as many potential voters as possible. When giving a stump speech he was a raw performer, frequently ignoring his prepared texts and speaking loudly and bluntly.

GERALD FORD   3
Gerald Ford was never a particularly good public speaker, but he made the most out of his modest speaking abilities. He was a plainspoken former jock who occasionally used poor grammar and mixed up words, but he was so likeable that voters usually forgave his speaking foibles. When delivering formal addresses, he sometimes spoke in a hesitating manner, occasionally emphasizing the wrong word or appearing uncertain of what to say. He was an unsophisticated orator who gave hundreds of simple, straightforward stump speeches and political addresses over his long legislative career.

GEORGE W. BUSH   3
George W. Bush was never a good public speaker. He was best when giving a set speech and working from a prepared text, but he struggled in extemporaneous speaking settings such as press interviews and debates. Before becoming Governor of Texas, he gave occasional speeches but was never a prolific speechmaker. He frequently displayed weak grammar and incorrect word usage, and often had a hesitating speaking style.

WILLIAM HENRY HARRISON   2
William Henry Harrison was not a talented or prolific public speaker or debater. His early speeches as governor of the Indiana Territory were to a legislative counsel of approximately a dozen members. In the campaigns of 1836 and 1840, he would occasionally give short, impromptu speeches which were well-received by audiences. His speaking manner was unaffected, probably due to the informality of governing he was used to from years in the western frontier.

MILLARD FILLMORE   2
Millard Fillmore was not a good public speaker. He spoke slowly and deliberately, using simple words in short, plain sentences. He was

usually logical, precise, and unembellished. He avoided extemporaneous speaking and impassioned rhetoric, and was considered plainspoken and sincere.

POOR

GEORGE WASHINGTON   1

Washington was never known for his public speaking ability. He had what John Adams once called the "gift of silence," and was accustomed to leading by listening and then making decisions. He rarely entered public debate and any speech he gave was short, formal, monotone, and often awkward. His painful wooden teeth made him prefer not to speak if he could avoid it. His "Newburgh Address" in 1783, where he refused any dictatorial powers at the closing of the Revolutionary War, remains his most famous public speech and it was less than ten minutes long.

THOMAS JEFFERSON   1

Thomas Jefferson could not speak in public. His natural shyness and discomfort in the spotlight led him to abhor conflict so much that he would not even disagree with anyone to his face. During his short career as a practicing attorney, he was at best an indifferent speaker. In politics, he never entered the public debate in any forum if he could help it, remaining at all times a listener and observer. If he did speak, he did so in a weak, almost inaudible voice.

ZACHARY TAYLOR   1

Zachary Taylor was never a public speaker. There is no indication that he ever gave a public speech. His whole life he had a hesitating manner of speaking, almost a stammer or stutter. Any time he did speak, he was brief and used simple language.

ULYSSES S. GRANT   1

Ulysses S. Grant had a clear, strong voice but acknowledged that he had no talent for public speaking. He had little occasion to speak publicly prior to becoming a famous general, and very rarely spoke publicly thereafter. Any remarks he did give were usually short (a minute or two at most) and gracious, never political. He never participated in a public debate. His presidential campaign in 1868 consisted of one public comment: "Let us have peace."

CHESTER A. ARTHUR   1

Chester A. Arthur was not a public speaker. He participated in his college debating society, but rarely spoke publicly thereafter. He was not a trial lawyer and therefore rarely spoke in public in his profession as an attorney. Any speech he did give on a public occasion was customarily non-substantive and brief.

OVERALL RESUME RANKINGS		
Resume Rank	**President**	**Resume Score**
Great	John Adams	69
	Richard Nixon	68
	John Quincy Adams	66
	Theodore Roosevelt	62
	Dwight Eisenhower	62
	James Monroe	60
	Thomas Jefferson	59
	George Washington	58
	James Madison	56
	Franklin Roosevelt	55
Near Great	Herbert Hoover	54
	George H.W. Bush	54
	Bill Clinton	50
Above Average	John F. Kennedy	49
	James Garfield	48
	Abraham Lincoln	47
	Benjamin Harrison	47
	William Howard Taft	46
	James K. Polk	45
	Woodrow Wilson	45
Average	William H. Harrison	44
	Franklin Pierce	44
	James Buchanan	44
	Jimmy Carter	44
	William McKinley	42
	Ronald Reagan	41
	Andrew Jackson	40
	Harry Truman	40
	Barack Obama	40
QUALIFIED THRESHOLD		
Below Average	John Tyler	39
	Ulysses S. Grant	39
	Martin Van Buren	38
	Rutherford B. Hayes	38
	Gerald Ford	38
	George W. Bush	38
	Andrew Johnson	36
	Lyndon Johnson	35
Poor	Calvin Coolidge	31
	Chester A. Arthur	29
	Warren G. Harding	29
	Millard Fillmore	26
	Grover Cleveland	24
	Zachary Taylor	23

TWELVE

The Qualified Threshold

While the individual man is an insoluble puzzle, in the aggregate he becomes a mathematical certainty. You can, for example, never foretell what any one man will be up to, but you can say with precision what an average number will be up to. Individuals vary, but percentages remain constant.

> – Sir Arthur Conan Doyle

Statistics may be defined as "a body of methods for making wise decisions in the face of uncertainty."

> – W.A. Wallis

QUALIFIED PRESENTS THE FIRST comprehensive analysis of every president's basic qualifications before he took office. The ultimate result of the analysis is the calculation of the QUALIFIED THRESHOLD: the minimum resume score necessary for a candidate to have a very high probability of becoming an Average or better president. Candidates who score below the QUALIFIED THRESHOLD have a low probability of presidential success and are unqualified to become president.

Calculation Methodology

The QUALIFIED THRESHOLD was calculated in the following manner.

1. Calculate each president's total resume score.
2. Compare the resume scores with the historical presidential ranking.
3. Determine the probability that a candidate with a particular resume score will become a president with a particular historical presidential ranking.
4. Determine the minimum resume score that has a very high probability of becoming an Average or better president and a high probability of becoming an Above Average or better president.

THE RESULTS

Based on the resume analysis, the QUALIFIED THRESHOLD is a score of 40 out of 100.

QUALIFIED THRESHOLD = **40 out of 100**

The following results show that a presidential candidate with a resume score of 40 or higher has a very high probability—a 76.92% chance—of becoming an Average or better president, and a high probability—a 57.69% chance—of becoming an Above Average or better president.

In stark contrast, a presidential candidate with a resume score of 39 or lower has only a fair probability—a 46.15% chance—of becoming an Average or better president, and only a slight possibility—a 15.38% chance—of becoming an Above Average or better president.

The results of the resume analysis clearly demonstrate that the better a presidential candidate's overall qualifications and resume score, the higher the probability that he or she will become a successful president. Determining whether a candidate's qualifications meet the QUALIFIED THRESHOLD, therefore, is a crucial second step in evaluating every presidential candidate.

Overall Breakdown

CHART 1 provides the overall breakdown of the resume analysis.

CHART 1

Resume Score	Resume Qualifications	# of Presidents	% of Presidents
55 or higher	Great	10	23.26%
50 to 54	Near Great	3	6.98%
45 to 49	Above Average	7	16.28%
40 to 44	Average	9	20.93%
35 to 39	Below Average	8	18.60%
34 or lower	Poor	6	13.95%

According to CHART 1:
- 30.24% of presidents have had Near Great or better qualifications upon taking office;
- 46.52% of presidents have had Above Average or better qualifications upon taking office;

- 67.45% of presidents have had Average or better qualifications upon taking office; and
- only 32.55% of presidents have had Below Average or Poor qualifications upon taking office.

These are fairly encouraging statistics. They mean that American voters elect presidents who meet the QUALIFIED THRESHOLD more than two-thirds of the time. Also encouraging is the fact that the most recent president who took office with a Poor resume score (34 or lower) was Calvin Coolidge in 1923, and only three presidents since then have had resume scores of Below Average (Lyndon Johnson, Gerald Ford, and George W. Bush). Hopefully, this modern trend of electing qualified presidents will continue through the twenty-first century.

Candidates with Great Resumes

The presidents with Great resume scores were, in chronological order:

Election	President	Resume Score	Historical Presidential Ranking
1789*	George Washington	58	Great
1796	John Adams	69	Above Average
1800	Thomas Jefferson	59	Near Great
1808	James Madison	56	Above Average
1816	James Monroe	60	Above Average
1824	John Quincy Adams	66	Average
1900	Theodore Roosevelt	62	Near Great
1932	Franklin Roosevelt	55	Great
1952	Dwight Eisenhower	62	Near Great
1968	Richard Nixon	68	Below Average

*Note: the first presidential election took place in early 1789, not 1788.

It is very encouraging that more presidents had resume scores of 55 or higher and took office with Great qualifications than any other resume ranking category (ten out of forty-three presidents). From an historical perspective, America clearly prefers presidents with excellent qualifications. Equally encouraging is the fact that most Great candidates ultimately become successful presidents.

CHART 2

		Near Great or Better	Above Average or Better	Average or Better	Below Average or Worse	
Rank	**Great**					**Failure**
Great (55+)	20% (2 of 10)	50% (5 of 10)	80% (8 of 10)	90% (9 of 10)	10% (1 of 10)	0% (0 of 10)

HISTORICAL PRESIDENTIAL RANKING

CHART 2 shows that a presidential candidate with a resume score of 55 or higher and Great qualifications has a very high probability—an 80% chance—of becoming an Above Average or better president, and an even probability—a 50% chance—of becoming a Near Great or better president. And almost every candidate with Great qualifications will become an Average or better president. This means that American voters should think long and hard about their decisions if they are considering not voting for a presidential candidate who has Great qualifications.

The first six presidents (discussed below) each entered the presidency with Great qualifications and established a very high standard of presidential excellence. Of course, the Nixon anomaly (discussed below) is a great reminder that even very talented and experienced politicians may have intangible personal characteristics that can cause poor presidential performance even when the probability of presidential success is very high.

Candidates with Near Great Resumes

The presidents with Near Great resume scores were, in chronological order:

Election	President	Resume Score	Historical Presidential Ranking
1928	Herbert Hoover	54	Below Average
1988	George H.W. Bush	54	Average
1992	Bill Clinton	50	Average

Only three presidents had resume scores between 50 and 54 that place them in the Near Great resume ranking, and none of them succeeded as impressively as his high resume score indicates that he could have.

CHART 3

HISTORICAL PRESIDENTIAL RANKING

Rank	Great	Near Great or Better	Above Average or Better	Average or Better	Below Average or Worse	Failure
Near Great or better (50+)	15.38% (2 of 13)	38.46% (5 of 13)	61.54% (8 of 13)	84.62% (11 of 13)	15.38% (2 of 13)	0% (0 of 13)

CHART 3 shows that a presidential candidate with a resume score of 50 or higher and Near Great or better qualifications has a very high probability—an 84.62% chance—of becoming an Average or better president, a high probability—a 61.54% chance—of becoming an Above Average or better president, and a fair probability—a 38.46% chance—of becoming a Near Great or better president. It is simply an oddity that none of the presidents with Near Great qualifications became Above Average or better presidents themselves. Voters should still carefully consider any candidate with such strong basic qualifications.

Based on his Near Great qualifications and his Below Average presidential ranking, Herbert Hoover (discussed below) is the second most underperforming president in American history behind Richard Nixon. The two other presidents who had Near Great qualifications, George H.W. Bush and Bill Clinton, did not underperform nearly as badly as some other presidents have, but neither was viewed as having performed spectacularly. In time, history may become more kind to Bush and/or Clinton when it comes to presidential rankings, but for now they remain historically Average presidents. Still, having Average presidential success is a very respectable accomplishment.

Candidates with Above Average Resumes

The presidents with Above Average resume scores were, in chronological order:

Election	President	Resume Score	Historical Presidential Ranking
1844	James K. Polk	45	Near Great
1860	Abraham Lincoln	47	Great
1880	James Garfield	48	Not Ranked
1888	Benjamin Harrison	47	Below Average
1908	William Howard Taft	46	Average
1912	Woodrow Wilson	45	Near Great
1960	John F. Kennedy	49	Above Average

Seven presidents had resume scores between 45 and 49 that place them in the Above Average resume ranking. The results are somewhat mixed but can generally be considered positive.

CHART 4

HISTORICAL PRESIDENTIAL RANKING						
Rank	Great	Near Great or Better	Above Average or Better	Average or Better	Below Average or Worse	Failure
Above Average or better (45+)	15.79% (3 of 19)	42.11% (8 of 19)	63.16% (12 of 19)	84.21% (16 of 19)	15.79% (3 of 19)	0% (0 of 19)

CHART 4 shows that a presidential candidate with a resume score of 45 or higher and Above Average or better qualifications has a very high probability—an 84.21% chance—of becoming an Average or better president, a high probability—a 63.16% chance—of becoming an Above Average or better president, and a fair probability—a 42.11% chance—of becoming a Near Great or better president. And significantly, there has never been a presidential candidate who had Above Average or better qualifications upon taking office who became a Failed president. While there is an outside possibility—a 15.79% chance—that a presidential candidate with Above Average or better qualifications will become a Below Average president, that candidate has the same chance of becoming a Great president.

Out of the six presidents listed in CHART 4 who received an historical presidential ranking (James Garfield was not ranked due to being assassinated early in his presidency), four of them performed as well or better than expected. Both James K. Polk and Woodrow Wilson slightly exceeded expectations by becoming Near Great presidents, and John F. Kennedy met expectations by becoming an Above Average president even though his presidential term was also cut short by an assassin's bullet. And Abraham Lincoln significantly exceeded expectations by becoming a Great president. It is important to note that only presidential candidates who took office with Above Average or better qualifications have ever become Great presidents.

Candidates with Average Resumes

The presidents with Average resume scores were, in chronological order:

Election	President	Resume Score	Historical Presidential Ranking
1828	Andrew Jackson	40	Near Great
1840	William H. Harrison	44	Not Ranked
1852	Franklin Pierce	44	Failure
1856	James Buchanan	44	Failure
1896	William McKinley	42	Above Average
1944	Harry Truman	40	Near Great
1976	Jimmy Carter	44	Below Average
1980	Ronald Reagan	41	Near Great
2008	Barack Obama	40	Not Ranked

Nine presidents had resume scores between 40 and 44 that place them in the Average resume ranking. At this point in the overall resume analysis, there is still a very high probability that a presidential candidate with Average or better qualifications becomes a successful president.

CHART 5

HISTORICAL PRESIDENTIAL RANKING

Rank	Great	Near Great or Better	Above Average or Better	Average or Better	Below Average or Worse	Failure
Average or better (40+)	11.54% (3 of 26)	42.31% (11 of 26)	57.69% (15 of 26)	76.92% (20 of 26)	23.08% (6 of 26)	7.59% (2 of 26)

CHART 5 shows that a presidential candidate who meets the QUALIFIED THRESHOLD with a resume score of 40 or higher and Average or better qualifications still has a very high probability—a 76.92% chance— of becoming an Average or better president, a high probability—a 57.69% chance—of becoming an Above Average or better president, and a fair probability—a 42.31% chance—of becoming a Near Great or better president. At this point there is a growing possibility—a 23.08% chance—that a presidential candidate who meets the QUALIFIED THRESHOLD will underperform and become a Below Average or Failed president, but it is still an unlikely enough possibility that American voters should not simply ignore or reject offhand presidential candidates with only Average qualifications.

History shows that some Average candidates rise to meet the challenges of the presidency and exceed their presidential expectations. Three presidents with Average qualifications significantly overachieved—Andrew Jackson, Harry Truman, and Ronald Reagan each became Near Great presidents. The logical conclusion is that a presidential candidate with Average qualifications still has a good chance of becoming a successful president.

Candidates with only Average qualifications still have a chance of becoming Failed presidents, however. Two of the four Failed presidents—Franklin Pierce and James Buchanan—took office with Average qualifications but were unable to effectively resolve the serious issues facing the nation (e.g., slavery and its expansion westward). It is easy to speculate (but impossible to know) whether a president with better qualifications could have prevented the Civil War which had become inevitable by 1860 and the election of the fairly highly qualified Abraham Lincoln.

Candidates with Below Average or Poor Resumes

The presidents with Below Average resume scores were, in chronological order:

Election	President	Resume Score	Historical Presidential Ranking
1836	Martin Van Buren	38	Average
1840	John Tyler	39	Below Average
1864	Andrew Johnson	36	Failure
1868	Ulysses S. Grant	39	Below Average
1876	Rutherford B. Hayes	38	Average
1960	Lyndon Johnson	35	Above Average
1973*	Gerald Ford	38	Below Average
2000	George W. Bush	38	Not Ranked

*Note: Gerald Ford was nominated for and appointed Vice President in 1973. He was not a candidate for the presidency or vice presidency in 1972.

Eight presidents had resume scores between 35 and 39 that place them in the Below Average resume ranking. The presidents with Poor resume scores were, in chronological order:

Election	President	Resume Score	Historical Presidential Ranking
1848	Zachary Taylor	23	Below Average
1848	Millard Fillmore	26	Below Average
1880	Chester A. Arthur	29	Average
1884	Grover Cleveland	24	Above Average
1920	Warren G. Harding	29	Failure
1920	Calvin Coolidge	31	Average

Only six presidents had resume scores 34 or lower that place them in the Poor resume ranking.

Presidential candidates with Below Average or Poor resume scores fail to meet the QUALIFIED THRESHOLD, have a significantly lower probability of becoming a successful president, and are therefore unqualified to become president. This should give every American voter serious concern when considering voting for an unqualified candidate.

CHART 6

HISTORICAL PRESIDENTIAL RANKING

Rank	Great	Near Great or Better	Above Average or Better	Average or Better	Below Average or Worse	Failure
Below Average or worse (39–)	0.00% (0 of 13)	0.00% (0 of 13)	15.38% (2 of 13)	46.15% (6 of 13)	53.85% (7 of 13)	15.38% (2 of 13)
Poor (34–)	0.00% (0 of 6)	0.00% (0 of 6)	16.67% (1 of 6)	50.00% (3 of 6)	50.00% (3 of 6)	16.67% (1 of 6)

CHART 6 shows that a presidential candidate who fails to meet the QUALIFIED THRESHOLD and has a resume score of 39 or lower has literally no possibility—a 0.00% chance—of becoming a Great or Near Great president, a very low possibility—a 15.38% chance—of becoming an Above Average or better president, and only a fair probability—a 46.15% chance—of becoming an Average or better president. Moreover, he or she has a disturbingly high probability—a 53.85% chance—of becoming a Below Average or Failed president. Candidates with Poor qualifications have an even worse chance of becoming successful presidents.

It is encouraging that American voters have elected only fourteen presidents who failed to meet the QUALIFIED THRESHOLD, and only six presidents whose qualifications were significantly below most presidents' qualifications and belong in the Poor resume ranking. Out of the seven historically ranked presidents with Below Average qualifications, only Lyndon Johnson (discussed below) significantly exceeded expectations. And out of the six presidents with Poor qualifications, only Grover Cleveland (discussed below) significantly exceeded expectations.

Moreover, three of the presidents with Poor qualifications were not first elected president but rather they ascended to the presidency (Millard Fillmore succeeded Zachary Taylor after he died in office, Chester A. Arthur succeeded James Garfield after he was assassinated, and Calvin Coolidge succeeded Warren G. Harding after he died in office). This indicates that Fillmore, Arthur, and Coolidge were not likely to have been initially elected president based on their own qualifications. This serves as a good reminder of how important it is that vice presidential candidates also meet the QUALIFIED THRESHOLD and are qualified to become president, if necessary.

Interestingly, four of the least qualified presidents in American history joined together on two dramatically unqualified presidential tickets. President Zachary Taylor (score of 23) and Vice President Millard Fillmore (score of 26) had a combined "ticket score" of only 49, not even as good as thirteen presidents' personal resume scores. And President Warren G. Harding (score of 29) and Vice President Calvin Coolidge (score of 31) had a combined "ticket score" of only 60, still lower than five presidents' personal resume scores.

OVERACHIEVERS AND UNDERACHIEVERS

There will always be a certain number of anomalies—results that do not follow the general rule—in a study of real world facts and imperfect people. In this study of presidential resumes and presidential success, several anomalies stand out where highly qualified presidential candidates became unsuccessful presidents and vice versa.

These anomalies help to emphasize the objective nature of the overall analysis and highlight the fact that intangible personal characteristics or other uncontrollable circumstances will occasionally create overachievers and underachievers.

Overachievers

The presidential anomalies include the following overachievers.

The First Six Presidents. Significantly, each of the first six American presidents took office with Great qualifications. Equally significant is the fact that three of the first six became Above Average presidents (J. Adams, Madison, and Monroe), one became a Near Great president (Jefferson), and one became a Great president (Washington). Only John Quincy Adams underperformed compared to his qualifications, and he still became an Average president. The Adams anomaly may be best explained by noting that his political party (the Democratic Republicans) was fracturing all around him, his was a disputed election where he did not win the popular vote, and no major national or world event occurred during his term that let him distinguish himself as an Above Average or better president.

The fact that each of the first six presidents had Great qualifications may be one of the most important reasons that the American experiment with representative government was so successful. Each man was already a well-known and widely respected politician and statesman (and in George Washington's case, a military hero and national icon) when he took office. For each of them the presidency was the natural next step in an already long and distinguished political career, not a premature "calling" or an aspiration for personal greatness. They each brought great experience, ability, knowledge, and a certain amount of gravitas to the presidency. No American voter or rival politician could claim that any of the first six presidents were unqualified for the presidency. They each helped create a strong foundation of American presidential leadership upon which every succeeding president has stood.

Grover Cleveland. Grover Cleveland was the most dramatic presidential overachiever. His success as president was primarily due to several very effective intangible personal characteristics. When speaking of Cleveland, no historian fails to note his political obscurity and inexperience just three years prior to becoming president. But historians then immediately comment on how his presidential success was largely due to his scrupulously honest character, his reformer's attitude, his willingness to be bipartisan, and his tremendous work ethic. He truly was an unexpected political phenomenon.

Lyndon Johnson. Lyndon Johnson's resume is particularly interesting when considered in hindsight from the perspective of his presidential successes and failures. His single greatest qualification was his Great legislative experience (he was probably the most influential legislator of the twentieth century and possibly in American history), and his biggest presidential successes were in proposing and passing his sweeping Great Society legislative agenda. Similarly, Johnson was least qualified in the areas of military and foreign experience, and he was least successful as president in managing foreign affairs and conducting the Vietnam War. Johnson thus exemplifies the idea that a presidential candidate's resume can both highlight strong qualifications and expose profound weaknesses, and that Americans should be diligent in reviewing a candidate's full set of qualifications (or lack thereof) when making voting decisions. If he had not presided somewhat unsuccessfully over the Vietnam War and the excessively partisan 1960s, he may have overachieved even more significantly.

Abraham Lincoln. Abraham Lincoln was more qualified for the presidency than many people have been taught to believe. Although he had only minimal service in government, particularly in the federal government, his exceptional intelligence and communication abilities and great private work experience made up for his lack of other experiences.

Theodore Roosevelt. Theodore Roosevelt is not so much an overachiever from a resume score and presidential ranking standpoint (he had Great qualifications that resulted in Near Great presidential success), as he is an overachiever simply in the sense of rising to the presidency with such exceptional qualifications at such a young age (42 years old). It is fun to imagine what his resume score would have been if he had become president four, eight, or twelve years later as was widely expected instead of in 1901.

John F. Kennedy. John F. Kennedy was the same type of overachiever as Theodore Roosevelt. Based on his relatively young age when he became president (43 years old), he has a surprisingly high resume score of 49. Many people speak casually about Kennedy's lack of experience upon taking office, but the historical facts show that he was actually a candidate with Above Average qualifications in 1960.

Underachievers

The presidential anomalies include the following underachievers.

Richard Nixon. Richard Nixon was one of the most qualified of all presidents when he took office, yet he became a Below Average president and the only president ever to resign the presidency. Many commentators, even those who rate him low in the historical presidential ranking, often note that he had great presidential potential and a number of positive presidential accomplishments before he became embroiled in Watergate, an appalling scandal of his own making. It is not a simplistic answer to conclude that, were it not for his personal demons and political indiscretions (i.e., his questionable intangible personal characteristics), Nixon very well could have become a successful president.

The Nixon anomaly is where a highly talented and experienced candidate crumbles under the pressures and responsibilities of the presidency primarily due to his or her intangible personal characteristics (in this case, a lack of good character).

227

John Quincy Adams. Most historians acknowledge that John Quincy Adams was one of the most qualified presidents in history. Yet he became only an Average president. There are many theories on why he underachieved. The three most convincing are: (i) that there were no major national or international events which he could have used to distinguish himself; (ii) that he was considered by many to be an illegitimate president because he lost the popular vote to Andrew Jackson (30.92% versus 41.35%) and only won in a very close vote in the House of Representatives; and (iii) that his Democratic Republican Party was collapsing around him and there was no way he could act as a party leader or maintain party loyalty.

Herbert Hoover. Herbert Hoover was a highly qualified candidate when he took office, yet he ended up becoming a Below Average president. This is primarily due to two interrelated facts: (i) that he prized individualism and free market principles above all others, and therefore tried to avoid dramatically expanding government's role in the national economy regardless of the consequences; and (ii) that no prior president had ever faced such a devastating economic collapse as the Great Depression. Even his many talents were not up to the unprecedented challenge, and perhaps he did as well or better than any other president would have done in the same circumstances. Nevertheless, because he presided over the most economically difficult years in American history, his failure to turn the tide of the crisis has, fairly or unfairly, left him with the rank of an unsuccessful and underachieving president.

STATISTICAL CORRELATIONS

In order to perform a statistical analysis of the presidential resumes, correlation coefficients were calculated by: (i) comparing each president's resume ranking (overall and for each category) with his historical presidential ranking; and (ii) determining whether there is a strong linear relationship between the two rankings. As shown below, the closer a correlation coefficient is to 0.00, the less statistical significance a particular resume score has with respect to presidential success (i.e., there is no relationship between the two rankings). In contrast, the closer a correlation coefficient is to 1.00 or -1.00, the more accurate the score is in predicting presidential success (i.e., there is a close relationship between the two rankings).

Correlation Coefficient*	Statistical Significance
0.00 to 0.20	Very Weak
0.20 to 0.40	Weak
0.40 to 0.60	Moderate
0.60 to 0.80	Strong
0.80 to 1.00	Very Strong

*Note: a correlation can also be negative, with the values ranging from 0.00 to -1.00

As predicted, the results of the statistical analysis show that a candidate's total resume score and resume ranking is a good indicator of his or her likely presidential success, while a candidate's score and ranking in any particular resume category is a weak or very weak indicator of his or her likely presidential success.

Moreover, the statistical significance of a candidate's total resume score is even stronger when the four "outlier" presidents are taken out of the equation. The outlier presidents are:

- John Quincy Adams (underachieved by three rankings);
- Grover Cleveland (overachieved by four rankings);
- Herbert Hoover (underachieved by three rankings); and
- Richard Nixon (underachieved by four rankings).

The successes or failures of each of these outlier presidents can be better explained by their intangible personal characteristics or uncontrollable outside influences than by their resume qualifications.

Resume Score	Correlation Coefficient	Statistical Significance
Total (Outliers Excluded)	0.61164	Strong
Total	0.46572	Moderate
Writing Ability	0.39085	Weak
Education/Intellect	0.28428	Weak
Executive Experience	0.19249	Very Weak
Legislative Experience	-0.17125	Very Weak
Public Speaking Ability	0.16952	Very Weak
Private Work Experience	0.14396	Very Weak
Foreign Experience	0.13556	Very Weak
Military Experience	0.13059	Very Weak

These statistical analysis results show that there is a strong relationship between receiving a high total resume score and receiving a high historical presidential ranking. To put it another way, statistics prove *Qualified*'s thesis that more qualified candidates become more successful presidents. Moreover, it is clear that a candidate's total resume score is far more significant in predicting presidential success than is his or her score in any single resume category.

Out of the eight resume categories, only Writing Ability and Education/Intellect have any statistically meaningful significance. But even they have only weak correlations, meaning that candidates with Great or Above Average scores in those categories have a slightly better chance of becoming successful presidents. The other six resume categories have very weak statistical correlations, meaning that candidates with Great or Above Average scores in those categories have essentially the same chance at becoming a successful president as candidates who have Below Average or Poor scores in the same categories.

Based on this statistical analysis, voters should pay much more attention to a candidate's total resume score and overall qualifications for the presidency and less attention to any particular qualification. Those candidates and commentators who believe that there is one "most important" presidential qualification (e.g., executive experience, foreign policy credentials, or communication ability) are simply incorrect. Because every president has numerous constitutional, historical, and practical responsibilities, it makes complete sense that no single experience or ability is significantly more important than the others. Only the totality of a candidate's qualifications is a good predictor of presidential success.

CONCLUSIONS

The foregoing resume analysis makes several things clear. First, America has a good track record in selecting qualified candidates for the presidency. A total of twenty-nine out of forty-three presidents, or more than two-thirds of all presidents, met the QUALIFIED THRESHOLD. And almost half of all presidents—twenty—had Above Average or better qualifications when they became president.

Second, there is a strong statistical correlation between a presidential candidate's qualifications and his or her actual performance as president. The general rule is the better the qualifications, the better the presidential performance.

- Presidential candidates with a Great resume score (55 or higher) have an 80.00% chance of becoming an Above Average or better president and a 90.00% chance of becoming an Average or better president.

- Presidential candidates with a Near Great or better resume score (50 or higher) have a 61.54% chance of becoming an Above Average or better president and an 84.62% chance of becoming an Average or better president.

- Presidential candidates with an Above Average or better resume score (45 or higher) have a 63.16% chance of becoming an Above Average or better president and an 84.21% chance of becoming an Average or better president.

- Presidential candidates with an Average or better resume score (40 or higher) have a 57.69% chance of becoming an Above Average or better president and a 76.92% chance of becoming an Average or better president.

There is an equally strong correlation in the other direction: the worse a presidential candidate's qualifications, the lower the probability that he or she will become a successful president.

- Presidential candidates with a Below Average or Poor resume score (39 or lower) have only a 15.38% chance of becoming an Above Average or better president and only a 46.15% chance of becoming an Average or better president. Moreover, they have little to no chance of becoming a Near Great or Great president.

Whenever a presidential candidate's resume score is 39 or lower and does not meet the QUALIFIED THRESHOLD, there is more than a 40% decrease in the candidate's probability of becoming an Above Average or better president and more than a 30% decrease in the candidate's probability of becoming an Average or better president.

Third, it is up to the American voters to acknowledge the fact that the QUALIFIED THRESHOLD draws a sharp line in the sand. To consider unqualified candidates is to risk presidential Failure with only a fair (at best) probability of presidential success. Why take a risk when the most likely result is an Average or worse president? Based on the resume analysis, voters should seriously consider those candidates who have a very high probability of becoming successful presidents, and they should be wary of supporting those candidates who have only a minimal chance of becoming successful presidents.

And finally, it is clear that a candidate's overall qualifications are much more statistically significant than his or her experiences or abilities in one particular area or another. Because statistical analysis shows that there is no one experience or ability that is more important than the others, voters should not value too highly a candidate's ability to give a speech, his or her intellect, or his or her other government or private work experiences.

If the resume challenge is successful and presidential candidates in the 2012 election and in future elections publicly release their official resumes, American voters will be more likely to continue the modern trend of selecting qualified candidates with a high probability of presidential success.

THIRTEEN
INTANGIBLES

Character is higher than intellect. A great soul will be strong to live as well as think.

— Ralph Waldo Emerson

No man can lead a public career really worth leading; no man can act with rugged independence in serious crises, nor strike at great abuses, nor afford to make powerful and unscrupulous foes, if he is himself vulnerable in his private character.

— Theodore Roosevelt

THE FIRST TWO STEPS

IN CONSIDERING A CANDIDATE for the presidency, the first step is always to determine whether he or she satisfies the CONSTITUTIONAL THRESHOLD. Without satisfying each of the six constitutional requirements, no presidential candidate is legally eligible to become president. The second step is to determine whether the candidate meets the QUALIFIED THRESHOLD. If the candidate's total resume score is 40 or higher, he or she has a high probability of becoming a successful president and deserves voters' serious consideration.

In many election cycles there will be a number of intelligent, experienced, and charismatic candidates who simply do not have the constitutional, historical, and practical qualifications to become president. Some low resume scores will be surprising or even shocking. Clearly the QUALIFIED THRESHOLD is a high bar for presidential success. However, in most election cycles there will be a number of candidates who meet or exceed the QUALIFIED THRESHOLD. This is where "intangible" personal characteristics should help voters differentiate between the qualified candidates.

The Third Step

Only *after* a candidate has already shown that he or she satisfies the CONSTITUTIONAL THRESHOLD and meets or exceeds the QUALIFIED THRESHOLD should voters move to step three. In contrast to a candidate's quantifiable experiences and abilities which can be described in a resume, measured against the QUALIFIED THRESHOLD, and compared with other candidates' and previous presidents' qualifications, a candidate's "intangibles" can only be measured by each voter's personal values and political preferences. This third step is where voters should ask:

> **Will this presidential candidate's intangible personal characteristics represent my values, ideals, and vision for America's future?**

In other words, does the candidate have certain personal attributes, political views, or other distinguishing features (apart from basic qualifications) that the voter values in a political leader? Based upon his or her personal characteristics, is the candidate likely to lead the country in the "right" direction?

Unlike the CONSTITUTIONAL THRESHOLD or the QUALIFIED THRESHOLD, there is no "intangibles threshold" a candidate needs to meet to have a high probability of becoming a successful president. To the contrary, each of these intangible considerations is wholly dependent on what each voter values most in a political leader, or what type of president the voter believes America needs at a particular moment in history. While the fundamental importance of selecting a legally eligible and qualified candidate to become president must remain paramount, the importance of the candidate's intangible personal characteristics will and should factor into every voter's decision-making process.

The Twelve Intangibles

Qualified sets forth twelve intangible personal characteristics and traits that qualified presidential candidates may have and that each voter may use to some extent (if they choose to) in making a voting decision. These twelve intangibles are not an exclusive list of intangible personal characteristics. For instance, a candidate's personal wealth or who a candidate's inner circle of advisors or cabinet members would be may also be characteristics that voters factor into their decisions. And each of these twelve intangibles will not be relevant to every voter or applicable in every presidential election. When the only qualified presidential candidates are elderly white men, using the candidates' race, gender, or age cannot help a voter differentiate between the candidates and therefore such intangibles become moot.

However, these intangibles are representative of the most important ways that qualified candidates can differentiate themselves from their opponents and that voters can use to make their voting decisions. Like the eight resume categories, these twelve intangibles are also worth a voter's serious consideration whenever he or she is faced with a difficult decision in choosing between two equally qualified presidential candidates.

The degree of importance for each intangible characteristic depends entirely on each individual voter's personal preferences. A single characteristic can stand on its own as the primary motivator of a voter's choice, or it can combine with other characteristics to form the collective basis for a voter's decision. One voter may value political ideology above all else and vote for the qualified candidate who is the most liberal or the most conservative. Another voter may simply pick the most qualified Democrat or Republican in the race. A third voter may believe that it is important to have an older male president who regularly practices the Christian or Jewish or Muslim religion because that voter specifically identifies with the teachings and values of a specific religion. And a fourth voter may decide that, all other things being equal, it is time for America to elect its first female, Hispanic, or openly gay president.

Voting based on the candidates' intangible personal characteristics is not a case where one voter is necessarily right by preferring one characteristic over another and the other voters are wrong. The Constitution protects every voter's ability to choose a president based on which candidate best represents his or her values and ideals, whatever those values and ideals may be.

Making voting decisions based on intangible personal characteristics such as religion, gender, sexual orientation, or race may be seen by some as crude or improper (even racist, intolerant, or worse), but may be seen by others as enlightened and uplifting (e.g., by electing the first Hispanic, female, or Jewish president). At the end of the day, the Constitution provides citizens with the right to vote for the candidate of their choice and trusts that most Americans will be thoughtful, fair-minded, and have the country's best interests at heart when they head to the polls to cast their votes.

1. CHARACTER

For many voters the most important intangible personal characteristic for a presidential candidate to possess is "character." Character is a person's mental or ethical traits. Other characteristics that fall under the "character" umbrella include:

Honesty	Candidness	Honor
Trustworthiness	Integrity	Morality
Loyalty	Forthrightness	Courage
Principles	Ethics	Faithfulness

Few can disagree that a candidate's character permeates who he or she is and what he or she believes in and stands for. A candidate's character also provides some insight into what type of president he or she will become if elected.

Because there are about as many ways a candidate can demonstrate that he or she has "good character" as an opponent can demonstrate he or she has "bad character," it is often in the eye of the beholder. Sometimes character is shown through the stance a candidate takes on a particular controversial issue. Other times it is displayed through the candidate's personal behavior and treatment of others. Often a candidate's views or actions will be interpreted by some voters as being high-minded and principled but by other voters as being immoral or unjust.

Abraham Lincoln serves as a good example. He was a presidential candidate in 1860 when the slavery issue had finally strained the nation to its breaking point. The views he expressed on the most important and most divisive issue in American history were, in many ways, equivocal. Often times his particular views on slavery were stated much differently depending on his audience. He was categorically opposed to the idea of slavery, but he would not go so far as to state that slaves should be or could ever be a white man's social equal. He refused to accept the spread of slavery to the western territories of the United States because it would only perpetuate the evil of slavery, but he entertained the idea of establishing a separate colony for former slaves. He condemned slavery as an institution, but he would not condemn slave owners.

Yet today, Lincoln is remembered as the Great Emancipator and one of the nation's three greatest presidents. But the "elements of greatness, combined with goodness" that General William T. Sherman recognized in him were not always recognized by his contemporaries. In 1860, many people knew Lincoln as Honest Abe, but others considered him immoral and unprincipled. Lincoln's stance on the slavery question is proof that good or bad "character" is often simply a matter of perspective.

There are countless ways voters determine a candidate's good or bad character. Naturally, some will carry more weight than others with particular voters. At the end of the day, these subjective determinations depend solely on the values of each individual voter. Consider the following examples.

Infidelity. Faithfulness by a presidential candidate to his or her spouse is seen by many voters as being a reflection of the faithfulness they can expect from that candidate if he or she is elected president. Being a faithful and loyal husband or wife is seen as a commitment made and a promise kept. Because making commitments and keeping promises is at the core of being a successful president, many voters place high value on what they consider to be the most important commitment and promise a person will make in life. But even when candidates fail the faithfulness test (as so many do), voters will often forgive him or her depending on the spouse's reaction, whether the candidate "came clean" and asked for forgiveness, and the recentness and extent of the infidelity.

History has confirmed that presidents who were unfaithful to their wives prior to being elected include at least James Garfield, Woodrow Wilson, Warren G. Harding, Franklin Roosevelt, Dwight Eisenhower (possibly), John F. Kennedy, Lyndon Johnson, and Bill Clinton. Unsubstantiated rumors often swirl around other presidents.

Sobriety. While some voters believe that drinking alcohol and drug use are vices that automatically reveal a certain character weakness, only a candidate's illegal drug use, drug abuse, or extreme drunkenness is the focus here.

The most famous example of a president who struggled with

sobriety was Ulysses S. Grant. While Grant was not a constant heavy drinker, he had a weakness for alcohol and went on occasional binges that negatively affected his judgment and actions. His drinking got him in trouble early in his military career, and he was accused (often without any evidence) of occasionally being drunk even as a top Union Army general. But when word reached President Lincoln of Grant's history and rumors of insobriety, Lincoln supported him because he recognized that Grant was otherwise a brilliant and effective general and could not be spared.

Presidents who used illegal drugs, abused other drugs, or had major bouts of drunkenness prior to being elected include: Franklin Pierce (alcohol), Andrew Johnson (alcohol), Ulysses S. Grant (alcohol), John F. Kennedy (pain killers), Bill Clinton (marijuana), George W. Bush (alcohol and possibly cocaine), and Barack Obama (marijuana and cocaine).

Truthfulness. A candidate's lack of truthfulness is demonstrated where he or she is proved to have lied or purposefully misrepresented a fact known to be true. Purposeful deception or conspiring behind someone's back also is a sign that a person lacks truthfulness. "Flip-flopping" on legislative votes or other such matters is not representative of a candidate's truthfulness without something more sordid or scandalous. Indeed, purposefully misrepresenting a candidate's voting record may be a better example of a lack of truthfulness.

Thomas Jefferson serves as a famous example of somewhat scandalous deception and dishonesty. While serving as Secretary of State under President Washington, Jefferson famously conspired to work against President Washington's policies while maintaining his position in the cabinet. He was covertly disloyal and at times acted directly against President Washington's wishes. Jefferson always stated that he was acting on principle to save America from heading in the wrong direction, but his excuse does not relieve him of the ignominy of purposeful deception and disloyalty. He eventually resigned his cabinet post and continued to act underhandedly as a private citizen and then as Vice President under President Adams.

Criminal history. A candidate's criminal history is always relevant information for voters to consider. Of course, context matters greatly. Was the candidate wrongly arrested? Was the crime violent or otherwise serious? What was the punishment, if any? How long ago was the crime committed? Did the candidate ever admit guilt and ask for forgiveness? Are there credible allegations of other illegal conduct that was not prosecuted?

History provides several examples of presidents who had some criminal history, both prosecuted and unprosecuted, prior to being elected. They include Andrew Jackson (killed at least one man in a duel), Chester A. Arthur (a corrupt Collector at the New York Customhouse) and George W. Bush (arrested for drunk driving in 1976).

Negative campaigning. To many voters, the art of negative campaigning appears to be a new phenomenon. But negative campaigning is at least two centuries old in America. It seems new and more extensive today simply because it is more prolific. Negative ads now appear on television, radio, the Internet, newspapers, magazines, bumper stickers, and yard signs, among many other places. So-called "personal attacks" now come straight out of opponents' mouths. A candidate's willingness to make negative, often inaccurate, statements about his or her opponent, or his or her willingness to denounce negative statements made by supporters, provides some insight into a candidate's character. But one person's negative ad or personal attack is another person's honest portrayal of the facts. Like so many other things, the truth is often in the eye of the beholder.

One sad thing about choosing which candidate to support for president based on the content of his or her character is that it is often a choice between the lesser of two evils. Of course, no candidate will ever be perfect, but a candidate's character should always be near the forefront of every voter's mind.

2.   POLITICAL IDEOLOGY OR PARTY AFFILIATION

The political ideology or party affiliation of a presidential candidate is frequently the indispensable or essential element that a candidate must possess for a voter to even consider him or her for president.

Liberal, Conservative, or Moderate. Judging a candidate's liberal or conservative credentials—his or her political ideas and beliefs, actions, voting history, and associations—is largely a subjective, issue-by-issue undertaking. Many voters claim that ideological consistency is extremely important to them and that certain compromises or conflicting ideological stances are unacceptable. The same candidate may be too liberal for some voters if he or she supports limited abortion options, and at the same time be too conservative for other voters if he or she favors additional tax cuts for corporations.

Other voters value "moderate" candidates who take somewhat liberal positions on some issues and somewhat conservative positions on other issues. Even though a presidential candidate's ability to seek compromise and act pragmatically is often an indispensable quality for becoming a successful president, it can be a burden when trying to please liberal or conservative supporters or ideology-driven commentators (particularly in party caucuses and primaries). And a few issues (such as slavery) may require a strong and uncompromising stance regardless of public opinion and the direction the political winds are blowing.

Political Party. A candidate's membership in a political party—Democratic, Republican, Independent, Tea, Green, Socialist, Communist, among others—is also a primary consideration for many voters and is often the best indicator of a candidate's overall political ideology. Many voters consider themselves to be party loyalists. They are so proud of their affiliation that they would never dream of breaking party ranks and voting for another party's candidate. However, using the Democratic and Republican parties as examples, history shows that each of the major parties has been on the "wrong" side of major issues (slavery, several wars, civil rights, etc.). This indicates that occasional compromise by loyal Democratic or Republican voters, especially when their party's stance is manifestly wrong, can be exactly what America needs.

With respect to the party affiliations of past presidents, history is fairly balanced overall, with several dominant periods by one party or another, including the Federalists (1789 to 1801), the Democratic Republicans (1801 to 1829), the Republicans (1861 to 1913, excluding Grover Cleveland's two terms), and the Democrats (1933 to 1953). The following are the number of presidents each political party has successfully elected:

Political Party	# of Presidents
Federalists	2
Democratic Republicans	4
Democrats	15
Whigs	4
Republicans	18

Note: George Washington is included as a Federalist and Andrew Johnson is included as a Democrat.

This historical balance is a good thing, and helps keep American politics safe from too frequent periods of excessive partisanship.

3. AGE

The Constitution does not permit voters to elect a candidate younger than 35 years old regardless of the candidate's qualifications or intangibles. But there is no corresponding maximum age for a president.

Old age is often associated with wisdom, experience, and judgment, yet many older candidates have been sorely lacking in wisdom and judgment, and their younger counterparts have had far more useful experiences. In contrast, youth is often associated with energy, idealism, and good health, yet many younger candidates have been sorely lacking in idealism and good health, and their older counterparts have shown far more energy and enthusiasm.

So what age is best? At what age is a candidate best prepared to utilize the virtues of wisdom, experience, and good judgment, while at the same time inspiring the nation with his or her energy, idealism, and good health?

The following are some of the presidents' vital statistics related to age.

- The average age of a president on the date he first took office—by inauguration, death, or resignation—is 54 years old.
- Nine presidents were in their 40s; twenty-four presidents were in their 50s; and ten presidents were in their 60s. No president has been in his 30s or 70s when he first took office.
- Theodore Roosevelt became the youngest president when he ascended to the presidency at 42 years old following President

William McKinley's assassination. He was later elected president in 1904 at 46 years old.

- John F. Kennedy was the youngest elected president at 43 years old, while Ronald Reagan was the oldest at 69 years old.

Age also factors into whether a candidate meets the QUALIFIED THRESHOLD. This is because younger candidates have fewer years to gain the valuable experiences and hone the natural abilities that will help them become increasingly qualified to become president.

Looking to the historical presidential ranking:

- the average age of the Great presidents at election was 53 (range is from 50 to 57);
- the average age of the Near Great presidents at election was 57 (range is from 42 to 69);
- the average age of the Above Average presidents at election was 53 (range is from 43 to 61);
- the average age of the Average presidents at election was 53 (range is from 46 to 64);
- the average age of the Below Average presidents at election was 54 (range is from 46 to 63); and
- the average age of the Failed presidents at election was 55 (range is from 48 to 65).

This shows that age is not a determinative factor in predicting whether a candidate will become a successful president as long as the candidate is between 40 and 70 years old at election. Older or younger candidates may be different, however. In some cases it may be reasonable for voters to prefer a younger candidate over an older candidate, but voters should not value youth so much that they are willing to sacrifice a qualified older candidate in favor of an unqualified younger candidate. Or vice versa. Candidates of every age must prove they are qualified.

Not discussed in detail but also important and somewhat related to a candidate's age is his or her physical health. Some older presidents were in relatively good health for most or all of their presidencies, while some younger presidents had serious health issues before and during their presidencies. It is important that whichever candidate is elected, he or she is physically healthy enough to serve the entire term with energy and vigor.

4. GENDER

Every president has been a man, placing America behind the international trend. In contrast, many other nations have had female heads of government, including the United Kingdom (Margaret Thatcher served as Prime Minister from 1979 to 1990) and Israel (Golda Meir served as Prime Minister from 1969 to 1974). America is behind the international trend. In 2008, Hillary Clinton was the first female presidential candidate in American history with a legitimate chance of being elected. Also in 2008, Sarah Palin was only the second female vice presidential candidate to be nominated by a major political party (Geraldine Ferraro was the first in 1984).

Whether there will be qualified female presidential candidates in the near future remains an open question. The 111th Congress (January 2009 to January 2011) had more women than at any time in history with seventeen senators and seventy-seven representatives (94 out of 535 congressional seats, or almost 18%). But twenty-four states have never elected a female governor and the most female governors serving at the same time was nine (once in 2006 and again in 2009). Finding qualified female candidates in the future will depend on electing more women as representatives, senators, and governors, selecting more women as cabinet officials, and persuading more women who are successful professionals to run for political office.

It may be reasonable for voters to prefer a qualified female candidate over an equally qualified male candidate. History has already demonstrated that women can be as competent as or more competent than men as the head of government, including during times of strife and war. However, like age, voters should not value breaking the gender barrier so highly that they are willing to sacrifice a qualified male candidate in favor of an unqualified female candidate. Or vice versa. Every candidate must still be qualified.

5. RACE

Racial and ethnic ancestry has a long and unpleasant history in America. Until the election of Barack Obama, every American president had been a white man. In fact, a number of presidents owned slaves during their lives, including George Washington, Thomas Jefferson, James Madison, James Monroe, Andrew Jackson, Martin Van Buren,

William Henry Harrison, John Tyler, Zachary Taylor, and Andrew Johnson. And before 2008, no major political party had ever even nominated a minority race candidate for president or vice president (rumors of there being some "negro blood" in Warren G. Harding's ancestry surrounded the 1920 presidential election, but no evidence supports this rumor).

The all-white tradition ended in 2008. Barack Obama was the son of a white woman and a black man, thereby technically making him a "mulatto"—a person of mixed white and black ancestry. Notwithstanding his skin color and half-black ancestry, some opponents have questioned whether it is proper to call Obama the first "black" president. This question is easily answered "yes."

America has always been a "one-drop-of-blood" nation with respect to race, particularly the black race. In fact, Supreme Court legal precedent confirms this. In the infamous 1896 case of *Plessy v. Ferguson*, the Supreme Court dealt with a challenge to a discriminatory Louisiana railroad law forcing black passengers to ride in separate cars from white passengers. Homer Plessy was a man who was one-eighth black (an "octoroon" in antiquated dialect) but who looked white. He announced his racial make-up and was subsequently thrown off the train and arrested for being a black man in the white railway car. This case affirmed the discriminatory doctrine of "separate but equal" (later overturned in 1954 by *Brown v. Board of Education*) and confirmed that America followed the one-drop-of-blood definition of a person's race (i.e., any amount of "black" ancestry made a person legally black and subject to segregation and discriminatory laws). It is therefore completely appropriate to consider Obama America's first black president.

Obama is America's first minority race president, but he will almost certainly not be its last. Racial and ethnic population trends generally predict that, by the 2050 Census, America will become a pluralistic White (non-Hispanic) nation. This means that whites will still be the largest racial/ethnic group but will no longer comprise more than 50% of the population.

According to the statistics collected by the U.S. Census Bureau, as of 2008 Americans belonged to the following racial groups (including approximate percentage of the total population):

- White (non-Hispanic) (66%);
- Hispanic or Latino (14%);
- Black or African American (12.4%);
- Asian American (4.4%);
- American Indian or Alaskan Native (0.8%);
- Native Hawaiian or Pacific Islander (0.14%); and
- Other or two or more races: (2.3%).

The racial make-up of Congress has failed to keep up with the minority population increases, however. In the 111th Congress (January 2009 to January 2011), the racial make-up included:

- Black—forty-two representatives and one senator (8% of Congress);
- Hispanic—twenty-five representatives and three senators (5% of Congress);
- American Indian—one representative and no senators (0.2% of Congress);
- Asian American, Hawaiian, or Pacific Islander—seven representatives and two senators (1.7% of Congress); and
- Total Minorities—seventy-five representatives and six senators (15% of Congress).

With the population trends breaking towards higher minority race populations, and with slowly increasing minority representation in Congress (and in recent presidents' cabinets), it is likely that America will see more qualified minority race candidates (and possibly more minority race presidents) in the near future.

President Obama's election broke the presidential race barrier. This achievement in overcoming historic racial prejudice should not be undersold. It also should not be oversold. It is impossible to tell how many voters made their voting decisions based on race or ethnicity. Race almost certainly had some impact on both sides of the question (in voting *for* Obama and in voting *against* Obama).

For better or worse, race and ethnicity (which also includes ancestries such as German American, Irish American, Swedish American, etc.) will continue to be one of the intangible personal characteristics that voters use to distinguish one candidate from the others. Like age and gender, voters should not value so highly breaking the presidential color barrier that they are willing to sacrifice a qualified candidate in favor of an unqualified candidate with a different racial or ethnic heritage.

6. RELIGION

Religion, similar to race, has had a long and at times difficult history in American politics. The Pilgrims settled in North America in the seventeenth century seeking freedom from religious persecution in Europe. The United States was founded mostly by Protestants who valued the right of religious freedom above almost all other individual rights. Article VI of the Constitution plainly stated that "no religious Test shall ever be required as a Qualification to any Office or public Trust under the United States." And the First Amendment to the Constitution enshrined religious freedom and the free exercise thereof as core American values. Religion has always been important in America.

While some presidents have been more devout than others, all but one have been at least nominally Protestant. The one exception was John F. Kennedy, a Catholic. Considering America's religious make-up, this is unsurprising. In 2007, the Pew Research Center surveyed the American public on the various religious traditions practiced in the United States. The results, by percentage of the population, were as follows:

- Christian Protestant (51.3%);
- Christian Catholic (23.9%);
- Christian Mormon (1.7%);
- Jewish (1.7%);
- Christian Orthodox or Christian Other (0.9%);
- Buddhist (0.7%);
- Muslim (0.6%);
- Hindu (0.4%);
- Other faiths or world religions (1.5%); and
- Unaffiliated (includes atheist, agnostic, or none) (16.1%).

As this survey indicates, a large majority of the electorate continues to identify with one Christian denomination or another, but there is a modern trend where some people are slowly leaving "organized religion" and are becoming what is popularly known as "secularists."

It is possible that someday America will no longer have a Christian majority. This would make it more likely that public support for qualified candidates from non-Christian religious traditions (or no religious tradition) will become much more common.

Thankfully, these are no longer the days of the Know Nothing

Party where, in the 1840s and 1850s, a strong nativist American political movement was hostile to Catholic immigrants and voted en bloc against any Catholic candidate. Today, religious acceptance and tolerance is on the rise and regular church attendance, while often preferred, is no longer expected of presidents.

Candidates from all religions (or no religion) must still be qualified to become president. But whether a voter chooses to require some level of devotion to one religious tradition or another is a personal choice that the voter must weigh alongside the other intangibles. Regardless of a voter's personal religious convictions or traditions, it should never be derogatory to say that a presidential candidate is Protestant, Catholic, Jewish, or Muslim.

7. **MARITAL AND PARENTAL STATUS**

Some voters may prefer presidential candidates who are married with families of their own. If a candidate can have a successful marriage and be a good head of household, perhaps he or she can also be a successful leader and a good Head of State. Other voters may believe that a married candidate will better understand the values of social and economic stability than an unmarried candidate, and that a candidate who is also a parent will be more concerned about the nation's education system, technological advancement, and the human costs of war than candidates who have no children. And others may just enjoy seeing parents with younger children (like the Kennedys or the Obamas) in the White House. Presumably these beliefs help them relate to the candidates in ways that policy discussions and political speeches often cannot. But many loyal spouses and good parents would be (and have been) unsuccessful presidents. A voter's way of relating to a particular candidate is subjective and personal.

Marriage. Thirty-nine out of forty-three presidents were married when they first took office. James Buchanan was the only "bachelor" president who never married. Thomas Jefferson's and Martin Van Buren's wives died years before their elections and they never remarried. And Grover Cleveland was unmarried when he was first elected president in 1884, but he was married in 1886 during his first term and became the first president to get married while in the White House. (He was also the first to become a parent while in office, and the Baby Ruth candy bar was named after his baby, Ruth.) Both John Tyler's and Woodrow Wilson's wives died during their first terms, and both remarried while still in office. Only one president, Ronald Reagan, has been divorced.

First Ladies and First Gentlemen. Not only does a successful marriage often create a connection between a candidate and certain voters who place a high value on marriage, but a wife or husband can often be an invaluable asset to a candidate and later to a president. Many presidential candidates' wives (and in the case of Hillary Clinton, her husband Bill) have been very effective campaigners, and have helped capture votes.

A spouse's ability to interact with voters, knowledgeably answer questions, demonstrate professional and social poise, and be a devoted companion, confidant, adviser, and partner can be hugely important for a presidential candidate. A spouse's indiscretions or failures to live up to the political or social protocol, however, can also become huge liabilities.

Several First Ladies have become respected or beloved national figures in their own right. Someday a First Gentleman or First Husband (or First Dude in the case of Todd Palin) will have large and fashionable shoes to fill. The first truly impressive First Lady was Abigail Adams. Like her husband John Adams, she was very intelligent and accomplished, and became one of his most influential political advisors. Eleanor Roosevelt, Rosalynn Carter, and Hillary Clinton also became known and admired for their political talents. Edith Wilson (Woodrow Wilson's second wife) exercised enormous influence as a sort of "gatekeeper" to her husband between 1919 and 1921 after he suffered a major stroke and was largely incapacitated. Unnervingly, in some ways she actually served as president when he was unable to do so. Other notable First Ladies, known particularly for their social graces, hospitality, and fashion sense, include Dolley Madison, Jacqueline Kennedy, and Nancy Reagan.

Parenthood. George Washington was unable to have children of his own (his wife had two from a previous marriage). Some historians believe that his lack of blood heirs was one reason why he was unanimously selected by his contemporaries to be the first American president: there was no chance of his trying to establish an hereditary monarchy. In stark contrast, Washington's immediate successor John

Adams had three sons, one of whom—John Quincy Adams—grew up to become president.

There have been several other families with multiple men who have been elected president: William Henry Harrison was Benjamin Harrison's grandfather; Theodore Roosevelt was an older distant cousin to Franklin Roosevelt; and George H.W. Bush was George W. Bush's father. Bill and Hillary Clinton would have been the first spouses who were each president had Hillary been successful in 2008. Clearly, America is not completely adverse to presidential family dynasties.

Only five presidents have never had children of their own: George Washington, James Madison, Andrew Jackson, James Polk, and James Buchanan. At least three presidents—Thomas Jefferson, Grover Cleveland, and Warren G. Harding—fathered at least one child out of wedlock. John Tyler had the most children (fifteen), followed by William Henry Harrison (ten), Rutherford B. Hayes (eight), James Garfield (seven), and Thomas Jefferson, Zachary Taylor, Franklin Roosevelt, and George H.W. Bush (each with six). Harry Truman and Bill Clinton each had one child.

Presidential Children. Several presidential children grew up to be successful politicians as well. John Quincy Adams and George W. Bush each became president like their fathers. Charles Francis Adams (son of John Quincy Adams) served in the House of Representatives and was nominated several times for president. Robert Todd Lincoln (son of Abraham Lincoln) became Secretary of War and Minister to Great Britain. Theodore Roosevelt, Jr. was a military hero in both World Wars and served as Assistant Secretary of the Navy (like both his father and his distant cousin Franklin Roosevelt). John Ellis "Jeb" Bush (son of George H.W. Bush and younger brother to George W. Bush) was a two term Florida Governor and is a possible future presidential candidate.

In politics just as in life, many voters understand that they don't just elect the candidate, they elect the whole family.

8. ATTRACTIVENESS

Physical attractiveness is the perception of a person's physical traits that is considered aesthetically pleasing or beautiful. The traits of body symmetry and proportion, athleticism, height, weight, hair color, hair style, smile, posture, appearance of youth or vitality, and countless others factor into a presidential candidate's perceived "attractiveness." Warren G. Harding is considered by some to have been America's most attractive president while Abraham Lincoln is considered to be America's most unattractive president.

Particularly in the modern age of television, the Internet, and color photography, what a candidate looks like is an inevitable intangible consideration for many voters. Perhaps some voters know that they will see the president's face daily or weekly for at least four years and prefer someone who is pleasing to look at. Remember that John F. Kennedy lost his first debate with Richard Nixon in 1960 according to radio listeners, but won according to the television audience, at least in part due to his being more tan, clean shaven, and telegenic.

Some presidents have been physically imposing or athletic men. George Washington was a tall, broad-shouldered man who looked impressive in a military uniform and on a horse. Thomas Jefferson and Lyndon Johnson were also quite tall. Abraham Lincoln was the tallest president at 6-feet-4-inches and was surprisingly athletic. Theodore Roosevelt was a weak child but as an adult he became known for being a vigorous athlete and fierce competitor (a skilled boxer, among other things). Gerald Ford was a great college football player at the University of Michigan and was offered contracts with two professional football teams, but he turned them down to coach boxing and football at Yale. Sometimes American voters prefer strong, tall, masculine men.

At other times, presidents' physical attributes have been less important to voters. John Adams, known by some as "His Rotundity," was fairly short and fat. James Madison was even shorter at about 5-feet-4-inches and very thin. Both Grover Cleveland and William Howard Taft weighed over 300 pounds (Taft peaked at around 355 pounds as president). And Abraham Lincoln was called "unfortunate looking" even by his admirers. None of these presidents would ever have won a beauty pageant.

Male and female candidates are also often judged, however unfairly, by completely different standards. Female candidates must navigate the infinitely more tricky social and professional standards for attire and personal style when they enter into the field of presidential politics. Some (particularly including Hillary Clinton and Sarah Palin in 2008) have already felt scrutiny no male candidate has ever had to face. Whether a female presidential candidate will be closely scrutinized for perceived attractiveness (to her advantage or disadvantage) is not a given, however. For instance, Golda Meir, Israel's female Prime Minister from 1969 to 1974, was a short, plump, grey-haired old lady who was admiringly called Israel's "Iron Lady" and the "grandmother" of the Jewish people.

An unqualified candidate is still unqualified even if he looks like Adonis or Carey Grant, and a qualified candidate is still qualified even if she looks like Mother Theresa or Medusa. Some Americans may hope for a president with movie star good looks such as a Harrison Ford, a Michael Douglas, or a Dennis Haysbert, but history has already proved that attractiveness is not a good predictor of presidential success. Physical health, stamina, and age do matter, but attractiveness rarely does. Hopefully voters will remember the differences between the ugly Abraham Lincoln and the handsome Warren G. Harding whenever they step into the voting booth.

9. SEXUAL ORIENTATION

America has never had an openly gay president. As far as historians know, America has never had a gay president, open or otherwise. Several commentators have speculated that James Buchanan (the "bachelor" president) or Abraham Lincoln may have been gay, but no reliable evidence has ever been brought forward. The most that these speculators have been able to point to is: (i) the common practice in the eighteenth and nineteenth centuries of men sharing rooms and beds (Benjamin Franklin and John Adams also did, and nobody claims they were gay); and (ii) occasional intimate language in letters with other male friends, none of which has ever been shown to have a sexual component or connection. While some may argue that the statistical odds favor the idea that at least one of the forty-three male presidents was gay, there is simply no proof.

Due to the social stereotypes and lingering stigma surrounding homosexuality for both men and women, it is impossible to know with a great degree of certainty what percentage of the American population is gay or lesbian. Unsubstantiated estimates range between 1% and 10% of adults.

Starting in the 1970s, there have been small yet slowly increasing numbers of elected officials and national figures who are openly homosexual. With the steadily increasing national acceptance of gay and lesbian candidates for public office, it is probably only a matter of time before a presidential candidate announces (or a president later reveals) that he or she is homosexual. Some voters adamantly maintain that a gay lifestyle and the "homosexual agenda" are anathema to their values, but the Constitution neither contains a sexual orientation test for the presidency nor adopts any particular religious tenets as the standard for presidential sexual behavior or lifestyles.

The same constitutional, historical, and practical qualification standards apply to straight candidates as they do to gay candidates. Being homosexual (or being heterosexual) does not make an otherwise qualified candidate unqualified. It remains up to the individual voter and his or her personal values and preferences whether sexual orientation will weigh in favor of or against a candidate (or will not be a factor at all).

10. HOME STATE

The Constitution requires that the president and the vice president not be residents of the same state. This essentially means that if there are two qualified candidates from the same state, they cannot be on the same ticket as president and vice president unless one of them moves. In any case, it is rare that two or more qualified candidates will hail from the same state at the same time.

However, voters sometimes prefer a candidate based on his or her home state. They may like their hometown boy and want to see him elected president as a point of state or personal pride. Other times they care about a candidate's "electability" and know that a candidate who is from a large population "swing state" (such as Florida, Ohio, or Pennsylvania) may be better able to defeat an opponent if that swing state is almost guaranteed to vote for its hometown hero. Other candidates who recently moved to a state may be seen by some voters as a "carpetbagger," in which case his or her home state may not be a positive factor at all.

Home state preferences for candidates formerly played a much larger role in American presidential politics, particularly due to the slavery divide between the northern and southern states and to the political bosses and early political party convention systems. But throughout much of the twentieth century and now in the twenty-first century, the home state of the presidential candidate has become far less important for most voters. Now, the most consideration home states typically receive is in the selection of the vice presidential running mate in order to "balance the ticket" geographically or win a questionable or swing state.

11. INTERNATIONAL APPEAL

During the Founding Era, the only ways people could travel were by foot, horse, or ship, and the only ways people could communicate were by speaking face-to-face or by writing letters, distributing pamphlets, or publishing books. Few Americans had ever ventured outside of the colony or state in which they were born, and far fewer had ever traveled to a foreign country.

Over 200 years later, technological advancements in travel and communications have created an increasingly connected global community. People can now travel across oceans and continents in mere hours. They can speak live to literally billions of people via television, the Internet, and radio. They can publish writings or pictures on the Internet and make them immediately available to any person with access to a computer or cellular phone.

In the twenty-first century, the American president cannot be isolated from the international community even if he or she would prefer to be. The world's population has reached almost seven billion people, only 310 million (or 4.6%) of whom live in the United States. The rest live in 191 other sovereign countries, Vatican City, or one of ten other partially-disputed states or territories (e.g., Palestine, Kosovo). As the leader of the world's most economically and militarily powerful nation, every word spoken and every action taken by an American president is scrutinized for signals of strength or weakness, indications of future actions, and global leadership in good times and in crises.

Throughout history, the citizens and the leaders of many other nations have cared greatly about who became America's president. In the early days, Great Britain, France, and Spain, all of whom had colonies and territorial claims in North America, South America,

Central America, and the Caribbean, held strong and often very different opinions of the early presidents. For instance, John Adams was known to favor England, while Thomas Jefferson, James Madison, and James Monroe were known to favor France.

Occasionally, presidential candidates have publicly expressed willingness to enter or to stay out of military conflicts, thereby sending clear signals to foreign leaders about America's possible future military actions if the candidate becomes president. In 1844, candidate James K. Polk was willing to fight Mexico for Texas and other southern and western territories. In 1860, candidate Abraham Lincoln stated he would not start a civil war but would fight to save the Union. In 1952, candidate Dwight Eisenhower stated he would seek a quick end to or a withdrawal from the Korean War. In 1980, candidate Ronald Reagan threatened that if Iran did not release the American hostages he would consider it an act of war. In 2000, candidate George W. Bush acknowledged that he believed Saddam Hussein may need to be removed by military force if Hussein did not comply with certain United Nations resolutions. And in 2008, candidate Barack Obama promised to end the Iraq War while he called the Afghanistan War a war of necessity. Of course, there are many ways apart from signaling future military plans that an American presidential candidate can appeal to, distress, or disappoint other nations.

In the summer of 2008, Barack Obama was the first presidential candidate to include official campaign stops outside of the United States. He visited France, Germany, Israel, Jordan, and Great Britain and gave speeches in each country. The stated purpose of his visits was to "assess the situation in countries that are critical to American national security." Many people also saw his trip as an attempt to bolster his foreign policy credentials and a way to showcase "Obamamania," a catchy term for his widely-recognized international appeal. In some foreign countries, polls showed that more than twice as many people had confidence that Obama "would do the right thing" in world affairs than would his Republican opponent John McCain.

American voters may appreciate or be inspired by a presidential candidate's international appeal. Some were likely inspired by Obama's appeal. Or they may become annoyed by or take offense at a candidate who seems to play up his or her popularity with foreign crowds when they think he or she should be focusing on domestic campaign issues and speaking to American voters. Only time will tell if the Obama precedent will be followed in future presidential election cycles.

12. PERSONALITY

"Personality" is the totality of a person's behavioral and emotional characteristics. In some ways it overlaps with "character." Personal characteristics like modesty, courage, a forgiving nature, decisiveness can fit into both a candidate's character and his or her personality.

But personality is more than just a person's character. It includes how a person relates to or connects with other people. Does a candidate demonstrate vigor or a love of life? Is he self-confident or arrogant or meek? Can she easily empathize with other people? What about his sense of humor? How talkative is she in conversations? Does he show great self-discipline? Is he charming? How "likeable" is she?

In 2000 and 2004, polls showed that voters preferred George W. Bush over his opponents Al Gore and John Kerry when asked the poll question, "Who would you prefer to have a beer with?" And in the days of the powerful political bosses and back-room deals, a candidate's likeability, charm, and number of powerful friends weighed heavily in presidential selection decisions. Other candidates have seemed to develop a special connection with voters and colleagues that sometimes seems to transcend politics. Ronald Reagan and Bill Clinton are two modern examples of candidates who could attract voters with their charm and empathy. Abraham Lincoln was perhaps the funniest president, being both a great storyteller and having an exceptional wit. Theodore Roosevelt, Calvin Coolidge, and Harry Truman were also known for their quick humor. Theodore Roosevelt and Lyndon Johnson were probably the two presidents with the most overwhelming personalities in terms of energy and magnetism.

Some presidential candidates must overcome their otherwise unlikeable personalities. John Adams was famously vain and irascible and could drive his colleagues up a wall. He was brilliant and incorruptible, but he had many detractors who disliked his personality. John Quincy Adams was very similar to his father. Richard Nixon could be very awkward and envied others (particularly John F. Kennedy) who had natural charm and charisma.

Personality is perhaps the most intangible of all of the intangible personal characteristics. A presidential candidate's personality can attract or aggravate voters. Like the indefinable personal connection we call love or adoration, some voters allow a candidate's personality to surpass all other considerations and develop an unbreakable, even blinding, loyalty to a candidate. Because the attraction of personality, or sometimes the "cult of celebrity," can be so vague yet so powerful, voters must take special care to remember that possessing a charming or larger-than-life personality does not make an otherwise unqualified candidate qualified to become president.

CONCLUSION

After a presidential candidate has satisfied the CONSTITUTIONAL THRESHOLD and met or exceeded the QUALIFIED THRESHOLD, voting decisions almost inevitably come down to each candidate's intangible personal characteristics. This is not necessarily a bad thing. If all of the candidates left standing on Election Day are qualified to become president, voters must choose one way or another to distinguish between the candidates and vote for one of them. And candidates must also find ways to differentiate amongst themselves. Hopefully, most voters will consider the various intangible characteristics in a thoughtful, well-intentioned manner and not from a perspective of racism, sexism, homophobia, or any other negative attitudes.

Ultimately, even highly qualified presidential candidates may sometimes be the wrong choice for America. A candidate with Great qualifications on paper may still be an unfaithful, deceitful, dishonest, frequently intoxicated, racist, or unethical person. Voters simply need to narrow the candidate field to only those who are objectively qualified to become president and then hope and pray that they have enough other information about the candidates' intangibles to make the best voting decision possible.

FOURTEEN
The Re-election Question

George Washington is the only president who didn't blame the previous administration for his troubles.

– Author Unknown

Hell, I never vote for anybody, I always vote against.

– W.C. Fields

ONE OF THE MOST important (and most difficult) questions for American voters is when to re-elect an incumbent president and when to choose a challenger instead.

Party Loyalists

Many Americans simply vote for or against an incumbent president's re-election based purely on the incumbent's and challenger's respective political parties. Republicans vote for Republicans and Democrats vote for Democrats, no questions asked. Whoever wins the party's nomination wins the voter's support, even if the voter did not originally support the candidate in the party caucuses and primaries. Unenthusiastic party loyalists may stay home instead of vote for their party's nominee, but they will never seriously consider voting for another party's candidate for president.

One potential danger to the party-loyalty approach, however, is that it could cause some voters whose preferred political party is out of power to disregard the challenger's qualifications and vote for him or her even if he or she fails to meet the QUALIFIED THRESHOLD. Hopefully, voters who follow this party-loyalty approach will participate early in the caucus and primary season and help ensure that the challenger is actually qualified to become president.

REFERENDUM VOTERS

Other Americans base their re-election decisions on their personal evaluations of the past four years and their perceptions as to whether the incumbent president was a good leader and generally did a good job. This approach to voting is often called a "referendum" on the incumbent president, where the voter's perspective regarding the incumbent's job performance is the most important factor. Most referendum voters are "independents" who do not identify strongly with one particular political party, or they are members of a party but are sometimes willing to support another party's candidate.

Voters who follow the referendum approach break down into three categories.

1. If they believe the incumbent has performed as well as or better than expected, they will vote for re-election regardless of the challenger's qualifications.
2. If they believe the incumbent has performed worse than expected, they will vote against re-election regardless of the challenger's qualifications.
3. If they have mixed perceptions as to whether the incumbent has performed well or poorly, they will carefully evaluate the challenger's qualifications to determine whether they believe he or she will be a better president than the incumbent.

The voters who fall into one of the first two categories are unlikely to be swayed by a challenger's qualifications. Thus, for voters in each of the first two categories, every re-election question boils down to a simple referendum.

It is the voters who fall into in the third category who remain open to persuasion as to whether a challenger will be a better, similar, or worse president than the incumbent.

HISTORICAL BREAKDOWN

Out of forty-three American presidents, nineteen were successful in their bids for re-election. This means that historically there is a 44.19% chance that a first-term president will be re-elected to a second term.

PRESIDENTS WHO WERE RE-ELECTED

Election	Re-elected President	Resume Score/ Resume Ranking	Historical Ranking
1792	George Washington	58 / Great	Great
1804	Thomas Jefferson	59 / Great	Near Great
1812	James Madison	56 / Great	Above Average
1820	James Monroe	60 / Great	Above Average
1832	Andrew Jackson	40 / Average	Near Great
1864	Abraham Lincoln*	47 / Above Average	Great
1872	Ulysses S. Grant	39 / Below Average	Below Average
1892	Grover Cleveland	24 / Poor	Above Average
1904	Theodore Roosevelt**	62 / Great	Near Great
1916	Woodrow Wilson	45 / Above Average	Near Great
1924	Calvin Coolidge**	31 / Poor	Average
1936			
1940	Franklin Roosevelt	55 / Great	Great
1944			
1948	Harry Truman**	40 / Average	Near Great
1956	Dwight Eisenhower	62 / Great	Near Great
1964	Lyndon Johnson**	35 / Below Average	Above Average
1972	Richard Nixon	68 / Great	Below Average
1984	Ronald Reagan	41 / Average	Near Great
1996	Bill Clinton	50 / Near Great	Average
2004	George W. Bush	38 / Below Average	Not Ranked

*Note: Abraham Lincoln was assassinated a little over one month into his second term and did not serve two full terms.

**Note: four presidents were "re-elected" after having been elected vice president and ascending to the presidency (Theodore Roosevelt, Calvin Coolidge, Harry Truman, and Lyndon Johnson).

History shows that American voters prefer to re-elect presidents who first took office with strong qualifications. Out of the nineteen presidents who were re-elected, eleven of them (57.89%) became president with Above Average, Near Great, or Great qualifications, and fourteen of them (73.68%) met the QUALIFIED THRESHOLD. Only five presidents who entered the presidency with Below Average or Poor qualifications (26.32%) have been re-elected.

All this makes one thing clear: presidential candidates who meet the QUALIFIED THRESHOLD not only have a very high probability of becoming a successful president, but they also have a much better chance of being re-elected. In other words, it is a win for the voters (they get a more successful president) and a win for the presidents themselves (they get re-elected).

INCUMBENTS VERSUS CHALLENGERS

Ten presidents have actively campaigned for re-election and lost to a challenger.

INCUMBENT PRESIDENTS WHO LOST RE-ELECTION			
Election	Incumbent President (Resume Score)	Successful Challenger (Resume Score)	Change in Historical Ranking
1800	John Adams (69)	Thomas Jefferson (59)	Improve
1828	John Quincy Adams (66)	Andrew Jackson (40)	Improve
1840	Martin Van Buren (38)	William H. Harrison (44)	Uncertain
1888	Grover Cleveland (24)	Benjamin Harrison (47)	Decline
1892	Benjamin Harrison (47)	Grover Cleveland (24*)	Improve
1912	William H. Taft (46)	Woodrow Wilson (45)	Improve
1932	Herbert Hoover (54)	Franklin Roosevelt (55)	Improve
1976	Gerald Ford (38)	Jimmy Carter (44)	No Change
1980	Jimmy Carter (44)	Ronald Reagan (41)	Improve
1992	George H.W. Bush (54)	Bill Clinton (50)	No Change

*Note: Grover Cleveland's resume was based on his 1884 qualifications. Because neither the party-loyalist approach nor the referendum approach depends upon a president's updated resume score (and because there are many inherent difficulties in trying to re-score a president's resume after his or her first term) the 1884 score is used.

Nine out of ten challengers who successfully defeated an incumbent president met the QUALIFIED THRESHOLD. Moreover, six of the successful challengers ended up being more successful presidents than the incumbents they replaced, and two had similar success. (Because William Henry Harrison died one month after his inauguration, it is uncertain whether he would have been an improvement to Martin Van Buren who was an Average president). In other words, six out of nine successful challengers (66.67%) were improvements, and eight out of nine successful challengers (88.88%) were as good as or better presidents than the defeated incumbents. Only Benjamin Harrison was less successful than Grover Cleveland, and in that unusual case Cleveland was subsequently re-elected to a second term in 1892, defeating the incumbent Harrison.

CONCLUSIONS

Several simple conclusions can be drawn from the historical facts. First, it is almost impossible (only a 10% chance) for a challenger who fails to meet the QUALIFIED THRESHOLD to defeat an incumbent president. The one historical exception was Grover Cleveland who had already served as president once and who lost a very close election as an incumbent president in 1888. Thus, if a voter supports an unqualified challenger running against an incumbent president, the voter is almost guaranteeing the incumbent's re-election.

And second, there is not a strong correlation between an unsuccessful incumbent's qualifications upon entering the presidency and the successful challenger's qualifications (other than the fact that the challenger meets the QUALIFIED THRESHOLD). In fact, seven out of ten incumbent presidents who lost their re-election bids met the QUALIFIED THRESHOLD when they first took office. The incumbents simply underperformed during the first four years and the voters decided to take a chance with a different president. This means that an incumbent's chances of being re-elected are almost entirely tied to his or her performance during the first four years. An incumbent who was perceived as successful during the first term will probably not be defeated regardless of the challenger's qualifications.

At the end of the day, history confirms two things: (i) only challengers whose qualifications meet the QUALIFIED THRESHOLD have a chance at defeating an incumbent president regardless of the incumbent's job performance; and (ii) every re-election contest is to a certain extent a referendum on the incumbent president's job performance during the first four years.

CONCLUSION

The President is merely the most important among a large number of public servants. He should be supported or opposed exactly to the degree which is warranted by his good conduct or bad conduct, his efficiency or inefficiency in rendering loyal, able, and disinterested service to the Nation as a whole. Therefore it is absolutely necessary that there should be full liberty to tell the truth about his acts, and this means that it is exactly necessary to blame him when he does wrong as to praise him when he does right. Any other attitude in an American citizen is both base and servile.

– Theodore Roosevelt

It behooves every man to remember that the work of the critic is of altogether secondary importance, and that in the end, progress is accomplished by the man who does things.

– Theodore Roosevelt

QUALIFIED HAS DEMONSTRATED THAT more qualified candidates become more successful presidents. Yet some American voters still get seduced by the draw of a particular presidential candidate's intellectual brilliance, great speechmaking abilities, long legislative career, high-level executive experience, prior military service, or foreign policy credentials. Others toe the partisan line and simply vote for whatever candidate is nominated by their preferred political party. But the foregoing analysis shows that no single experience or ability (or party affiliation) is significantly more important than the others in predicting presidential success.

Voters should therefore be wary of supporting popular candidates who may have one or two Above Average or Great experiences or abilities but who fail to meet the QUALIFIED THRESHOLD. They should also be wary of supporting candidates simply because they generally like or agree with them, without also looking to the candidates' basic qualifications for the presidency. History shows that a candidate's overall qualifications—as shown by his or her total resume score—is the most important factor when predicting whether he or she will become a successful president.

VICE PRESIDENTS

In every presidential election season, voters should remember that the qualifications of vice presidential candidates, like those of presidential candidates, should meet not only the CONSTITUTIONAL THRESHOLD as mandated by the Twelfth Amendment, but also the QUALIFIED THRESHOLD. Because a vice president could unexpectedly ascend to the presidency at any time, he or she should also have a high probability of becoming a successful president.

There have been forty-seven vice presidents in American history. For the first four presidential elections, there was no presidential/vice presidential "ticket" and the candidate with the most electoral votes became president while the candidate with the second most electoral votes became vice president. This original electoral process was intended to ensure that highly qualified candidates would become vice president as well as president. However, after the famous election of 1800 where Thomas Jefferson and Aaron Burr tied in the electoral college vote count, the Twelfth Amendment created the current system of separate balloting for presidential candidates and vice presidential candidates. This change created the presidential "ticket" system and made it less likely that vice presidents would themselves be highly qualified to become president.

Five former vice presidents were elected to the presidency and nine vice presidents have ascended to the presidency due to the death (eight times) or resignation (once) of their predecessor.

The fourteen vice presidents who became president are:

President (Resume Score)	Tenure as Vice President	Became President	Reason
John Adams (69)	1789–1797	1797	Election
Thomas Jefferson (59)	1797–1801	1801	Election
Martin Van Buren (38)	1833–1837	1837	Election
John Tyler (39)	1841	1841	Death of Harrison
Millard Fillmore (26)	1849–1850	1850	Death of Taylor
Andrew Johnson (36)	1865	1865	Lincoln Assassination
Chester A. Arthur (29)	1881	1881	Garfield Assassination
Theodore Roosevelt (62)	1901	1901	McKinley Assassination
Calvin Coolidge (31)	1921–1923	1923	Death of Harding
Harry Truman (40)	1945	1945	Death of Roosevelt
Richard Nixon (68)	1953–1961	1969	Election
Lyndon Johnson (35)	1961–1963	1963	Kennedy Assassination
Gerald Ford (38)	1973–1974	1974	Nixon Resigned
George H.W. Bush (54)	1981–1989	1989	Election

Out of the five vice presidents who were later elected president, four of them (80.00%) met the QUALIFIED THRESHOLD (three with Great qualifications and one with Near Great qualifications). The same number also became Average or better presidents.

What is unsettling is the fact that only one out of the nine vice presidents (11.11%) who ascended to the presidency had a resume that exceeded the QUALIFIED THRESHOLD when he became vice president (Theodore Roosevelt). Seven out of nine (77.78%) entered the vice presidency with Below Average or Poor qualifications, and the eighth (Harry Truman) was right on the qualified bubble with a score of 40. Unlike the five vice presidents who later became president for the first time by election, the nine vice presidents who ascended to the presidency had a very mixed record of presidential success. Four of them were ranked as Below Average or Failed presidents, and two others overachieved when they became Average presidents.

Ultimately, seven out of the fourteen Below Average or Failed presidents (50%) were vice presidents who ascended to the presidency, and only three of them became Average or better presidents. These historical facts make clear that America's general trend of selecting qualified presidents has not extended to the almost equally important task of selecting qualified vice presidents. This is not encouraging, especially when nine out of forty-three presidents (20.93%) have either died in office or resigned.

Modernly, each party's vice presidential candidate has been handpicked by the party's presidential nominee. In making their decisions they have weighed various factors including: (i) creating regional balance between the candidates; (ii) creating an ideological balance between the candidates; (iii) the vice presidential candidate's potential to influence the voting outcome in a particular state or states; (iv) the vice presidential candidate's perceived popular appeal; and (v) the vice presidential candidate's qualifications for becoming president, if necessary.

Because there is a better than 20% chance that a vice president will unexpectedly ascend to the presidency mid-term, it is imperative that reason (v) above is the primary (if not the only) criterion used to select a party's vice presidential candidate. While the modern vice presidency certainly provides excellent experiences for a future president, that office should not be used simply as a training position for candidates who are otherwise unqualified for the presidency. It simply is not worth the risk.

COVER LETTERS

Secondary in importance to a professional resume, but not to be ignored, is a professional cover letter. Presidential candidates should also consider drafting a cover letter addressed to the American public and submitting it along with their resumes.

Cover letters are meant to supplement and complement a candidate's resume, not to duplicate or replace it. The greatest value it has is its ability to highlight several of the most impressive parts of the candidate's resume while at the same time adding a personal touch to the bare facts. Rather than simply repeating the factual information of the resume, it should tell a story and establish a theme for a candidate (the dependable candidate, the visionary candidate, the war hero candidate, etc.). At its core, the cover letter should attempt to convince the reader that he or she is the best person for the job and make the reader want to interview the candidate.

A cover letter is also a great way for a candidate to answer several basic questions. Does he or she have enough relevant experiences and abilities to be successful? Is he or she the best prospect out of all of the candidates? What are his or her goals and vision for the position? And why does he or she want the job in the first place?

Presidential candidates already frequently deliver what could be considered oral cover letters. Many stump speeches touch on all of the same cover letter themes—best qualifications, best candidate, and goals and vision for the country—but take a half hour or longer to do so. And many media interview answers simply recite what would otherwise be a good written cover letter. Essentially, a great cover letter is simply the written version of a great two-minute answer to the question: why will you be a successful president? The smartest approach is for presidential candidates to put the answer in writing in the first place.

Perhaps the most famous botched "cover letter answer" was then-Senator Ted Kennedy's answer to CBS journalist Roger Mudd's simple interview question on November 4, 1979. Kennedy's two-minute answer can only be described as rambling, vague, and somewhat incoherent.

Mudd: Why do you want to become president?

Kennedy: Well I'm ... uh ... were I to, to make the, uh, the announcement ... to run, the reasons that I would run is because I have a great belief in this country that it is, there's more natural resources than any nation in the world, there's the greatest educated population in the world, the greatest technology of any country in the world, uh, the greatest capacity for innovation in the world, and the greatest political system in the world. And yet, uh, I see, at, uh, the current time, that, uh, most of the industrial nations of the world are exceeding us in terms of productivity, are doing better than us in terms of meeting the problems of inflation, that they're dealing with their problems of energy and their problems of unemployment, and it just seems to me that, uh, this nation can cope and deal with its problems in a way that it has in the past. We are facing complex issues and problems in this nation at this time. But we have faced similar challenges at other times. And the energies and the resourcefulness of this nation I think should be focused on these problems in a way that brings a sense of restoration, uh, in this country by its people in dealing with the problems that we face, primarily the issues on the economy, the problems of inflation and the problems of, uh, uh, energy. And, uh, I would uh, basically, uh, feel that, uh, that it's imperative for this country to either move forward that it can't stand still or otherwise it moves backward.

Perhaps if Senator Kennedy had written (and then memorized) a precise and professional cover letter, he would have been better prepared and more persuasive in answering this simple, straightforward, and altogether predictable interview question. Many commentators believe that his unconvincing answer helped to sink his 1980 presidential campaign before it had ever formally begun.

Every presidential candidate will have a unique story to tell, and should tailor the cover letter message to fit his or her particular personality, experiences, reason for seeking the presidency, and vision for America's future. But a cover letter should never serve as a replacement for the candidate's official resume.

The Resume Challenge Revisited

Presidential candidates are, by definition, professional politicians. They actively seek a high pay, high stress job that manages a large staff and has globally significant responsibilities. Every American voter is therefore, by definition, a prospective employer vested by the Constitution with the responsibility of helping to select which candidate to hire and whether to offer one or two four-year terms of employment. From this perspective at least, it makes complete sense for American voters to treat every presidential candidate like a typical professional job applicant and insist on reviewing a candidate's official resume at the beginning of the hiring process. It is high time that presidential candidates join every other American professional and submit an official resume to his or her prospective employer, the American voters.

The benefits that would flow from accepting *Qualified*'s resume challenge would be manifold and immediate. Voters could quickly weed out all of the clearly unqualified candidates, saving time and money and leaving only candidates who meet the QUALIFIED THRESHOLD. In reviewing the presidential resumes, voters could also better compare the various candidates with each other and with past presidents, providing additional insights into what type of president the candidate may become.

As discussed throughout this book and shown in Appendix A, the presidents have had a wide range of experiences and abilities, and more than two-thirds of them have met the QUALIFIED THRESHOLD. Hopefully, this encouraging trend will continue with the 2012 presidential election and beyond. The sample resumes of the seventeen current and potential candidates provided in Appendix B show that the current presidential field also has a wide range of experiences, abilities, and other intangible characteristics.

Several current candidates—e.g., Sarah Palin, Michele Bachmann, and Chris Christie—are unqualified to become president (at least in 2012). Other current or potential candidates—e.g., Hillary Clinton, Condoleezza Rice, Newt Gingrich, and Ron Paul—are highly qualified to become president, but they either may not run or may have intangible personal characteristics that make them unfit or otherwise unelectable. Moreover, President Obama barely met the QUALIFIED THRESHOLD in 2008, and, from an historical perspective, appears vulnerable against a qualified challenger. As is almost always the case in presidential elections, the American voters have some difficult choices to make in 2012.

Ultimately, there is great upside and no downside to accepting the resume challenge and working to make the resume submission process and QUALIFIED THRESHOLD evaluation a standard part of all future campaigns and elections. Once one presidential candidate releases his or her professional resume, other candidates will almost certainly follow suit until it becomes a basic part of the political hiring process. In this manner, voters can begin participating in the process from the very start, and begin to better evaluate candidates based on the presidency's constitutional, historical, and practical responsibilities. Hopefully, voters will choose to support only those candidates who meet the QUALIFIED THRESHOLD and who have a high probability of becoming successful presidents. In the end, electing a president who becomes successful is the overarching goal of every presidential election.

Total Score	President	Resume Ranking	Historical Success
	PRESIDENTIAL RESUMES		
58	George Washington	Great	Great
69	John Adams	Great	Above Average
59	Thomas Jefferson	Great	Near Great
56	James Madison	Great	Above Average
60	James Monroe	Great	Above Average
66	John Quincy Adams	Great	Average
40	Andrew Jackson	Average	Near Great
38	Martin Van Buren	Below Average	Average
44	William H. Harrison	Average	Not Ranked
39	John Tyler	Below Average	Below Average
45	James K. Polk	Above Average	Near Great
23	Zachary Taylor	Poor	Below Average
26	Millard Fillmore	Poor	Below Average
44	Franklin Pierce	Average	Failure
44	James Buchanan	Average	Failure
47	Abraham Lincoln	Above Average	Great
36	Andrew Johnson	Below Average	Failure
39	Ulysses S. Grant	Below Average	Below Average
38	Rutherford B. Hayes	Below Average	Average
48	James Garfield	Above Average	Not Ranked
29	Chester A. Arthur	Poor	Average
24	Grover Cleveland	Poor	Above Average
47	Benjamin Harrison	Above Average	Below Average
42	William McKinley	Average	Above Average
62	Theodore Roosevelt	Great	Near Great
46	William H. Taft	Above Average	Average
45	Woodrow Wilson	Above Average	Near Great
29	Warren G. Harding	Poor	Failure
31	Calvin Coolidge	Poor	Average
54	Herbert Hoover	Near Great	Below Average
55	Franklin Roosevelt	Great	Great
40	Harry Truman	Average	Near Great
62	Dwight Eisenhower	Great	Near Great
49	John F. Kennedy	Above Average	Above Average
35	Lyndon Johnson	Below Average	Above Average
68	Richard Nixon	Great	Below Average
38	Gerald Ford	Below Average	Below Average
44	Jimmy Carter	Average	Below Average
41	Ronald Reagan	Average	Near Great
54	George H.W. Bush	Near Great	Average
50	Bill Clinton	Near Great	Average
38	George W. Bush	Below Average	Not Ranked
40	Barack Obama	Average	Not Ranked

APPENDIX A
PRESIDENTIAL RESUMES

APPENDIX A PROVIDES PRESIDENTIAL resumes for each of the forty-three American presidents, drafted as of the date they were either elected president or elected or appointed vice president prior to ascending to the presidency due to the death or resignation of their predecessor.

In each resume, *Qualified* has diligently attempted to provide the most factually accurate information and assessments, and believes it has provided reasonable scores and rankings of the presidents based on careful historical analysis. Nevertheless, readers are encouraged to perform their own evaluations of the presidents based on the historical evidence provided in the detailed summaries sections of Chapters Four through Eleven if they disagree with any of this book's scorings, rankings, or conclusions.

The forty-three presidential resumes are provided in chronological order, beginning with George Washington and ending with Barack Obama.

GEORGE WASHINGTON

58

Election: 1789	**Party**: None (Federalist)	**Opponent**: None
Age: 57	**Home State**: Virginia	**Running Mate**: None

LEGISLATIVE EXPERIENCE 8

1759–1775: member of the Virginia House of Burgesses; leader starting in 1769
1774: delegate to First Continental Congress; played only a minor role
1775: delegate to Second Continental Congress; chaired several military
committees
1787: delegate to and President of the Constitutional Convention; presided daily

EXECUTIVE EXPERIENCE 8

1754–1759, 1775–1783: high-ranking military officer
1759–1775, 1783–1788: personally managed properties and business operations
Known to be a great talent scout; good at delegation while keeping overall control

MILITARY EXPERIENCE 15

1754–1759: during French and Indian War was a Lieutenant Colonel in the
Virginia Militia; then Captain and aide-de-camp to British General Braddock;
then Colonel in the Virginia Militia; highest ranking military officer in Virginia
in 1759
Fought multiple battles/skirmishes during the French and Indian War
1775–1783: Commander in Chief of the Continental Army; commanded up to
16,000 troops and 28 generals; spent all eight years in the field with the Army
Fought many battles during the Revolutionary War, including at Long Island,
Trenton, and Yorktown

FOREIGN EXPERIENCE 6

Born and lived in British Empire (French and Indian and Revolutionary Wars)
1751: traveled to Barbados as a teenager
1754–1788: fought with/against the British, French, and Indians; had many
commercial dealings within the British mercantile system

PRIVATE WORK EXPERIENCE 7

1759–1775, 1783–1788: assiduous hands-on management of extensive properties
Plantation included 20,000+ acres, crops, flour mill, trade ships

EDUCATION/INTELLECT 7

Grade school equivalent formal education; no classical curriculum or college
Personal advisers on policy and politics: Benjamin Franklin, John Adams, Thomas
Jefferson, James Madison, Alexander Hamilton, George Mason, and John Jay

WRITING ABILITY 6

Drafted thousands of letters and military orders; meticulous attention to detail
Writing steadily improved with help from brilliant advisers and much practice

PUBLIC SPEAKING ABILITY 1

Rarely spoke publicly; speeches lasted only a few minutes; uninspired and awkward

INTANGIBLES

Tall and athletic; physical bravery; great self-control and judgment

JOHN ADAMS 69

Election: 1796   **Party**: None (Federalist)   **Opponent**: Jefferson
Age: 61   **Home State**: Massachusetts   **Running Mate**: None

LEGISLATIVE EXPERIENCE 13

1768–1774: representative in colonial Massachusetts legislature
1774: delegate to First Continental Congress; modest influence
1775–1778: delegate to Second Continental Congress; the most active and effective leader; served on 26+ committees; head of the Board of War
1779: delegate to Massachusetts Constitutional Convention; primary drafter
1789–1796: Vice President; presided daily over Senate; cast 31 tie-breaking votes

EXECUTIVE EXPERIENCE 2

Some executive duties as a foreign minister and Vice President

MILITARY EXPERIENCE 2

Never served in any military capacity
1776–1777: headed of the Second Continental Congress's Board or War

FOREIGN EXPERIENCE 13

Born and lived in the British Empire (French and Indian and Revolutionary Wars)
1778–1780: Commissioner and then Minister to France (became fluent in French)
1780–1782: Minister to Holland; negotiated a major loan (fluent in Dutch)
1783–1788: Commissioner and then Minister to Great Britain

PRIVATE WORK EXPERIENCE 9

1755–1758: school teacher while studying law at night and under an attorney
1759–1778: became Boston's busiest and most respected trial lawyer; successfully defended British soldiers accused of murder in the "Boston Massacre" (1770)
1760s–1790s: owned and farmed 40+ acres in Massachusetts

EDUCATION/INTELLECT 10

Was tutored as a youth by his father, a Harvard educated farmer
1750–1755: received great classical education at Harvard College; was an excellent student who was very hard-working
1755–1758: read law under a local Boston attorney
Possessed a brilliant intellect; one of the most widely-read men of the generation

WRITING ABILITY 10

An excellent and prolific writer, essayist, and correspondent; publications include: *Dissertation* (1765), *Braintree Instructions* (1765), *Novanglus* (1774), *Thoughts on Government* (1776), *Defence of the Constitution* (1787), and *Discourses on Davila* (1790)
1779: primary drafter (sub-subcommittee of one) of Massachusetts Constitution
Wrote thousands of long letters full of wit and insight; could have been a novelist

PUBLIC SPEAKING ABILITY 10

An exceptional and polished orator and debater; known for eloquence and passion
Accomplished at extemporaneous speaking (rarely used notes or a text); witty
Spoke with a clear, sonorous voice; most effective advocate for independence

INTANGIBLES

Politically independent; scrupulously honest; devout Christian; wife Abigail

273

THOMAS JEFFERSON — 59

Election: 1800   **Party**: Democratic Republican   **Opponent**: Adams
Age: 57   **Home State**: Virginia   **Running Mate**: Burr

LEGISLATIVE EXPERIENCE — 12

1769–1775: member of the Virginia House of Burgesses; only modest influence
1776: delegate to Second Continental Congress; primary role was drafter of reports
1776–1779: member of the Virginia General Assembly; a fairly effective leader
1783–1784: delegate to the Confederation Congress; accomplished little
1797–1800: Vice President; presided daily over Senate; no executive
  responsibilities

EXECUTIVE EXPERIENCE — 8

1779–1781: Governor of Virginia; few executive powers; commanded the militia
1790–1794: Secretary of State; capable administrator; feud with A. Hamilton
Some executive duties as a foreign minister

MILITARY EXPERIENCE — 2

Never served in any military capacity
Made several poor military decisions as Governor and head of the Virginia Militia

FOREIGN EXPERIENCE — 10

Born and lived in the British Empire (French and Indian and Revolutionary Wars)
1784–1789: Minister to France; close partner with John Adams; very able diplomat
Responsible for foreign relations and policy as Secretary of State (1790–1794)

PRIVATE WORK EXPERIENCE — 6

1767–1769: briefly practiced law; a capable researcher; not a good trial attorney
A fairly hands-off manager of his extensive properties; always deeply in debt
1790s: became the first leader of the opposition party (Democratic Republican)

EDUCATION/INTELLECT — 10

Boarded with a local schoolmaster to prepare for a classical college education
1760–1762: received great classical education at the College of William and Mary;
  a very hard-working and talented student; also diligently practiced the violin
1762–1765: studied law as an apprentice to the renowned attorney George Wythe
Possessed a brilliant intellect; one of the most widely-read men of the generation

WRITING ABILITY — 10

A brilliant, beautiful, and prolific writer and correspondent; great style and
  rhetoric
Publications include: *A Summary View* (1774), *Declaration of Causes* (1775), *Declaration
  of Independence* (1776), *Act for Religious Freedom* (1779), *Notes on Virginia* (1781),
  Report on Trade (1793), and the *Kentucky Resolutions* (1798)
Writings were elegant and eloquent; used clear, descriptive, and poetic language

PUBLIC SPEAKING ABILITY — 1

A nervous, awkward, almost inaudible speaker; never debated or made speeches

INTANGIBLES

A master of rhetoric; political visionary; had a child with his slave Sally Hemings

JAMES MADISON   56

Election: 1808   **Party**: Democratic Republican   **Opponent**: Clinton
Age: 57   **Home State**: Virginia   **Running Mate**: Gerry

LEGISLATIVE EXPERIENCE   15

1774–1775: member of the Committee of Safety for Orange County, Virginia
1776: delegate to the Virginia constitutional convention; played only a minor role
1778–1779: member of the Virginia Council of State; started gaining prominence
1779–1783: delegate to the Confederation Congress; became influential
1784–1786: member of the Virginia General Assembly; very influential
1786: delegate to the Annapolis Convention; one of the most effective leaders
1787: delegate to the Constitutional Convention; became the most influential leader
1789–1797: member of the U.S. House of Representatives; acted as floor leader

EXECUTIVE EXPERIENCE   8

1801–1808: Secretary of State; dealt with Louisiana Purchase and Napoleonic Wars
Closest advisor to President Jefferson; a co-architect of the administration

MILITARY EXPERIENCE   1

1775: commissioned and drilled briefly with the Virginia Militia; never fought

FOREIGN EXPERIENCE   5

Born and lived in the British Empire (young adult during the Revolutionary War)
Responsible for foreign relations and policy as Secretary of State (1801–1809)

PRIVATE WORK EXPERIENCE   1

No real career outside of government service and politics
1790s: became a co-founder of the opposition party (Democratic Republican)

EDUCATION/INTELLECT   10

1762–1769: excellent private tutors preparing for a classical college education
1769–1772: received great classical education at College of New Jersey at Princeton (now Princeton University); a hardworking and intense student
1784–1786: self-studied law but had no intention of becoming a practicing lawyer
Brilliant intellect and accomplished scholar; widely read on government and politics

WRITING ABILITY   10

Excellent and prolific writer; publications include: *Vices of the Political System* (1787), *Notes on the Constitutional Convention* (1787); on the Constitutional Convention Committee of Style (1787); 29 out of 85 essays in THE FEDERALIST (1787); *Virginia Resolutions* (1798); *1800 Report* (1800); *Examination of British Doctrine* (1805)
Best at careful and reasoned analysis of complex issues; persuasive and effective

PUBLIC SPEAKING ABILITY   6

Effective and analytical speaker and debater with unmatched command of issues
Quiet and reserved speaker; never passionate or political; not a great orator

INTANGIBLES

Practical; not tied to ideology; deliberate; very small stature; stylish wife Dolley

JAMES MONROE   60

Election: 1816   **Party**: Democratic Republican   **Opponent**: King
Age: 58   **Home State**: Virginia   **Running Mate**: Tompkins

LEGISLATIVE EXPERIENCE   9

1782–1783: member of the Virginia Council of State; only modest influence
1783–1786: delegate to the Confederation Congress; slowly gained prominence
1787–1788: member of the Virginia General Assembly; modest influence
1788: delegate to the Virginia ratifying convention; voted against the Constitution
1790–1794: member of the U.S. Senate; resigned to be minster to France
1810–1811: member of the Virginia General Assembly; most prominent member

EXECUTIVE EXPERIENCE   12

1799–1802: Governor of Virginia; far more influential than previous governors
1811: Governor of Virginia; resigned to become Secretary of State
1811–1816: Secretary of State; dealt with War of 1812 and Napoleonic Wars
1812, 1814–1815: Acting Secretary of War; managed much of the War of 1812

MILITARY EXPERIENCE   7

1776–1780: fought as a Lieutenant in the Virginia sharpshooters at the Battles
of Long Island and Trenton (wounded and cited for conspicuous gallantry
at Trenton); promoted to Major and aide-de-camp to General Lord Stirling
(camped at Valley Forge; fought at Monmouth)
Commanded some troops as Secretary of War in Washington during War of 1812

FOREIGN EXPERIENCE   12

Born and lived in the British Empire (young adult during the Revolutionary War)
1794–1797: Minister to France during the French Revolution (fluent in French)
1803–1807: Commissioner to France (negotiated the Louisiana Purchase), then
Minister to Spain (for a short time) and Great Britain
Responsible for foreign relations and policy as Secretary of State (1811–1816)

PRIVATE WORK EXPERIENCE   4

1786–1811: private attorney; practiced only intermittently due to public service

EDUCATION/INTELLECT   6

Early education at a rural Virginia school (classmates with John Marshall)
1774–1776: received a good classical education at College of William and Mary
1780–1782: studied law as an apprentice to then-Governor Thomas Jefferson

WRITING ABILITY   6

A respectable writer; published multiple essays under the name Aratus (1791)
Published *A view of the Conduct of the Executive in Foreign Affairs* (1797)

PUBLIC SPEAKING ABILITY   4

A modest, slow and deliberate speaker; steadily improved as a debater and orator

INTANGIBLES

Good-hearted; very friendly; excellent judgment; very beautiful wife Elizabeth

JOHN QUINCY ADAMS   66

Election: 1824   **Party**: Democratic Republican   **Opponent**: Jackson
Age: 57   **Home State**: Massachusetts   **Running Mate**: Calhoun

LEGISLATIVE EXPERIENCE   6

1802–1803: member of the Massachusetts Senate; was somewhat effective
1803–1808: member of the U.S. Senate; modest influence; was bothersome
  to some colleagues by insisting that legislation was properly spelled and
  grammatical

EXECUTIVE EXPERIENCE   11

1817–1824: Secretary of State; negotiated the Treaty of 1818 with Great Britain
  and the Transcontinental Treaty with Spain; main proponent of the Monroe
  Doctrine
Some executive duties as a foreign minister

MILITARY EXPERIENCE   0

Never served in any military capacity

FOREIGN EXPERIENCE   15

1778–1785: traveled through Europe as a teenager (France, Spain, Great Britain,
  Belgium, Holland, Germany, Russia, Finland, Sweden, Denmark); Secretary to
  the Commissioner to Russia (1781) and Minister to Great Britain (1783–1785)
1794–1801: Minister to Holland and Prussia, then Commissioner to Great Britain
1809–1817: Minister to Russia; then chief negotiator of the Treaty of Ghent (1814)
  ending the War of 1812; then Minister to Great Britain
Responsible for foreign relations and policy as Secretary of State (1817–1824)

PRIVATE WORK EXPERIENCE   6

1790–1794, 1801–1809: modest and intermittent private law practice in Boston
1805–1809: well-respected professor of rhetoric and oratory at Harvard College

EDUCATION/INTELLECT   10

Attended French boarding schools and lectures at Leyden University in Holland
1786–1787: received great classical education at Harvard College; 2nd in class
1788–1790: studied law under the renowned attorney Theophilus Parsons

WRITING ABILITY   10

An excellent and prolific writer on many subjects and in multiple languages
Published letters, books, and reports include *Letters of Publicola* (1791), translation
  of *Oberon* into English (1800), *Serious Reflections* (1804), *Lectures on Rhetoric and
  Oratory* (1809), *Report on Weights and Measures* (1821), and *The Duplicate Letters*
  (1822)
Had a graceful, formal, and eloquent writing style; also wrote poems and hymns

PUBLIC SPEAKING ABILITY   8

A sought-after and respected public speaker beginning in 1780s
A very formal orator with expert delivery; spoke fluently in multiple languages
Not as quick or passionate as some debaters; not a great extemporaneous speaker

INTANGIBLES

Personally familiar with many world leaders; very hard working; vain personality

ANDREW JACKSON   40
Election: 1828   **Party**: Democratic   **Opponent**: J.Q. Adams
Age: 61   **Home State**: Tennessee   **Running Mate**: Calhoun

LEGISLATIVE EXPERIENCE   5
 1796: delegate to the Tennessee Constitutional Convention; emerged as a leader
 1796–1797; member of the U.S. House of Representatives; resigned in 1797
 1797–1798: member of the U.S. Senate; resigned in 1798
 1823–1825: member of the U.S. Senate; resigned in 1825

EXECUTIVE EXPERIENCE   5
 1821: appointed the Military Governor of Florida; resigned later in 1821
 Executive responsibilities as a high-ranking military officer (1811–1820)

MILITARY EXPERIENCE   12
 1790s: served as the judge advocate of the Tennessee Militia
 1801–1814: Major General in Tennessee Militia (several skirmishes with Indians)
 1814–1820: Major General in the U.S. Army; commanded up to 10,000 troops;
   fought in several skirmishes with Indians; won the Battle of New Orleans
   (1815), seized Florida from Spain at Pensacola (1817)
 No formal military training; spent about four years in the field with the troops

FOREIGN EXPERIENCE   3
 Born and lived in the British Empire (youth during the Revolutionary War)
 Fought against Indians, British, and Spanish

PRIVATE WORK EXPERIENCE   8
 1787–1797: started a private law practice in rural North Carolina and Tennessee
 1798–1804: served as a judge on the Tennessee Superior Court
 1798–1828: owned and managed a farm and business with a general store, horses
   and stables, race track, tavern, and boatyard

EDUCATION/INTELLECT   2
 Early education in a rural school; learned to read, write, and calculate
 Never learned proper grammar or spelling; accused by opponents of being
   illiterate
 1785–1787: rudimentary legal training in a rural Tennessee law office

WRITING ABILITY   2
 Never a good writer; always had poor spelling and poor grammar
 Wrote many letters; presented poorly written and misspelled bills in Congress

PUBLIC SPEAKING ABILITY   3
 A slow, forceful speaker who spoke rapidly when excited; not polished or eloquent
 A dramatic and bold performer when speaking; known for fluency in profanity

INTANGIBLES

 A natural leader of men; violent temper (multiple duels); considered a war hero

MARTIN VAN BUREN   38

Election: 1836   **Party**: Democratic   **Opponent**: Harrison
Age: 53   **Home State**: New York   **Running Mate**: Johnson

LEGISLATIVE EXPERIENCE   12

1812–1815: member of the New York Senate (2nd youngest ever elected)
1821: delegate to the New York Constitutional Convention; an influential moderate
1821–1828: member of the U.S. Senate; became a behind-the-scenes leader
1833–1837: Vice President; presided daily over Senate; advisor to President Jackson

EXECUTIVE EXPERIENCE   6

1815–1819: New York Attorney General; removed by rival Governor in 1819
1829: Governor of New York; resigned to become Secretary of State
1829–1831: Secretary of State; President Jackson's closest adviser; negotiated trade
    agreement with Great Britain and large indemnity payments from France
One of the few early vice presidents with some executive influence (1833–1837)

MILITARY EXPERIENCE   0

Never served in any military capacity

FOREIGN EXPERIENCE   3

1831–1832: traveled to Great Britain and Holland; not confirmed by U.S. Senate
Responsible for foreign relations and policy as Secretary of State (1829–1831)

PRIVATE WORK EXPERIENCE   7

1803–1828: very successful private attorney; practiced intermittently after 1812
1800–1820: acknowledged master of New York politics; created a political machine
1821–1836: created national political organization with local and state committees,
    caucuses, and party discipline which became the modern Democratic Party
Political virtuoso who created parties unattached to specific candidates

EDUCATION/INTELLECT   4

Early education in a one-room schoolhouse in rural New York until 1796
1796–1803: an apprentice in a law office; only a rudimentary legal education
Always insecure about his lack of reading and formal education as an adult

WRITING ABILITY   3

Wrote many letters to friends and colleagues; never published any writings
Helped draft President Jackson's famous *Maysville Road Veto* (1830)

PUBLIC SPEAKING ABILITY   3

Never a strong orator or debater; with practice became a decent trial lawyer
Lost his place and sat down in first Senate speech; embarrassed to speak thereafter

INTANGIBLES

Political visionary; personally charming and entertaining; noncommittal on issues

WILLIAM HENRY HARRISON 44
Election: 1840   **Party**: Whig   **Opponent**: Van Buren
Age: 67   **Home State**: Ohio   **Running Mate**: Tyler

LEGISLATIVE EXPERIENCE   7
1799–1801: first delegate to Congress from the Northwest Territory
1816–1819: member of the U.S. House of Representatives; minimal influence
1819–1821: member of the Ohio Senate; only modest influence
1825–1828: member of the U.S. Senate (elected to complete a partial term)

EXECUTIVE EXPERIENCE   10
1798–1799: first Secretary of the Northwest Territory
1801–1812: first Governor of the Indiana Territory; helped write, adopt, and
enforce the laws; organized the militia; negotiated land treaties with Indian
tribes
Some executive responsibilities as a military officer and foreign minister

MILITARY EXPERIENCE   11
1791–1799: commissioned as an Ensign in the U.S. Army; promoted to Lieutenant
and aide-de-camp to General Anthony Wayne; served primarily on patrols of the
Northwest Territory frontier; promoted to Captain before resigning in 1799
1811–1814: General of Indiana Militia and then promoted to U.S. Army Brigadier
General (1812) and Major General (1813); commanded the Battle of Tippecanoe
(1811), defended the Siege of Fort Meigs (1812), and commanded the Battle of
Thames River (1813); resigned due to a dispute with Secretary of War in 1814
1814–1815: Peace Commissioner to the Indian tribes to negotiate treaties

FOREIGN EXPERIENCE   3
Born and lived early life in the British Empire (child during Revolutionary War)
1828–1829: Minister to Colombia; only minor accomplishments; recalled in 1829

PRIVATE WORK EXPERIENCE   3
1799–1840: owned and managed a farm in Ohio; faced poverty several times
1834–1840: served as clerk of court in Cincinnati to help make ends meet

EDUCATION/INTELLECT   4
Early education in rural Virginia schools
1787–1790: received part of a classical college education by attending Hampden
Sidney College and Southampton College; wanted to study medicine
Quit school for financial reasons; considered moderately intelligent as an adult

WRITING ABILITY   4
Wrote many letters; drafted many bills as Governor and a state legislator
Wrote and published a pamphlet describing his role in the War of 1812

PUBLIC SPEAKING ABILITY   2
Not a good public speaker; improved by 1836 and gave a few campaign speeches

INTANGIBLES
Had great compassion for the poor and for the Indian tribes; lived very modestly

JOHN TYLER 39

Election: 1840	Party: Whig	Opponent: Van Buren
Age: 50	Home State: Virginia	Running Mate: Harrison

LEGISLATIVE EXPERIENCE   13

1811–1814: member of the Virginia General Assembly; had considerable influence

1815–1816: member of the Virginia Council of State

1816–1822: member of the U.S. House of Representatives; gained prominence

1823–1825: member of the Virginia General Assembly; resigned to be Governor

1827–1836: member of the U.S. Senate; moderately effective; became Whig in 1834

1829–1830: delegate to the Virginia Constitutional Convention; played minor role

1838–1839: member of the Virginia General Assembly; elected Speaker

EXECUTIVE EXPERIENCE   2

1825–1827: Governor of Virginia; had few powers and exercised little influence

MILITARY EXPERIENCE   0

Never served in any military capacity

FOREIGN EXPERIENCE   0

Never traveled outside of the United States

PRIVATE WORK EXPERIENCE   5

1809: established a private law practice; was very successful for several years but practiced only intermittently during many periods of public service

Owned a 600+ acre farm; never personally managed the farm

EDUCATION/INTELLECT   7

Early education at Virginia schools and then a preparatory academy (1802–1804)

1804–1807: received a good classical education at the College of William and Mary

1807–1809: studied law under his father (a judge and later Governor) and under Edmund Randolph (former Attorney General and Secretary of State)

Intelligent; read extensively on history, government, literature, and law

WRITING ABILITY   5

A good but not prolific writer; carefully wrote out most of his public speeches

Writing style in letters and other state papers was always clear and persuasive

PUBLIC SPEAKING ABILITY   7

A very good but not great orator; always spoke fluently and sometimes eloquently

A capable debater who had a pleasant speaking manner and used strong logic

Spoke often and well as a federal and state legislator

INTANGIBLES

A polished, courteous southern gentleman; politically shortsighted; principled

JAMES KNOX POLK 45

Election: 1844	**Party**: Democratic	**Opponent**: Clay
Age: 49	**Home State**: Tennessee	**Running Mate**: Dallas

LEGISLATIVE EXPERIENCE 14

1819–1823: served as clerk of the Tennessee Senate

1823–1825: member of the Tennessee House of Representatives; very influential

1825–1839: member of the U.S. House of Representatives; very influential; served as Speaker for two terms (1835–1839); worked closely with President Jackson

EXECUTIVE EXPERIENCE 2

1839–1841: Governor of Tennessee; focused largely on national, not state, issues

MILITARY EXPERIENCE 1

Colonel in the Tennessee Militia in the 1820s during peacetime

FOREIGN EXPERIENCE 2

Never traveled outside of the United States

Member of the House Foreign Relations Committee from 1825 to 1835

PRIVATE WORK EXPERIENCE 4

1820: established a successful private law practice in Tennessee but practiced only intermittently during many periods of public service

EDUCATION/INTELLECT 8

1813–1816: attended a distinguished North Carolina college preparatory academy

1816–1818: received a good classical education at the University of North Carolina; an excellent student and president of the debating society

1819–1820: studied law as an apprentice to renowned attorney Felix Grundy

Very intelligent and scholarly; known for being a policy wonk

WRITING ABILITY 6

A good but not prolific writer; wrote many letters to friends and colleagues

Wrote out weekly essays for his college debating society; good analytical writer

While running for governor, published an *Address to the People of Tennessee* (1839)

PUBLIC SPEAKING ABILITY 8

Became an excellent debater and skilled extemporaneous speaker while in college

Always spoke fluently and confidently; sometimes spoke eloquently

Beginning in the 1830s, was considered one of the best Democratic stump speakers

INTANGIBLES

Very close relationship with Andrew Jackson; politically shrewd and insightful

ZACHARY TAYLOR   23

Election: 1848   **Party**: Whig   **Opponent**: Cass
Age: 63   **Home State**: Louisiana   **Running Mate**: Fillmore

LEGISLATIVE EXPERIENCE   0

Never served in any legislative capacity

EXECUTIVE EXPERIENCE   5

Some executive responsibilities as a military officer

MILITARY EXPERIENCE   12

1808–1848: served in the U.S. Army during the War of 1812, the Indian Wars, and
the Mexican-American War; nicknamed "Old Rough and Ready"

Commissioned a First Lieutenant (1808); promoted to Captain (1810), Major
(1816), Lieutenant Colonel (1819), Colonel (1832), Brigadier General (1837), and
finally Major General (1846)

Saw limited action in the War of 1812; fought in multiple skirmishes with Indian
tribes in Florida including the Battle of Lake Okeechobee (1837); commanded
up to 8,000 troops in Texas and Mexico during the Battles of Palo Alto (1846),
Resaca de la Palma (1846), Monterrey (1846), and Buena Vista (1847)

Never a great soldier or inspiring leader, but loved and respected by his troops

FOREIGN EXPERIENCE   2

1846–1847: served in Mexico during the Mexican-American War

PRIVATE WORK EXPERIENCE   1

No real career outside of the military

Owned a farm (grew to 10,000+ acres) but was never a hands-on manager

Made investments and accumulated over $1 million (modernly) by 1848

EDUCATION/INTELLECT   1

Very little formal education as a youth; attended a rural Kentucky school

Considered by many to be uneducated and generally ignorant in public affairs

Had a limited intellectual capacity and was never intellectually curious

WRITING ABILITY   1

Never learned proper grammar or spelling; handwriting was virtually illegible

Never published any writings; wrote fewer letters than his contemporaries

Arguments in letters were unclear, convoluted, illogical, and very long

Agreed to stop writing letters as they were hurting his 1848 presidential campaign

PUBLIC SPEAKING ABILITY   1

A poor public speaker who gave very few (if any) speeches

Had an unfortunate hesitating speech pattern (almost a stammer or stutter)

INTANGIBLES

Considered a military hero; uncommitted on public issues; kind and
straightforward

MILLARD FILLMORE   26

Election: 1848   **Party**: Whig   **Opponent**: Scott
Age: 50   **Home State**: New York   **Running Mate**: Taylor

LEGISLATIVE EXPERIENCE   9
  1828–1831: member of the New York State Assembly; in the Anti-Mason Party
  1832: member of the committee which drew up the charter for the City of Buffalo
  1833–1835: member of the U.S. House of Representatives (Anti-Mason Party)
  1837–1843: member of the U.S. House of Representatives (Whig Party)

EXECUTIVE EXPERIENCE   1
  1848: Comptroller of New York; was a competent administrator

MILITARY EXPERIENCE   0
  Never served in any military capacity

FOREIGN EXPERIENCE   0
  Never traveled outside of the United States

PRIVATE WORK EXPERIENCE   8
  1823–1830: established the only law practice in the small town of East Aurora,
    NY
  1830–1833: moved to Buffalo and joined a larger and more successful law practice
  1833–1848: started a new practice which became the preeminent Buffalo law firm;
    a very successful private attorney; practiced intermittently during public service
  A New York Whig Party leader and co-founder in 1834

EDUCATION/INTELLECT   3
  Early education in rural New York schools; learned reading, writing, and
    arithmetic
  1819–1822: studied law intermittently under a local judge; gained only a
    rudimentary legal education but tried to improve it by reading
  Always insecure about his lack of a good formal education

WRITING ABILITY   3
  An adequate but unremarkable writer; never widely published
  1832: published a series of letters against Masons in a Buffalo newspaper

PUBLIC SPEAKING ABILITY   2
  Spoke slowly and deliberately with a loud, low voice; methodical
  Never a strong orator or debater; a poor extemporaneous speaker

INTANGIBLES
  Had good common sense; gained a good knowledge of finance and economics

FRANKLIN PIERCE   44

Election: 1852	**Party**: Democratic	**Opponent**: Scott
Age: 48	**Home State**: New Hampshire	**Running Mate**: King

LEGISLATIVE EXPERIENCE   11

1828–1832: moderator of the Hillsborough, New Hampshire town meetings

1829–1832: member of the New Hampshire legislature; Speaker from 1831 to 1832

1833–1837: member of the U.S. House of Representatives; only modest influence

1837–1843: member of the U.S. Senate; somewhat effective

1850–1851: presided over the New Hampshire Constitutional Convention

EXECUTIVE EXPERIENCE   1

Some executive responsibilities as a military officer

MILITARY EXPERIENCE   4

1831–1846: Colonel in the New Hampshire Militia; twice annual muster of troops

1847: commissioned a Brigadier General in the U.S. Army; fought in several minor battles during the Mexican-American War; returned home injured and resigned

FOREIGN EXPERIENCE   1

1847: served for several months in Mexico during the Mexican-American War

PRIVATE WORK EXPERIENCE   8

1827–1852: established a private law practice; became an excellent trial lawyer who was famous in New Hampshire for his great oral advocacy and speaking manner; practiced intermittently during public service

1829–1852: a Democratic Party leader in New Hampshire; chairman (1842–1845)

EDUCATION/INTELLECT   7

Attended good local schools and a preparatory academy; private tutor for one year

1820–1824: received a classical education at Bowdoin College; an average student

1824–1829: studied law as a clerk to several local judges; became a diligent worker

Considered a well-educated and intelligent person

WRITING ABILITY   4

A respectable writer but never prolifically published; wrote many letters

Wrote occasional pro-Democrat editorials in New Hampshire newspapers

PUBLIC SPEAKING ABILITY   8

A very good public speaker who gained fame in New Hampshire as a trial lawyer known for eloquent, passionate, and persuasive jury arguments

A good extemporaneous speaker; one of the best Democratic stump speakers

As a legislator, tried to preserve influence by only speaking on important questions

INTANGIBLES

Charming and friendly; uncompromising party loyalist; a heavy drinker

JAMES BUCHANAN 44

Election: 1856   **Party**: Democratic   **Opponent**: Fremont
Age: 65   **Home State**: Pennsylvania   **Running Mate**: Breckinridge

LEGISLATIVE EXPERIENCE   12

1814–1820: member of the Pennsylvania State Assembly (Federalist)

1821–1831: member of the U.S. House of Representatives; became a Democrat in
1829; fairly effective legislator

1834–1845: member of the U.S. Senate; modest influence; a loyal Democrat but
never more than a peripheral player in Congress

EXECUTIVE EXPERIENCE   4

1845–1849: Secretary of State; dealt with issues surrounding the admission of Texas
into the Union, the Mexican-American War, issues surrounding the Oregon
Territory, and tariffs on foreign trade; President Polk was a micromanager

Some executive responsibilities as a foreign minister

MILITARY EXPERIENCE   0

Never served in any military capacity

FOREIGN EXPERIENCE   8

1832–1834: Minister to Russia; negotiated an important commercial treaty

1853–1856: Minister to Great Britain; dealt with British seizure of the Bay Islands
in Honduras and Canadian fishing rights; negotiated a trade treaty with Canada

Served on the Senate Foreign Relations Committee (chairman for five years)

Responsible for foreign relations and policy as Secretary of State (1845–1849)

PRIVATE WORK EXPERIENCE   5

1812–1856: established a private law practice in Lancaster, Pennsylvania; slowly
became a successful attorney; practiced intermittently during public service

Never a great trial lawyer; was a diligent and competent researcher

EDUCATION/INTELLECT   7

Early education at a Pennsylvania college preparatory academy

1807–1809: received a classical education at Dickinson College; hard working;
graduated near the top of his class of nineteen; was intellectually vain

1810–1812: studied law as a clerk to a local attorney; was a diligent worker

Considered well-educated and quite intelligent

WRITING ABILITY   4

A respectable and meticulous writer; wrote mostly letters to friends and colleagues

Reports were always very long and thorough, well-reasoned, and heavy on data

PUBLIC SPEAKING ABILITY   4

A good but not great public speaker; made logical arguments filled with data

Had a sonorous voice; very long-winded and methodical; not a good stump speaker

INTANGIBLES

Scrupulous; formal and vain; sought compromise; guided by reason, not passion

ABRAHAM LINCOLN   47

Election: 1860   **Party**: Republican   **Opponent**: Breckinridge
Age: 51   **Home State**: Illinois   **Running Mate**: Hamlin

LEGISLATIVE EXPERIENCE   5
  1834–1842: member of the Illinois state legislature; became a Whig Party leader
  1847–1849: member of the U.S. House of Representatives; only modest influence

EXECUTIVE EXPERIENCE   0
  Never served in any executive capacity

MILITARY EXPERIENCE   2
  1832: served as a Captain in the Illinois Militia during the Black Hawk War;
    mustered out after several months after seeing no combat

FOREIGN EXPERIENCE   0
  Never traveled outside of the United States

PRIVATE WORK EXPERIENCE   10
  1837–1860: established a very successful private law practice in Springfield,
    Illinois; became a renowned trial lawyer with great talents in persuading juries
  Also was an impressive appellate advocate, arguing over 175 arguments before the
    state supreme court
  1834–1854: a leader in the Illinois Whig Party
  1854–1860: a founder and leader of the Illinois Republican Party

EDUCATION/INTELLECT   10
  Received less than one year of formal education in a rural Kentucky school
  Became a voracious reader of everything he could get his hands on as a youth
  Self-taught many subjects including grammar, geometry, trigonometry, and law
  1834–1837: self-studied law at night; became a member of the Illinois bar in 1837
  Exceptionally intelligent with a great memory, powerful concentration abilities,
    and acute reasoning skills; was personally modest but had the intellectual self-
    confidence of someone who had never met his equal

WRITING ABILITY   10
  A brilliant writer with a great ability to write clearly, concisely, and beautifully
  Remarkable power of literary expression and a great sense of style and word use
  Habit of reading aloud helped develop a good understanding of rhythm and
    pacing
  During the 1830s, 1840, and 1850s, drafted hundreds of legal briefs, newspaper
    essays and editorials, and major speeches
  Would labor over his choice of words in order to express his exact meaning

PUBLIC SPEAKING ABILITY   10
  An extraordinary public speaker who used humor, charm, and logic to persuade
  A great stump speaker, accomplished in oratory and extemporaneous speaking
  Famous speaking occasions include: *Lyceum Address* (1838), *Temperance Address*
    (1842), *Eulogy of Henry Clay* (1852), *Peoria Speech* (1854), *House Divided Speech*
    (1854), Lincoln-Douglas debates (1858), and *Cooper Union Speech* (1860)

INTANGIBLES
  Great at understanding the public mood; legendary storyteller; kind; very friendly

ANDREW JOHNSON   36

| **Election**: 1864 | **Party**: Union (Democrat) | **Opponent**: McClellan |
| **Age**: 56 | **Home State**: Tennessee | **Running Mate**: Lincoln |

LEGISLATIVE EXPERIENCE   13
1829–1833: served as an Alderman for Greeneville, Tennessee
1835–1836, 1839–1841: member of the Tennessee House of Representatives
1841–1853: member of the U.S. House of Representatives; independent Democrat
1857–1862: member of the U.S. Senate; only Southern Senator loyal to the Union;
   resigned in 1862 to become Military Governor of East Tennessee

EXECUTIVE EXPERIENCE   7
1834, 1836: served as Mayor of Greeneville, Tennessee
1853–1857: Governor of Tennessee; modest success at reforming the education
   system and making good appointments; used office for self promotion
1862–1864: appointed Military Governor of East Tennessee after it was once again
   under Union control; worked with military leaders to begin Reconstruction

MILITARY EXPERIENCE   4
1830s: Colonel in the Tennessee Militia during peacetime; never saw combat
As Military Governor of East Tennessee, worked with military officers to restore
   order, recruit troops, and begin the process of reconstruction; moderate success

FOREIGN EXPERIENCE   0
Never traveled outside of the United States

PRIVATE WORK EXPERIENCE   5
1824–1860: after apprenticing in a tailor shop, became a journeyman tailor and
   eventually opened his own tailor business; became fairly successful and known
   for making high quality clothes; worked intermittently during public service

EDUCATION/INTELLECT   2
Never attended a day of school; learned to read as a tailor's apprentice
Always desired a better education; read fairly often, especially while in Congress
Considered fairly uneducated and not particularly intelligent

WRITING ABILITY   1
A very poor writer; never learned proper grammar or spelling
Wrote many letters; had a dull, convoluted style; rarely wrote out speeches

PUBLIC SPEAKING ABILITY   4
A successful but not great speaker; enjoyed combative public debates
Took frequent speaking tours for self promotion; fluent speaker but never eloquent
Known as a demagogue with a sharp, aggressive, ad hominem style of speaking
For his inaugural speech as Vice President in 1865, gave a long and drunken rant

INTANGIBLES
Shrewd politician; called a "maverick;" a wholly self-made man; strong convictions

ULYSSES S. GRANT   39

Election: 1868   **Party**: Republican   **Opponent**: Seymour
Age: 46   **Home State**: Illinois   **Running Mate**: Colfax

---

LEGISLATIVE EXPERIENCE   0

Never served in any legislative capacity

EXECUTIVE EXPERIENCE   9

1866–1868: Acting Secretary of War; second most influential person in the country
Took a simple, "big picture" approach to leadership and decision-making; a skilled
  delegator of responsibilities who remained willing to take ultimate responsibility
Many executive responsibilities as a high-ranking military officer

MILITARY EXPERIENCE   15

1843–1854: Second Lieutenant and Quartermaster in charge of logistics; fought in
  most of the battles in the Mexican-American War; resigned as a Captain in 1854
1861–1865: joined the Illinois Militia at start of Civil War and was soon promoted
  to Brigadier General (1-star, 1861) and ultimately to General (4-star, 1865)
Major military victories during the Civil War include the Battles at Shiloh,
  Vicksburg, Chattanooga, the Wilderness, and Petersburg; accepted General
  Robert E. Lee's surrender at Appomattox
1865–1868: 4-Star General in Chief (first ever); commanded over 500,000 troops at
  war's end; oversaw the five military districts in the South during reconstruction
Leadership based on having a clear conception and precise execution
A military genius who never lost a battle or ran from a fight; developed the military
  doctrine of total war and unconditional surrender

FOREIGN EXPERIENCE   3

1846–1848: served in Mexico during the Mexican-American War; learned to speak
  Spanish fairly well; loved the Mexican people and culture

PRIVATE WORK EXPERIENCE   1

1854–1861: faced severe poverty trying and failing at multiple low-level jobs

EDUCATION/INTELLECT   5

Early education at local schools; considered intelligent but never a great student
1839–1843: received a college education at West Point Military Academy which
  focused exclusively on military and civil engineering; was an average student
One of the best equestrians in military history; a superb artist and map-drawer

WRITING ABILITY   5

A good writer with strong command of the English language; wrote with precision
  and nuance; every military order was crisp, concise, and always very clear
Wrote many military orders but little else; wrote quickly

PUBLIC SPEAKING ABILITY   1

A poor public speaker; rarely gave any public remarks; never participated in debate
Any comments were straightforward, plainspoken, and very brief

INTANGIBLES

  Kind and generous; honest; an occasional binge drinker; "big picture" thinker

RUTHERFORD BIRCHARD HAYES   38
Election: 1876   **Party**: Republican   **Opponent**: Tilden
Age: 54   **Home State**: Ohio   **Running Mate**: Wheeler

LEGISLATIVE EXPERIENCE   2
1865–1867: member of the U.S. House of Representatives; resigned near the
  beginning of a second term to become Governor of Ohio
EXECUTIVE EXPERIENCE   7
1867–1871, 1875–1876: Governor of Ohio for three terms
Was a good but not great Governor; relatively non-partisan; civil service reformer
Some executive responsibilities as a military officer
MILITARY EXPERIENCE   7
1846: trained briefly with Ohio Militia but never served in Mexican-American War
1861–1865: began Civil War as a Major in an Ohio volunteer infantry regiment;
  fought in several minor battles including at Cedar Creek; wounded multiple
  times; promoted steadily and resigned as a Major General in 1865
FOREIGN EXPERIENCE   1
Never traveled outside of the United States; spoke some German and French
PRIVATE WORK EXPERIENCE   5
1845–1850: established a small private law practice in Sandusky, Ohio
1850–1859: moved to Cincinnati and became a highly successful attorney; known
  as a lawyer's lawyer (hired by other lawyers for careful research)
1859–1861: elected the Cincinnati city attorney; was competent and respected
EDUCATION/INTELLECT   8
Attended Norwalk Academy as a teenager; excelled in Latin and Greek
1838–1842: received a good classical education at Kenyon College; became a very
  diligent scholar and graduated 1st in class
1843–1845: attended Harvard Law School; continued to be a diligent student
Considered very intelligent and well-educated
WRITING ABILITY   5
An average, unremarkable writer; wrote many letters to friends and colleagues
Wrote out most of his public speeches; not prolifically published
PUBLIC SPEAKING ABILITY   3
Good speaker as a youth; performed famous speeches by memory for crowds
Never participated in debates in Congress; delivered some speeches as Governor
  but was never known as a great orator or debater
INTANGIBLES
Always very dignified; champion of moderation and non-partisanship; very friendly

JAMES ABRAM GARFIELD   48

Election: 1880   **Party**: Republican   **Opponent**: Hancock
Age: 49   **Home State**: Ohio   **Running Mate**: Arthur

LEGISLATIVE EXPERIENCE   13

1859–1861: member of the Ohio Senate; had a habit of speaking on every matter

1863–1880: member of the U.S. House of Representatives; became very influential

Steadily gained power and prominence during seventeen years in Congress;
  served as chairman of the banking and currency and later the appropriations
  committees

EXECUTIVE EXPERIENCE   1

Some executive responsibilities as a military officer

MILITARY EXPERIENCE   8

1861–1863: raised a volunteer Ohio regiment of his former students and was made
  a Lieutenant Colonel; promoted steadily up to Major General

Helped to re-secure Kentucky for the Union in 1862; became chief of staff for
  General Rosecrans in 1863; fought at Battle of Chickamauga Creek

The quintessential political general; preferred volunteers over West Point
  graduates

FOREIGN EXPERIENCE   2

1867: traveled on a seventeen-week tour of Europe with his wife

Learned to speak German fairly well as a youth and college student

PRIVATE WORK EXPERIENCE   4

Pre-1851: held various jobs including on a canal ship and as a carpenter and
  teacher

1857–1861: professor and president of the Eclectic School (now Hiram College)

1853–1859: a celebrated Disciples of Christ preacher during the Revival Era

1865: became a practicing attorney after casually self-studying the law for several
  years; argued occasional cases but never made practicing law a real career

EDUCATION/INTELLECT   5

1848–1849: attended two local Ohio college preparatory academies

1851–1854: a top student at the Eclectic School; exhausted all of the class
  offerings by 1853 and started teaching several classes before graduation in 1854

1854–1856: received a classical education at Williams College; popular on campus;
  excelled in debating; an average student but considered fairly intelligent

WRITING ABILITY   6

Wrote clearly and precisely; his writings often used elegant literary flourishes

A slow, painstaking writer; occasionally published political papers

Published *Review of the Credit Mobilier* (1880), a well-written defense of his actions

PUBLIC SPEAKING ABILITY   9

A famous orator and accomplished debater and stump speaker

Always fluent but sometimes bordered on glibness; habit of speaking too often

Could give powerful prepared speeches and also polished extemporaneous
  speeches; had great ability to persuade and inspire audiences

INTANGIBLES

Linked to several scandals; had a marital affair; supported civil service reform

CHESTER ALAN ARTHUR 29
Election: 1880   **Party**: Republican   **Opponent**: Hancock
Age: 51   **Home State**: New York   **Running Mate**: Garfield

LEGISLATIVE EXPERIENCE   0
Never served in any legislative position
EXECUTIVE EXPERIENCE   7
1871–1877: Collector of the New York Customhouse (powerful federal position)
Responsible for the administration of the country's largest customhouse which had
   over 1,000 employees and collected close to $100 million in annual revenue
Suspended from the position by President Hayes due to corruption allegations
Some executive responsibilities as a military officer
MILITARY EXPERIENCE   4
1861–1863: joined the New York Militia at start of the Civil War; commissioned a
   Brigadier General and Engineer-in-Chief due to political connections
Due to administrative talents, became Acting Assistant Quartermaster General
   responsible for large amounts of paperwork, contract negotiations, and auditing
Never received military training or fought in a battle; resigned in 1863
FOREIGN EXPERIENCE   1
Never traveled outside of the United States; learned French fairly well
PRIVATE WORK EXPERIENCE   7
1849–1853: teacher and eventually acting principle of a small Vermont school
1854–1871: joined a private law practice in New York City; became a moderately
   successful transactional attorney (not trial attorney)
1869–1870: appointed counsel to the New York City Tax Commission
1877–1880: returned to private law practice; remained fairly successful
EDUCATION/INTELLECT   5
Early education by his preacher father and at a preparatory academy in Vermont
1845–1848: received a respectable classical education at Union College
1848–1853: began studying law at a newly-opened law school in New York but
   soon returned to Vermont and self-studied law while teaching school
WRITING ABILITY   4
Edited the college newspaper; a proficient writer but was never widely published
Wrote many letters; published a letter response to charges of corruption in 1877
PUBLIC SPEAKING ABILITY   1
Joined the debating club in college; did not distinguish himself as a speaker
Rarely gave speeches as an adult; and public remarks were unremarkable and brief
INTANGIBLES
Linked to the corrupt spoils system; never a hard worker; very loyal Republican

STEPHEN GROVER CLEVELAND   24

Election: 1884   **Party**: Democratic   **Opponent**: Blain
Age: 47   **Home State**: New York   **Running Mate**: Hendricks

LEGISLATIVE EXPERIENCE	0

Never served in any legislative capacity

EXECUTIVE EXPERIENCE	3

1882: served as Mayor of Buffalo, New York; known for honesty and fiscal reform; called the "veto mayor" for vetoing measures not in the public good

1883–1884: Governor of New York; developed a national reputation for willingness to veto legislation that does not help the general public; exhorted public officials as the trustees of the people

Was a prodigiously hard worker who carefully studied every word of every bill

MILITARY EXPERIENCE	0

Never served in any military capacity

Avoided service in the Civil War by paying for another man to serve in his place

FOREIGN EXPERIENCE	0

Never traveled outside of the United States

PRIVATE WORK EXPERIENCE	8

1850s: worked as a laborer on the Erie Canal; taught at the Institute for the Blind in New York City in 1853

1859–1882: became a successful attorney in Buffalo; known as a good trial lawyer

1862–1865: served as the assistant district attorney for Buffalo

1871–1873: elected sheriff of Buffalo; considered a very fair and effective public official and public servant; reformed the relatively corrupt department

Was a very popular Democrat in a heavily Republican county

EDUCATION/INTELLECT	4

Early education at local New York schools; not a particularly good student

Never attended college; gained a modest education through extensive reading

1855–1859: studied law as a clerk in a Buffalo attorney's office

WRITING ABILITY	4

A respectable writer; wrote clearly and concisely but rarely original or profound

Took painstaking care in drafting any public address, then committed it to memory

Wrote many letters to friends and colleagues

PUBLIC SPEAKING ABILITY	5

A capable public speaker; always spoke from memory and without any notes

Could occasionally be eloquent; was usually forceful and straightforward

Had a strong, clear voice slightly higher than people expected from a large man

INTANGIBLES

Honest; independent; reform-minded; unmarried; fathered a child out of wedlock

BENJAMIN HARRISON   47

Election: 1888   **Party**: Republican   **Opponent**: Cleveland
Age: 55   **Home State**: Indiana   **Running Mate**: Morton

LEGISLATIVE EXPERIENCE   6
1881–1887: member of the U.S. Senate; a modestly influential and loyal Republican
Excelled as a party spokesman but was never a Senate leader
Replaced by the Democratic state legislature in 1887

EXECUTIVE EXPERIENCE   1
Some executive responsibilities as a military officer

MILITARY EXPERIENCE   8
1862: commissioned a Second Lieutenant and quickly promoted to Colonel
1862–1865: recruited an Indiana volunteer regiment; joined the Atlanta Campaign
    led by General William T. Sherman; experienced hard fighting, including at
    Golgotha Church in Georgia; gained notice for his leadership abilities
Resigned commission in 1865 as a Brigadier General

FOREIGN EXPERIENCE   0
Never traveled outside of the United States

PRIVATE WORK EXPERIENCE   9
1854–1888: became a prominent and successful attorney in Indiana; considered the
    best trial lawyer in Indiana and one of the best in the country
Argued at trial the famous *Ex Parte Milligan* and the *Whiskey Ring* cases
Served as court reported for the Indiana Supreme Court (published the opinions)

EDUCATION/INTELLECT   9
1847–1850: attended Farmers' College near Cincinnati to prepare for college
1850–1852: received a strong classical education at Miami University in Ohio;
    distinguished himself as a brilliant student and an excellent public speaker and
    debater; graduated 3rd in class
1852–1854: studied law as a clerk for the renowned Ohio attorney Bellamy Storer

WRITING ABILITY   5
Strong writing abilities, drafting occasional analytical essays and superb speeches
Personal writings replete with penetrating analysis and strong persuasion
Never published many of his writings

PUBLIC SPEAKING ABILITY   9
A great orator and debater, both extemporaneously and from prepared texts
Honed his speaking abilities in college; became renowned as a trial lawyer
Beginning in the 1860s, considered the country's best Republican stump speaker

INTANGIBLES
Grandson of a president; devoutly religious; a cold man with few friends

WILLIAM McKINLEY 42
Election: 1896 **Party**: Republican **Opponent**: Bryan
Age: 53 **Home State**: Ohio **Running Mate**: Hobart

LEGISLATIVE EXPERIENCE 13
1877–1891: member of the U.S. House of Representatives; became a very
  influential congressman who was respected on both sides of the aisle; served as
  floor leader and became chairman of the Ways and Means Committee
Very collegial with both Republicans and Democrats; a great peacemaker
Became a nationally-known figure for championing tariff reform in the 1880s
Gerrymandered out of his congressional district in the 1890 election

EXECUTIVE EXPERIENCE 5
1892–1896: Governor of Ohio; was an effective and successful administrator
Dealt effectively with many "capital v. labor" issues, including using troops to halt
  the violence surrounding coal miners' strikes; used position as a platform on
  which to speak about national issues
Some executive responsibilities as a military officer

MILITARY EXPERIENCE 6
1861–1865: enlisted in an Ohio volunteer regiment; promoted steadily from
  Commissary Sergeant to First Lieutenant and finally to Major
Fought in many battles including the Battle of South Mountain; noted for
  gallantry
Served on future-President Hayes's staff; Hayes became his supporter and mentor

FOREIGN EXPERIENCE 0
Never traveled outside of the United States

PRIVATE WORK EXPERIENCE 5
1860–1861: teacher at a local Ohio school; resigned to serve in the Civil War
1867–1891: became a successful attorney based in Canton, Ohio; practiced only
  intermittently during many public service positions
Reputation for being a clear, methodical, well-prepared advocate

EDUCATION/INTELLECT 4
Early education in a rural New York school and later in an Ohio academy
1859–1860: attended Allegheny College; not a great student but a hard worker; did
  not complete college due to illness and lack of finances
1865–1867: studied law under a local attorney; briefly attended Albany Law School

WRITING ABILITY 4
A respectable writer who carefully drafted all of his speeches, reports, and
  messages
Wrote simply, clearly, and concisely; considered writing anything formal an ordeal

PUBLIC SPEAKING ABILITY 5
A strong, simple, unembellished speaker; gave spirited but methodical speeches
Campaigned extensively throughout Ohio and other states beginning in the 1870s
Typically spoke from a prepared text; not a great extemporaneous speaker

INTANGIBLES
Loyal Republican but favored compromise; had a certain personal magnetism

THEODORE ROOSEVELT   62
Election: 1900   **Party**: Republican   **Opponent**: Bryan
Age: 42   **Home State**: New York   **Running Mate**: McKinley

LEGISLATIVE EXPERIENCE   2
   1882–1884: member of the New York State Assembly; quickly became influential
   Three one-year terms; was Minority Leader in 1883 and lost Speakership in 1884
EXECUTIVE EXPERIENCE   13
   1889–1895: federal Civil Service Commissioner; immediately became the *de facto*
      leader of the Commission; made it a powerful and effective political force
   1895–1897: NYPD Commissioner; ended widespread corruption in the NYPD
   1897–1898: Assistant Secretary of the Navy; energetic and effective administrator
   1898–1900: Governor of New York; passed admirable progressive legislation
   Some executive responsibilities as a military officer
MILITARY EXPERIENCE   5
   1898: Lieutenant Colonel (later Colonel) commanding the Rough Riders regiment
   Fought in the Spanish-American war in the Battles of Las Guasimas and San Juan
FOREIGN EXPERIENCE   6
   1869–1870: one-year family educational trip; visited nine European countries
   1872–1873: one-year family educational trip; visited Europe, Africa, Middle East
   1881, 1887: five-month and four-month trips throughout Europe
   Became fluent in both French and German
PRIVATE WORK EXPERIENCE   7
   1880–1900: became a well-respected and prolific professional author
   1884–1886: became a cattle rancher in the Badlands (now North Dakota)
EDUCATION/INTELLECT   10
   Exceptionally intelligent and probably a genius; legendary photographic memory
   1876–1880: attended Harvard University; graduated magna cum laude
   1880–1882: attended Columbia Law School; decided not to graduate
   An amazing range of reading; a speed reader who read about 500 books a year
WRITING ABILITY   10
   1880–1900: published: *The Naval War of 1812* (1880); *Hunting Trips of a Ranchman*
      (1885); *The Life of Thomas Hart Benton* (1887); *Ranch Life and the Hunting Trail*
      (1887); *Essays in Practical Politics* (1887); *The Winning of the West* (four volumes,
      1889 (2), 1894, 1896); *The History of New York* (1891); *The Wilderness Hunter* (1893);
      Hero Tales from American History (1895; collaboration with Henry Cabot Lodge);
      American Ideals (1897); *The Rough Riders* (1899); and *Oliver Cromwell* (1899)
   Also published hundreds of essays and articles in magazines and newspapers
PUBLIC SPEAKING ABILITY   9
   A great public speaker; spoke to more audiences than anyone in his generation
   Gave thousands of campaign speeches, academic lectures, and political addresses
   A passionate and very persuasive speaker; good at extemporaneous speaking
INTANGIBLES
   Most famous man in America; overwhelming personality; a true moral crusader

WILLIAM HOWARD TAFT 46

Election: 1908   **Party**: Republican   **Opponent**: Bryan
Age: 51   **Home State**: Ohio   **Running Mate**: Sherman

LEGISLATIVE EXPERIENCE 0

Never served in any legislative capacity

EXECUTIVE EXPERIENCE 8

1900: President of the Philippine commission; traveled to the Philippines

1901–1904: Governor of the Philippines (a U.S. protectorate); established a new
civil government by drafting and enforcing new laws including a criminal code,
internal revenue code, a corporations code, and a land use and settlement code

1904–1908: Secretary of War; jack-of-all-trades advisor to President Roosevelt

MILITARY EXPERIENCE 2

Never served in a military capacity

Secretary of War during peacetime; a hands-off manager of the War Department

FOREIGN EXPERIENCE 8

1900–1904: lived in Philippines; also traveled to Japan, Hong Kong, and Italy

1905–1908: all purpose Secretary of War; sometimes dispatched to foreign
countries as a goodwill ambassador; strong knowledge of foreign affairs

1907: sent on an around-the-world trip covering 24,000 miles and eight countries

PRIVATE WORK EXPERIENCE 9

1880: joined private law practice in Cincinnati; moved in and out of private practice

1881–1883: served as an assistant prosecuting attorney in Cincinnati

1883: served as Collector of Internal Revenue for Cincinnati

1887–1890: served as a judge on the Ohio Superior Court; loved judicial work

1890–1892: U.S. Solicitor General; argued eighteen cases before the Supreme Court

1892–1900: federal appellate judge in Cincinnati; became a highly respected judge

EDUCATION/INTELLECT 8

1874: graduated from Woodward High School in Cincinnati; 2nd in class

1874–1878: attended Yale University; excelled as a student; graduated 2nd in class

1878–1880: attended Cincinnati Law School; again performed well

Known as being a very intelligent but not quite brilliant man

WRITING ABILITY 8

As a judge, wrote hundreds of carefully researched and argued legal opinions; habit
of always providing a thorough and painstaking analysis in a logical presentation

Drafted many of the new civil and criminal laws as Governor of the Philippines

PUBLIC SPEAKING ABILITY 3

Disliked public speaking; very long-winded and uninspiring; read directly from text

A respectable oral advocate, but never enjoyed or excelled at arguing cases in court

Gave few speeches during the 1908 campaign; those he gave were dry and boring

INTANGIBLES

Hand-picked successor to Roosevelt; modest; avoided controversy; procrastinator

THOMAS WOODROW WILSON   45

Election: 1912   **Party**: Democratic   **Opponent**: Roosevelt, Taft
Age: 55   **Home State**: New Jersey   **Running Mate**: Marshall

LEGISLATIVE EXPERIENCE   0
Never served in any legislative capacity

EXECUTIVE EXPERIENCE   6
1911–1912: Governor of New Jersey; had a very legislatively successful first year
Passed a number of major bills that addressed a wide variety of issues
Many executive responsibilities as president of Princeton University

MILITARY EXPERIENCE   0
Never served in any military capacity

FOREIGN EXPERIENCE   2
1906: vacationed in Great Britain for the summer to hike in the Lake Districts
1907, 1908: vacationed in Bermuda during the winter of both years

PRIVATE WORK EXPERIENCE   10
1882–1883: started private law practice in Atlanta; soon turned to academia instead
1885–1910: became a nationally renowned political science professor at Bryn Mawr
     College (1885–1888), Johns Hopkins University (1887–1890, part-time), Wesleyan
     College (1888–1890), and Princeton University (1890–1910)
1902–1910: president of Princeton University; made visionary improvements
The leading political scientist of the era and a widely-published author

EDUCATION/INTELLECT   9
1873–1874: attended Davidson College; member of the debating society
1875–1879: attended Princeton University; graduated in top 25% of the class
1879–1882: studied law for 1½ years at University of Virginia, then self-studied
     back home in Georgia; received the top score on the 1882 Georgia bar exam

WRITING ABILITY   9
An excellent writer and prolific published author; wrote primarily on government
Books include: *Congressional Government* (1884); *History of Political Economy in the United
     States* (textbook, never published); *The State* (1889); *A History of the American People*
     (1907); and *Constitutional Government* (1908)
Starting in the early 1880s, published hundreds of articles, essays, and speeches

PUBLIC SPEAKING ABILITY   9
Excellent public speaker; known as an inspiring and very popular academic lecturer
Was always articulate and often eloquent; early political speeches were stiff and
     overly formal but quickly became passionate and hard-hitting
An accomplished extemporaneous speaker; rarely spoke from a prepared text

INTANGIBLES
Intellectual visionary; consummate academic; personal loner; marital affair in 1908

WARREN GAMALIEL HARDING   29

Election: 1920   **Party**: Republican   **Opponent**: Cox
Age: 55   **Home State**: Ohio   **Running Mate**: Coolidge

LEGISLATIVE EXPERIENCE   8
1900–1903: member of the Ohio Senate; gained modest influence quickly
1904–1906: Lieutenant Governor of Ohio; presided over the Ohio Senate
1915–1920: member of the U.S. Senate; very popular but minimally effective

EXECUTIVE EXPERIENCE   3
Some executive responsibilities as a small town newspaper owner and publisher

MILITARY EXPERIENCE   0
Never served in any military capacity

FOREIGN EXPERIENCE   2
1907, 1909: traveled to Europe and the Mediterranean for several-month vacations
1911: traveled to Bermuda and Europe for vacation; uninterested in foreign culture

PRIVATE WORK EXPERIENCE   6
1882–1884: several short jobs including as a teacher and as an insurance agent
1884–1920: reporter, editor, and owner/publisher of the *Star* newspaper in Marion,
    Ohio; increased circulation from several hundred to several thousand by 1900
Was a hands-on reporter and editor until 1894, then became a hands-off publisher

EDUCATION/INTELLECT   3
Early education in rural Ohio was rudimentary: reading, writing, and arithmetic
1880–1882: attended Iberia College; graduated with only two other students
1883: self-studied law casually and quickly became disinterested
Poorly educated; rarely read any books; had no intellectual or academic interests

WRITING ABILITY   3
Was a prolific local news writer but was not very articulate, eloquent, or insightful
Began writing articles and editorials in 1884; most were "bloviated" and often
    uninformed opinions on state and national issues from a Republican perspective

PUBLIC SPEAKING ABILITY   4
Spoke with a clear and resonant voice; a very smooth and soothing speaker
1880s-1910s: traveled the rural speaking circuit giving a set speech about patriotism
    and his heroes: Alexander Hamilton, Napoleon, and Caesar
In the U.S. Senate, learned he was simply a glib, unspectacular, and often
    uninformed speaker with very little substance; stopped giving many speeches

INTANGIBLES
Very good looking; friendly; had two marital affairs; had a child out of wedlock

JOHN CALVIN COOLIDGE   31

Election: 1920   **Party**: Republican   **Opponent**: Cox
Age: 50   **Home State**: Massachusetts   **Running Mate**: Harding

LEGISLATIVE EXPERIENCE   4
  1897–1900: a Northampton, Massachusetts, ward member and councilman
  1907–1909: member of the Massachusetts State Assembly; only modest influence
  1912–1916: member of the Massachusetts Senate; had considerable influence
  Became a popular and respected state senator; Senate President from 1914 to 1915

EXECUTIVE EXPERIENCE   5
  1909–1912: Mayor of Northampton; hard worker; competent administrator
  1917–1918: Lieutenant Governor of Massachusetts; popular but not powerful
  1919–1920: Governor of Massachusetts; ably handled the Boston police strike
  Believed strongly that enforcing current laws was better than writing new laws

MILITARY EXPERIENCE   0
  Never served in any military capacity

FOREIGN EXPERIENCE   2
  Never traveled outside of the United States; learned to speak French and Italian

PRIVATE WORK EXPERIENCE   4
  1897–1916: established a small private law practice in Northampton, Massachusetts;
     in 1899 also became counsel and vice president of a local bank
  A moderately successful and well-respected local attorney; reputation for integrity
  City solicitor from 1900 to 1902; clerk of courts starting in 1903

EDUCATION/INTELLECT   7
  1887–1890: early education at Black River Academy in Vermont
  1991–1895: attended Amherst College; good student; graduated cum laude
  1895–1897: studied law as a clerk in a Northampton, Massachusetts, law office
  Intelligent; an avid reader of philosophy, history, political science, and literature

WRITING ABILITY   5
  A respectable but not great writer; notable for his concise and straightforward style
  Published *Have Faith in Massachusetts* (1919), a collection of his speeches

PUBLIC SPEAKING ABILITY   4
  A capable public speaker, but not an outgoing or talkative person
  Very witty; delivered the college graduation speech intended to be humorous
  A fairly stiff and slightly awkward speaker; spoke very concisely and deliberately

INTANGIBLES
  Very politically shrewd and astute; often received widespread bipartisan support

HERBERT CLARK HOOVER   54

Election: 1928   **Party**: Republican   **Opponent**: Smith
Age: 54   **Home State**: California   **Running Mate**: Curtis

LEGISLATIVE EXPERIENCE   0
Never served in any legislative capacity

EXECUTIVE EXPERIENCE   15
1914–1917: head of the Commission for Relief in Belgium (massive food program)
1917–1920: top U.S. Food Administrator; oversaw all aspects of the food industry
1921–1928: Secretary of Commerce; focused on all areas of economic development
Extensive executive responsibilities as an international businessman

MILITARY EXPERIENCE   2
Never served in any military capacity
Managed food relief program in Europe during World War I

FOREIGN EXPERIENCE   15
1897–1902: worked as a mining engineer and businessman in Australia and China
1902–1907: traveled around the world five times, each time taking several months
1903–1917: lived and worked most of each year in London
Between 1897 and 1928 traveled to six continents and dozens of countries
International businessman who frequently interacted with top foreign officials

PRIVATE WORK EXPERIENCE   8
1895–1914: became a famous mining engineer and international businessman
A talented engineer and business manager; a consummate technocrat
Forcefully persuasive negotiator; strong principles of individualism and efficiency

EDUCATION/INTELLECT   5
Early education in Iowa and Oregon; average student; never graduated high school
1891–1895: attended Stanford University (inaugural class); focused on geology
As a student, started a profitable laundry business; class treasurer; entrepreneurial
Intuitively intelligent and a very hard worker

WRITING ABILITY   6
Good technical writing abilities; prose suffered due to unwillingness to accept edits
Most writings focused on engineering, mining, business, and management
Published many professional articles; wrote the textbook *Principles of Mining* (1909)

PUBLIC SPEAKING ABILITY   3
Gave many lectures; had a very technical vocabulary and weak grammar
Campaign speeches were generally dull and delivered in a flat, monotone voice

INTANGIBLES
Very self-confident; focused on efficiency; very intense; an optimistic progressive

301

FRANKLIN DELANO ROOSEVELT   55

Election: 1932   **Party**: Democratic   **Opponent**: Hoover
Age: 50   **Home State**: New York   **Running Mate**: Garner

LEGISLATIVE EXPERIENCE   1

1911–1913: member of the New York Senate; gained modest influence

EXECUTIVE EXPERIENCE   13

1913–1920: Assistant Secretary of the Navy; youngest ever at only 31 years old; responsible for developing naval policy and overseeing the naval fleet

Disliked paperwork and micromanagement; showed energy, flexibility, decisiveness, and a willingness to delegate responsibilities as an administrator

1929–1932: Governor of New York; dealt with early years of the Great Depression

MILITARY EXPERIENCE   6

Never served in any military capacity

Oversaw massive naval operations throughout World War I as Assistant Secretary of the Navy, supervising and working closely with top naval commanders

FOREIGN EXPERIENCE   9

1882–1896: visited and studied in Europe eight times for several months each time

1901, 1905: traveled several months through Europe in college and on honeymoon

1918: traveled to the Western Front near the end of WWI to oversee operations

PRIVATE WORK EXPERIENCE   4

1907–1910: associate at Carter, Ledyard & Milburn, a top law firm in NYC

Had little passion for the practice of law; worked on minor cases and admiralty law

1921–1928: vice president of a major surety bonding company and top partner at a self-named law firm founded in 1922; spent time recovering from Polio

EDUCATION/INTELLECT   7

Became fluent in French and German during frequent trips and studies in Europe

1896–1900: attended Groton School, then the nation's most prestigious academy

1900–1903: attended Harvard University; only an average student; became President of the Harvard *Crimson* newspaper

1904–1907: attended Columbia Law School; failed several classes during first year due to lack of attendance and disinterestedness; graduated slightly below average

WRITING ABILITY   6

Strong writer; great at describing complicated subjects using simple language

Developed strong editing abilities as President of the Harvard *Crimson* newspaper

Began receiving speechwriting help as Governor; maintained editorial control

PUBLIC SPEAKING ABILITY   9

Delivered thousands of public speeches between 1910 and 1932

A great speaking cadence, strong speaking voice, sophisticated yet casual delivery

Delivered "fireside chats" as Governor; famous speeches include *Forgotten Man* (1932), *New Deal* (1932), and *Four Horseman of the Republican Apocalypse* (1932)

INTANGIBLES

Exuded optimism and confidence; great at feeling political nuance; marital affair

HARRY S. TRUMAN   40

Election: 1944   **Party**: Democratic   **Opponent**: Dewey
Age: 60   **Home State**: Missouri   **Running Mate**: Roosevelt

LEGISLATIVE EXPERIENCE   10

1935–1944: member of the U.S. Senate; started out somewhat tainted due to close
  ties to corrupt political bosses in Missouri; steadily gained influence
Very loyal, hard-working, and productive; one of the most popular senators
Headed the "Truman Committee" investigating military spending and contracts

EXECUTIVE EXPERIENCE   5

1923–1925, 1927–1935: served as "judge," a top administrative, not judicial,
  position, for Jackson County (which included Kansas City); responsible for 700
  county employees and $7 million operations budget
1933–1935: Missouri Director of the Federal Reemployment Service

MILITARY EXPERIENCE   5

1917–1919: served as an Army officer in France during World War I
Formed a volunteer artillery battery from Missouri; commissioned First
  Lieutenant
Discovered leadership abilities; promoted to Captain; returned from France in
  1919

FOREIGN EXPERIENCE   3

1918–1919: served and traveled throughout France during World War I
1940: visited multiple Central American countries on a Senate "fact-finding" trip

PRIVATE WORK EXPERIENCE   5

1901–1906: worked as a timekeeper for a construction crew and as a bank teller
1906–1917: worked on and managed the 600-acre family farm
1919–1922: opened a haberdashery store in Kansas City which ultimately failed

EDUCATION/INTELLECT   5

Attended local Independence schools through high school; was an average student
Never attended college; was a true book worm and read extensively on history

WRITING ABILITY   4

An adequate writer; used respectable grammar but was a fairly bad speller
Never widely published; wrote many letters because he disliked the telephone

PUBLIC SPEAKING ABILITY   3

A plainspoken country boy who used simple language and common sense
Disliked public speaking; spoke with a flat, high-pitched voice; never a good
  orator

INTANGIBLES

Never self-important; very hard-working; physically fit; great conversationalist

DWIGHT DAVID EISENHOWER · 62

Election: 1952   **Party**: Republican   **Opponent**: Stevenson
Age: 62   **Home State**: New York   **Running Mate**: Nixon

LEGISLATIVE EXPERIENCE · 0
Never served in any legislative capacity

EXECUTIVE EXPERIENCE · 15
Extensive executive duties as a high-ranking military office and university president

MILITARY EXPERIENCE · 15
1915–1952: military officer during World War I and World War II; became Supreme Allied Commander in Europe in 1943; top NATO commander in 1951
During WWII, was top commander for multiple major battles including Operation Torch in North Africa and the Mediterranean (1942), Operation Overlord in France (1944), Operation Market Garden in Belgium and Holland (1944)
Served under three brilliant generals for over fifteen years: Fox Conner (1922–1925), Douglas MacArthur (1929–1939), and George C. Marshall (1941–1945)
1945–1948: served as Army Chief of Staff in Washington
1951–1952: the Supreme Allied Commander of NATO, headquarters in France

FOREIGN EXPERIENCE · 15
1922–1925: served in the Panama canal zone under General Fox Conner
1935–1939: served in the Philippines under General Douglas MacArthur
1942–1945: served in Europe during WWII; headquarters in London
1951–1952: lived and traveled throughout Europe as top NATO commander

PRIVATE WORK EXPERIENCE · 1
1948–1950: served as President of Columbia University in NYC; disliked the job

EDUCATION/INTELLECT · 8
1911–1915: attended West Point Military Academy; fairly disinterested in scholarship; graduated as only an average student; excelled in English
1922–1925: read serious military history with General Fox Conner
1925–1926: Army's Command and General Staff School; 1st in class of 275
1927–1929: attended the Army War College; studied the Army's history in France

WRITING ABILITY · 5
Showed strong writing abilities in many college essays and military reports
Strongest subject in school was English; published memoir *Crusade in Europe* (1948)

PUBLIC SPEAKING ABILITY · 3
Never a good public speaker; gave a number of speeches after 1945
Emphasized his image (which he liked) as a plainspoken, simple country boy

INTANGIBLES
Decisive; self-confident but not arrogant; possibly had a marital affair in London

JOHN FITZGERALD KENNEDY 49
Election: 1960 **Party:** Democratic **Opponent:** Nixon
Age: 43 **Home State:** Massachusetts **Running Mate:** Johnson

LEGISLATIVE EXPERIENCE 12
1947–1953: member of the U.S. House of Representatives; minimal influence
1953–1960: member of the U.S. Senate; modest influence, mostly in foreign affairs
One of the first "celebrity politicians;" had few legislative accomplishments

EXECUTIVE EXPERIENCE 1
Some executive duties as a military officer in World War II

MILITARY EXPERIENCE 6
1941–1942: served stateside in the Navy's foreign intelligence office
1942–1943: became a patrol-torpedo (P-T) boat officer in the Pacific Theater
On August 1, 1943, P-T boat was rammed by Japanese; rescued several crewmates
Considered a war hero; recuperated for several months; left Navy in early 1945

FOREIGN EXPERIENCE 7
1935, 1937–1939: traveled and studied in Europe for four summers, visiting many
    foreign embassies and meeting with many American and foreign diplomats
1941: traveled throughout much of South America for several months
1942–1943: spent 17 months on a P-T boat in the Pacific Theater during WWII
1951: two several-month trips through Europe, the Middle East, and much of Asia
Member of the Senate Foreign Relations Committee from 1957 to 1960

PRIVATE WORK EXPERIENCE 1
1945: spent several months as a correspondent for the United Nations conference
1940–1960: wrote several books (with considerable help) that became bestsellers

EDUCATION/INTELLECT 7
Early education at the Canterbury School and Choate; slightly below average grades
1936–1940: attended Harvard University; generally a disinterested student with
    average grades; enjoyed and excelled in government classes
1940: took several classes at Stanford University during the fall semester; no degree
Had a very clever, individualist mind; always well-informed on current events

WRITING ABILITY 7
Wrote a 148-page senior thesis (with help of a research assistant); New York Times
    writer Arthur Krock edited it to become the book *Why England Slept* (1940)
1945–1960: published hundreds of articles focusing on foreign affairs and politics
Wrote (with help) a Pulitzer Prize-winning book *Profiles in Courage* (1956)
Had significant help in most writings, but always maintained total editorial control

PUBLIC SPEAKING ABILITY 8
Improved greatly from 1945 to 1960 to become an accomplished public speaker
Early speeches were awkward and poorly crafted; practiced diligently to improve
Delivered thousands of speeches as a politician; developed a great delivery and style
1960: evenly matched with Richard Nixon in four televised presidential debates

INTANGIBLES
Political visionary; gift for rhetoric; multiple marital affairs; serious health problems

LYNDON BAINES JOHNSON   35

Election: 1960   **Party:** Democratic   **Opponent:** Nixon
Age: 55   **Home State:** Texas   **Running Mate:** Kennedy

LEGISLATIVE EXPERIENCE   15

1931–1935: legislative aide to a Texas congressman; a natural political operator
1937–1949: member of the U.S. House of Representatives; quickly gained influence
1949–1960: member of the U.S. Senate; Minority Whip from 1951 to 1953; Minority
    Leader from 1953 to 1955; Majority Leader from 1955 to 1960
Collected legislative power in many ways, including giving office and committee
    assignments, scheduling votes, directing campaign finances, moving forward or
    stopping legislation, exercising great personal persuasion with individual senators
Consulted legislators at all stages to find consensus and avoid unhelpful debates

EXECUTIVE EXPERIENCE   2

1935–1937: Texas Director of the National Youth Administration, a jobs program
The youngest and most effective program administrator in the country

MILITARY EXPERIENCE   2

1941–1942: served 12 months as a Naval Commander; recalled home to Congress
Awarded a silver star for gallantry, although he was only an inspector and observer

FOREIGN EXPERIENCE   1

1942: briefly toured the Pacific Theater as a naval inspector and observer

PRIVATE WORK EXPERIENCE   4

1924–1927: worked odd labor jobs like grape-picking, dish-washing, and road work
1928–1929, 1930–1931: taught school for two years in Cotulla, Texas, and Houston
1943–1960: bought Austin, Texas radio station; became wealthy with investments

EDUCATION/INTELLECT   5

Early education in Johnson City, Texas; mediocre student; graduated in 1924
1927–1930: attended Southwest Texas State Teachers College; active on campus
    becoming a student politician and newspaper editor; graduated with honors
As an adult, read national and local newspapers, congressional reports, and bills
Great intuition for evaluating other people's intelligence, strengths, and weaknesses

WRITING ABILITY   3

An adequate writer; wrote occasional editorials; not widely published

PUBLIC SPEAKING ABILITY   3

Disliked public speaking or debating; preferred personal persuasion in small groups
Participated in high school and college debates, but was a constant "mumbler"
Nervous in large audiences; believed public speeches prevented good compromises

INTANGIBLES

Hard-working; very personally persuasive; politically shrewd; several marital affairs

RICHARD MILHOUS NIXON   68

Election: 1968   **Party**: Republican   **Opponent**: Humphrey
Age: 55   **Home State**: New York   **Running Mate**: Agnew

LEGISLATIVE EXPERIENCE   10
1947–1951: member of the U.S. House of Representatives; quickly gained influence
1951–1953: member of the U.S. Senate; maintained legislative prominence
1953–1961: Vice President; a very effective congressional liaison
Split time between legislative responsibilities and executive responsibilities

EXECUTIVE EXPERIENCE   9
1942: very effective administrator in the federal office of price administration
1953–1961: the first Vice President with real executive responsibilities, including
    chairing presidential commissions and acting as a foreign goodwill ambassador
Some executive responsibilities as a military officer

MILITARY EXPERIENCE   6
1942–1946: commissioned a Lieutenant in the Navy; served stateside first 7 months
1943–1945: air transport command officer; directed troop logistics in the Pacific
Commanded about 20 men; promoted to Lieutenant Commander; resigned in 1946

FOREIGN EXPERIENCE   14
1943–1945: served in the Pacific Theater during World War II
1947: visited Great Britain, Greece, and Italy on a congressional fact-finding trip
1953–1961: met with foreign leaders in dozens of countries as Vice President
1961–1968: continued to be a frequent world traveler, visiting dozens of countries
Acknowledged as a foreign policy expert; had friendships with foreign leaders

PRIVATE WORK EXPERIENCE   6
Worked in the family's general store as a youth and through high school
1937–1942: private attorney in Whittier, CA; became a respectable trial lawyer
1961–1968: a "rainmaker" and top partner at a major New York law firm

EDUCATION/INTELLECT   8
Educated in Yorba Linda and Whittier schools; graduated 3rd in high school class
1930–1934: attended Whittier College; champion debater; graduated 2nd in class
1934–1937: attended Duke Law School; very hard worker; graduated 3rd in class
Had a great memory; loved reading about history and foreign affairs

WRITING ABILITY   7
Very good writer; published hundreds of articles and editorials starting in 1945
Remained intimately involved in speechwriting more than most top politicians
Published a memoir titled *Six Crises* (1961) covering six major political events

PUBLIC SPEAKING ABILITY   8
Talented public speaker; a better debater than orator, but accomplished at both
Hard-hitting stump speaker; always fluent and articulate; often spoke without notes
Major speeches included *Checkers* (1952) and the Nixon/Kennedy debates (1960)

INTANGIBLES
Very partisan Republican; awkward personality; dealings with shady individuals

GERALD RUDOLPH FORD, JR.   38

Election: 1973   **Party**: Republican   **Opponent**: None
Age: 60   **Home State**: Michigan   **Running Mate**: None

LEGISLATIVE EXPERIENCE   14

1949–1973: member of the U.S. House of Representatives; steadily gained influence
  as chairman of the Republican Caucus from 1963 to 1965 (#3 leadership
  position), and as Minority Leader from 1965 to 1973
Served (fairly inactively) on the Warren Commission in 1963 and 1964
Well liked on both sides of the aisle; instituted strict party discipline

EXECUTIVE EXPERIENCE   1

Some executive responsibilities as a military officer

MILITARY EXPERIENCE   6

1942–1946: started as Navy Ensign; promoted to Lieutenant Commander by 1946
1942–1943: served stateside as a physical fitness instructor and specialist
1943–1944: commanded a light carrier anti-aircraft gun crew in the Pacific
Received 10 battle stars; almost killed/sunk in a typhoon in December 1944

FOREIGN EXPERIENCE   1

Served in the Pacific Theater during World War II

PRIVATE WORK EXPERIENCE   2

1935–1938: boxing and football coach at Yale University
1941–1942: clothing model in New York City, then attorney in Grand Rapids, MI
1946–1948: private law practice in Grand Rapids; active in the Republican Party

EDUCATION/INTELLECT   7

Early education in Grand Rapids public schools; a good but not great student
1931–1935: attended University of Michigan; a solid B student; star football player
1938–1941: attended Yale Law School; a slightly above average student

WRITING ABILITY   4

A respectable writer but never widely published; wrote occasional editorials
1965: co-authored book refuting conspiracy theories of the Kennedy Assassination

PUBLIC SPEAKING ABILITY   3

Never a great public speaker; very plainspoken and sometimes used poor grammar
An unsophisticated orator; sometimes awkward hesitations and improper emphasis

INTANGIBLES

Known for personal integrity; liked everyone; very likable; sought compromise

JAMES EARL CARTER, JR.   44

Election: 1976   **Party**: Democratic   **Opponent**: Ford
Age: 52   **Home State**: Georgia   **Running Mate**: Mondale

LEGISLATIVE EXPERIENCE   3
1956–1962: member of the Sumter County school board; chairman starting in 1961
1963–1967: member of the Georgia Senate; steadily became influential

EXECUTIVE EXPERIENCE   7
1971–1975: Governor of Georgia; proved to be an effective administrator
Led by example; disliked group meetings, preferring meeting with individuals
Some executive responsibilities as a military officer and small business owner

MILITARY EXPERIENCE   5
1946–1953: served as a junior naval officer immediately following World War II
1946–1948: stationed on the U.S.S. Wyoming battleship
1948–1951: joined the prestigious submarine program; assigned to U.S.S. Pomfret
1951–1953: engineering officer in the nuclear submarine development program
Received high marks from superior officers; resigned in 1953 as a Lieutenant

FOREIGN EXPERIENCE   4
Several brief trips on a submarine, including to Hong Kong and the Bahamas
1971–1975: went on "trade missions" as governor to multiple foreign countries
     including Mexico, Brazil, Great Britain; West Germany, Japan, Canada, and
     Israel
Studied Spanish in college and spoke Spanish moderately well

PRIVATE WORK EXPERIENCE   7
1953–1976: owned and managed a successful peanut farming business in Georgia
Worked diligently to utilize modern farming technologies
A hands-on, detail-oriented businessman; became fairly wealthy by the mid-1960s
Very active in the Georgia community, holding multiple civic leadership positions

EDUCATION/INTELLECT   7
Early education in rural Georgia schools; graduated near top of high school class
1941–1943: attended classes at Georgia Southwestern College and Georgia Tech
1943–1946: attended U.S. Naval Academy; a good but not great student
1948: graduated 3rd in class in the summer submarine officers school
Took two nuclear reactor and physics classes as a submarine officer

WRITING ABILITY   5
Respectable writer but not widely published; writing was clear and straightforward
Published occasional editorials in the 1970s; wrote autobiography in 1975

PUBLIC SPEAKING ABILITY   6
A capable public speaker but never a great orator; a fairly strong debater
Very dynamic in smaller groups; struggled to connect with larger audiences
Debated President Ford to a draw in 1976; speeches were politely received

INTANGIBLES
Tenaciously competitive; devout Christian; preferred principle over compromise

RONALD WILSON REAGAN   41

Election: 1980   **Party**: Republican   **Opponent**: Carter
Age: 69   **Home State**: California   **Running Mate**: Bush

LEGISLATIVE EXPERIENCE   0
Never served in any legislative capacity

EXECUTIVE EXPERIENCE   9
1967–1975: Governor of California; became a popular and effective politician
Dealt effectively with student rebellions, race riots, anti-Vietnam War protests
Effectively avoided partisan extremism and sought bipartisan compromise

MILITARY EXPERIENCE   3
1937–1942: served in the Army Reserve; called to active duty in 1942
1942–1946: served in the Army's public relations department making movies

FOREIGN EXPERIENCE   1
Visited Great Britain as president of the screen actors guild in the 1950s

PRIVATE WORK EXPERIENCE   8
1932–1937: popular radio announcer and sports broadcaster in Iowa
1937–1957: became a successful Hollywood "B movie" actor; over 50 films
1940s–1950s: board member of the Screen Actors Guild; president for several
   terms
1954–1962: vice president of General Electric, giving hundreds of speeches at GE
   plants; popular host of the *General Electric Theater* television program

EDUCATION/INTELLECT   5
Early education in Dixon, IL; a popular and politically involved high school
   student
1928–1932: attended Eureka College; involved in theater, student government,
   yearbook, student newspaper; was an economics major and average student
An intelligent, thoughtful man; read a lot of newspapers, magazines, and books

WRITING ABILITY   6
A good writer who became widely published with frequent articles and editorials
Hand-wrote hundreds of essays and speeches beginning in the 1940s
1975–1980: published a political opinion column in hundreds of newspapers

PUBLIC SPEAKING ABILITY   9
Excellent public speaker; comfortable on television and before large audiences
Powerful and persuasive orator; developed a very compelling delivery style
A good but not great extemporaneous speaker and competitive debater
Gave thousands of public speeches beginning in 1946; known for his relaxed and
   witty manner; famous political debut speech was *A Time For Choosing* (1964)

INTANGIBLES
Optimistic political visionary; big picture leader; not detail-oriented; once divorced

GEORGE HERBERT WALKER BUSH   54

Election: 1988   **Party**: Republican   **Opponent**: Dukakis
Age: 64   **Home State**: Texas   **Running Mate**: Quayle

LEGISLATIVE EXPERIENCE   6
1967–1971: member of the U.S. House of Representatives; an effective legislator
1981–1988: Vice President; maintained some legislative responsibilities

EXECUTIVE EXPERIENCE   9
1976–1977: Director of the Central Intelligence Agency; an effective administrator
1981–1988: Vice President; had considerable executive responsibilities including
    chairing many national security councils, committees, and task forces
Exercised more executive influence than any vice president in history to that point

MILITARY EXPERIENCE   6
1942: enlisted in the U.S. Navy; became the Navy's youngest pilot at 18 years old
1943–1944: had 58 torpedo bomber missions in the Pacific; shot down in 1944
1945: mustered out after receiving a distinguished flying cross and two gold stars

FOREIGN EXPERIENCE   11
1971–1973: U.S. Ambassador to the United Nations; showed talent in diplomacy
1974–1976: head liaison to the newly-opened China diplomatic office in Beijing
1978: around-the-world trip; met many foreign leaders preparing for 1980 election
1981–1989: significant travels and foreign policy responsibilities as Vice President
Served in the Pacific during WW II; foreign policy experience as CIA Director

PRIVATE WORK EXPERIENCE   7
1949–1988: successful business owner and executive in the Texas oil industry
1949–1959: partner in Midland, Texas, oil company called Zapata Petroleum
1959–1988: sole owner of Zapata; top executive when not in public service
1963–1967: chairman of the Harris County, Texas (Houston) Republican Party
1973–1974: chairman of the Republican National Committee

EDUCATION/INTELLECT   6
1937–1941: attended high school at Phillips Academy in Andover, Massachusetts
1946–1949: fourth generation of family to attend Yale University; average student
A thoughtful and intelligent adult; never particularly philosophical or conceptual

WRITING ABILITY   4
Respectable writer; never widely published; editor of the high school newspaper
Straightforward writing style; resisted speechwriter efforts at more elegant
    language
Co-wrote the book *Looking Forward: An Autobiography* (1988)

PUBLIC SPEAKING ABILITY   5
A respectable public speaker; never a great orator or a particularly skilled debater
A somewhat awkward speaking style and rhythm; sometimes used garbled syntax
Gave thousands of public speeches beginning in the 1960s

INTANGIBLES
Modest; very competitive; politically moderate; generally had prudent judgment

WILLIAM JEFFERSON CLINTON 50

Election: 1992 **Party**: Democratic **Opponent**: Bush
Age: 46 **Home State**: Arkansas **Running Mate**: Gore

LEGISLATIVE EXPERIENCE 1
1966–1968: clerk for Senator Fulbright on the Senate Foreign Relations Committee
EXECUTIVE EXPERIENCE 14
1977–1979: Attorney General of Arkansas; closely connected to President Carter
1979–1981: Governor of Arkansas; youngest governor in the country
1983–1992: Governor of Arkansas; had matured after the first term and became
    one of the country's longest serving governors; held national leadership
    positions
Showed a flexible and pragmatic ideology; sought practical political solutions
MILITARY EXPERIENCE 0
Never served in any military capacity; avoided service in the Vietnam War
FOREIGN EXPERIENCE 7
1968–1970: studied at Oxford University in Great Britain as a Rhodes Scholar;
    traveled extensively throughout Europe including Ireland, France, Belgium,
    Germany, Austria, Norway, Finland, Russia, and Spain
As an adult, traveled to multiple foreign countries including Spain, Mexico, Haiti
Exposure to foreign policy as a clerk for the Senate Foreign Relations Committee
PRIVATE WORK EXPERIENCE 4
1966–1976: worked on multiple Democratic political campaigns across the country
1973–1976: full-time professor at the University of Arkansas Law School; also
    taught criminal justice classes to law enforcement part-time
1981–1983: private attorney ("of counsel") for a top Little Rock law firm
EDUCATION/INTELLECT 9
Early education at Hot Springs High School; graduated 4th in class in 1964
1964–1968: attended Georgetown University; honor student; student politician
1968–1970: one of thirty-two Rhodes Scholars; studied at Oxford University
1970–1973: attended Yale Law School; a very good student
A very intelligent adult; considered a "policy wonk;" avid reader on many subjects
WRITING ABILITY 7
Strong writer with good command of the English language; fairly widely published
Best at writing longer essays or articles that showcase strong analytical abilities
During the 1992 presidential campaign published *Putting People First* (1992)
PUBLIC SPEAKING ABILITY 8
An accomplished public speaker beginning as a high school student
Developed a comfortable, confident speaking style; great extemporaneous speaker
Good but not great at passionate rhetorical oratory delivered from prepared texts
Excelled at informal, off-the-cuff speaking opportunities like town hall meetings
INTANGIBLES
    Great networker; fairly moderate; several marital affairs; smoked marijuana

GEORGE WALKER BUSH 38

Election: 2000 **Party**: Republican **Opponent**: Gore
Age: 54 **Home State**: Texas **Running Mate**: Cheney

LEGISLATIVE EXPERIENCE 0
Never served in any legislative capacity

EXECUTIVE EXPERIENCE 9
1995–2000: Governor of Texas; successfully cut taxes, increased funding for
    education, pushed for tort reform and stricter criminal laws, fairly moderate
Executive experience as a businessman

MILITARY EXPERIENCE 3
1968–1974: commissioned as an officer in the Texas Air National Guard; pilot who
    flew missions stateside; joined the Alabama Air National Guard from 1972 to
    1973; honorably discharged in November 1974; accused of irregular attendance

FOREIGN EXPERIENCE 4
Occasional travel outside of the United States, including to Mexico; developed
    close relationships with Mexican officials while Governor of Texas
Learned to speak Spanish relatively well but not fluently

PRIVATE WORK EXPERIENCE 7
1975–1988: returned to Midland, Texas, and entered the oil business; started the
    company Arbusto Energy, later named Bush Exploration; became chairman after
    a merger with Spectrum 7; sold to Harken Energy Corp. in 1986
1988–1989: full-time consultant and adviser on father's presidential campaign
1989–1994: managing partner of the Texas Rangers baseball team
Adviser to his father, who was both Vice President and President (1981–1993);
    member of various corporate boards and committees from 1986 to 1994

EDUCATION/INTELLECT 7
1959–1964: attended The Kinkaid School in Houston, Texas, and then Phillips
    Academy in Andover, Massachusetts; was a popular and average student
1964–1968: attended Yale University; average student; president of the fraternity
    Delta Kappa Epsilon; received a degree in history
1973–1975: attended Harvard Business School; received an M.B.A.

WRITING ABILITY 5
Respectable writer; occasionally published opinion editorials and other articles
Wrote and published an autobiography *A Charge to Keep* (1999)

PUBLIC SPEAKING ABILITY 3
A below average public speaker; speaks fairly fluently from prepared scripts but
    struggles in extemporaneous speaking; comfortable with smaller audiences
Had occasional poor grammar and incorrect word usage; hesitating speaking style
Not a prolific speechmaker until the mid-1990s; campaigned for his father

INTANGIBLES
Arrested for DUI in 1976; son of a president; brother of the Florida Governor

BARACK HUSSEIN OBAMA 40

Election: 2008 **Party**: Democratic   **Opponent**: McCain
Age: 47   **Home State**: Illinois   **Running Mate**: Biden

LEGISLATIVE EXPERIENCE   6
1997–2005: member of the Illinois Senate; had modest influence the last few years
2005–2008: member of the U.S. Senate; loyal Democrat; minimally effective
Started campaigning for the Senate in 2003 and the presidency in 2007

EXECUTIVE EXPERIENCE   0
Never served in any executive capacity

MILITARY EXPERIENCE   0
Never served in any military capacity

FOREIGN EXPERIENCE   7
1967–1971: lived and attended 1st through 4th grades in Jakarta, Indonesia
1981, 1983, 1988: traveled for several weeks during three summers to Pakistan,
    Indonesia, Great Britain, France, Spain, and Kenya
2005, 2006: traveled for Senate Foreign Relations Committee to Europe and Africa
2008: visited and made speeches in France, Germany, Israel, Jordan, Great Britain

PRIVATE WORK EXPERIENCE   5
1983–1985: researcher and report writer for publishing company in New York City
1985–1988: community organizer for the developing communities project
1993–2004: associate and later "of counsel" at a Chicago civil rights law firm
1992–2004: part-time professor at the University of Chicago Law School

EDUCATION/INTELLECT   8
Early education split between Hawaii and Indonesian elementary schools
1975–1979: attended prestigious Punahou High School; graduated with B average
1979–1981: attended Occidental College near Los Angeles; was an average student
1981–1983: attended Columbia University; became a more serious student
1988–1991: attended Harvard Law School; graduated magna cum laude; was
    President of the Harvard Law Review and a research assistant to Lawrence Tribe

WRITING ABILITY   7
Strong writing abilities; fairly widely published; tendency towards wordiness
Developed good editing skills as President of the Harvard Law Review
Published dozens of opinion articles as an Illinois and U.S. Senator
Published: *Dreams From My Father* (1995) and *The Audacity of Hope* (2006)

PUBLIC SPEAKING ABILITY   7
Steadily improved as a public speaker to become an accomplished orator
Speeches in the 1990s tended to be awkward and overly professorial
Worked hard to become more conversational; best speaking from a prepared text
2008: lost debates to Hillary Clinton but won debates against John McCain

INTANGIBLES
Very self-confident; personally charming and funny; used marijuana and cocaine

APPENDIX B

CURRENT CANDIDATE RESUMES

APPENDIX B PROVIDES SAMPLE presidential resumes for seventeen current or potential candidates for the 2012 presidential election. Each candidate has either announced that he or she is seeking his or her party's nomination, or has received significant media attention and speculation as to whether he or she will in fact become a candidate for the presidency in 2012. Just like the presidential resumes provided in Appendix A, each of the candidates' resumes was drafted, scored, and ranked using a standardized presidential resume template.

Resume Score	Candidate	Political Party	Home State
61	Hillary Clinton	Democratic	New York
59	Condoleezza Rice	Republican	California
51	Newt Gingrich	Republican	Virginia
51	Ron Paul	Republican	Texas
48	Joe Biden	Democratic	Delaware
46	Rick Perry	Republican	Texas
44	Mitt Romney	Republican	Massachusetts
43	Mitch Daniels	Republican	Indiana
43	Mike Huckabee	Republican	Arkansas
42	Tim Pawlenty	Republican	Minnesota
42	Jon Huntsman, Jr.	Republican	Utah
QUALIFIED THRESHOLD			
39	Donald Trump	Republican	New York
39	Herman Cain	Republican	Georgia
36	Rick Santorum	Republican	Pennsylvania
32	Chris Christie	Republican	New Jersey
29	Michele Bachmann	Republican	Minnesota
28	Sarah Palin	Republican	Alaska

Some readers will be surprised at the scores and rankings of some of the above candidates. Several candidates' resumes score very high while several others' resumes score surprisingly low. Encouragingly, eleven out of the seventeen candidates' resumes meet the QUALIFIED THRESHOLD (not counting the incumbent President Obama, whose resume is drafted as of 2008 and provided in Appendix A). These resumes show that there are certainly qualified candidates in the 2012 presidential election field.

Several results of the candidate resume analysis stand out and deserve particular attention. The two most qualified candidates—Hillary Clinton and Condoleezza Rice—are women and are from different political parties. Sadly, neither is likely to run for the presidency, but both may be considered as vice presidential running mates. The three lowest scoring candidates—Sarah Palin, Michele Bachmann, and Chris Christie—are each very popular within the Republican Party, but they fail to meet the QUALIFIED THRESHOLD. Their intangible personal characteristics seem to be the sole drivers of their popularity. And the most probable Republican nominees—at least according to early polling and press accounts—are clustered in the Average/Above Average resume rankings. This simply means that they will need to find other ways (i.e., intangible personal characteristics) to differentiate themselves from each other.

It was fairly difficult to accurately and comprehensively describe each of these candidates' presidential qualifications, primarily because none of them has made public his or her official resume. This is one of the problems caused by the current backwards system of selecting presidents. The only way a voter can get a clear picture of a candidate's actual qualifications is to try to piece together information from newspaper articles, Internet websites, speeches, campaign advertisements, autobiographies, biographies, and various other sources. No professional hiring manager or employer would stand for such an inefficient and unhelpful system, and American voters should not stand for it either. The onus should be on the candidate who wants the job to proactively submit his or her resume qualifications for scrutiny by the voter/employer. As it is, the descriptions in the candidate resumes have been drafted by using whatever sources were already easily available to the public.

If any current or potential candidate whose resume appears in Appendix B would like to correct or clarify his or her experiences or abilities, he or she should feel free to accept the resume challenge and release an official resume to the American public. This would be the best result possible: the candidate's resume would be accurate and complete, and the public would have all of the information necessary to evaluate the candidate's qualifications and make an informed voting decision.

HILLARY RODHAM CLINTON 61

Election: 2012   **Party**: Democratic   **Opponent**: Uncertain
Age: 65   **Home State**: New York   **Running Mate**: Uncertain

LEGISLATIVE EXPERIENCE 9
  1974: attorney on the House Judiciary Committee focusing on Watergate
  2001–2009: member of the U.S. Senate; quickly gained influence; fairly bipartisan

EXECUTIVE EXPERIENCE 4
  2009–2012: Secretary of State; considered a very competent administrator; dealt
    with foreign issues related to Iraq, Afghanistan, Libya, Egypt, Syria, Israel

MILITARY EXPERIENCE 0
  Never served in any military capacity

FOREIGN EXPERIENCE 14
  1970s–1980s: occasional foreign travel including to Spain, Mexico, and Haiti
  1990s: frequent foreign travel as First Lady, including trips to Asia (1995), South
    America (1995, 1997), Africa (1997), Eastern Europe (1997, 1998)
  2009–2012: visited over 75 countries and met with dozens of world leaders

PRIVATE WORK EXPERIENCE 10
  1974–1976: professor at the University of Arkansas Law School
  1977–1992: became first female partner of the Rose Law Firm in Little Rock in
    1979; member of several corporate boards and committees (e.g., Walmart); twice
    named one of America's 100 most influential lawyers
  1979–1981, 1983–1993: First Lady of Arkansas; held numerous substantive roles
    including chairwoman of state committees focused on children and education
  1993–2001: First Lady of the United States; numerous substantive roles including
    head of a healthcare taskforce and policy adviser to President Bill Clinton

EDUCATION/INTELLECT 9
  1961–1965: Maine East High School; graduated near the top of the class; National
    Merit Scholar; participated on the school newspaper and student government
  1965–1969: attended Wellesley College; graduated near the top of the class; degree
    in political science; active in student government and political organizing
  1969–1973: attended Yale Law School; an outstanding student; an editor of the Yale
    Review of Law and Social Action; spent an extra year studying at the Yale Child
    Study Center before graduating in 1973

WRITING ABILITY 8
  Strong and prolific writer; published hundreds of editorials as First Lady, Senator,
    and Secretary of State; several scholarly articles including *Children Under the Law*
    (1973); and several books including *It Takes a Village* (1996), *An Invitation to the
    White House* (2000), and an autobiography *Living History* (2003)

PUBLIC SPEAKING ABILITY 7
  Strong, experienced public speaker; delivered thousands of speeches since 1969
  2008: considered by many to have won multiple debates against Barack Obama

INTANGIBLES
  Wife of Bill Clinton; fairly liberal; considered by some to be a "polarizing figure"

CONDOLEEZZA RICE 59

Election: 2012   **Party**: Republican   **Opponent**: Obama
Age: 57   **Home State**: California   **Running Mate**: Uncertain

LEGISLATIVE EXPERIENCE   0

Never served in any legislative capacity

EXECUTIVE EXPERIENCE   10

1986: Special Assistant to the Director of the Joint Chiefs of Staff
1989–1991: National Security Council Director of Soviet and East European
   affairs
2001–2005: National Security Advisor; responsible for analyzing international data
   and developing and implementing a comprehensive foreign policy; first female
2005–2009: Secretary of State; dealt with issues surrounding Afghanistan and Iraq
Also had executive responsibilities as provost of Stanford University

MILITARY EXPERIENCE   0

Never served in any military capacity

FOREIGN EXPERIENCE   14

Widely acknowledged as a foreign policy expert; visited dozens of foreign countries
Learned French and Spanish from a very young age; also fluent in Russian

PRIVATE WORK EXPERIENCE   10

1981–1989, 1991–1993: professor of political science at Stanford University;
   specializing in the Cold War and the Soviet Union
1993–1999: provost of Stanford University (chief budget and academic officer);
   senior fellow of the institute for international studies and the Hoover institution
1999–2001: foreign policy advisor to presidential candidate George W. Bush
2009–2012: Stanford University professor; senior fellow at the Hoover Institution
Also a board member for several corporations and other organizations

EDUCATION/INTELLECT   9

A child prodigy; skipped several grades growing up in Birmingham, Alabama
1971–1974: attended the University of Denver; graduated with honors at 19 years
   old; received a degree in political science, also studied classical piano
1974–1975: attended the University of Notre Dame; received a master's degree in
   political science; started specializing in the Cold War and Eastern Europe
1981: received a Ph.D. from University of Denver; dissertation on Czechoslovakia

WRITING ABILITY   9

An excellent and prolific author; has published many academic and opinion articles
Published multiple books including *Uncertain Allegiance* (1984), *The Gorbachev Era*
   (1986), *Germany Unified and Europe Transformed* (1995), *Belarus and the Flight from
   Sovereignty* (2001), *Individuals Matter* (2003), and *Extraordinary, Ordinary People*
   (2010)

PUBLIC SPEAKING ABILITY   7

An accomplished and very articulate public speaker; comfortable and direct
Has delivered hundreds of speeches; classroom professor for two decades

INTANGIBLES

Moderate; loves football; single black female; accomplished pianist; fashionable

NEWTON LEROY GINGRICH   51

Election: 2012   **Party**: Republican   **Opponent**: Obama
Age: 69   **Home State**: Virginia   **Running Mate**: Uncertain

LEGISLATIVE EXPERIENCE   14

1979–1999: member of the U.S. House of Representatives; served in multiple
legislative leadership positions including Minority Whip (1989–1995) and
Speaker of the House (1995–1999); became a very influential legislator

Co-author and proponent of the "Contract with America," a campaign and policy
document which was promoted during the 1994 election and which helped win a
Republican majority; became the first Republican Speaker since 1955

Negotiated with President Clinton for welfare reforms, tax cuts, and budget
balancing; voted to impeach Clinton; resigned in 1999

EXECUTIVE EXPERIENCE   1

Some executive responsibilities as a private businessman

MILITARY EXPERIENCE   0

Never served in any military capacity

FOREIGN EXPERIENCE   3

Lived on a U.S. Army base in Orleans, France, as a teenager

[Not enough information on travel]

PRIVATE WORK EXPERIENCE   8

1970–1978: history and environmental studies professor at West Georgia College

1999–2012: author; founder and chair of multiple policy organizations and
companies including American Solutions, Center for Health Transformation, and
Gingrich Productions; part-time professor of history

Served on multiple political boards and committees; commentator on Fox News

EDUCATION/INTELLECT   9

Attended multiple schools as a youth with an army officer father; graduated from
Baker High School in Columbus, Georgia, in 1961; was a very good student

1961–1965: attended Emory University; was a good student; degree in history

1965–1971: attended Tulane University; continued to be a strong student; received
a master's degree and Ph.D. in European history; wrote a dissertation titled
Belgian Education Policy in the Congo: 1945–1960 (1971)

Considered a policy wonk; very intelligent and often times an original thinker

WRITING ABILITY   9

An accomplished and prolific writer of at least 23 historical fiction and non-fiction
(often bestselling) books; including many books on military history

Has published hundreds of editorials, policy articles, and book reviews

PUBLIC SPEAKING ABILITY   7

An accomplished public speaker; delivered thousands of lectures and speeches

A good extemporaneous speaker; not particularly passionate or inspirational

INTANGIBLES

Republican Party strategist; considered a "polarizing" figure; two marital affairs

319

RONALD ERNEST PAUL   51
Election: 2012   **Party**: Republican   **Opponent**: Obama
Age: 77   **Home State**: Texas   **Running Mate**: Uncertain

LEGISLATIVE EXPERIENCE   13
1976–1977: member of the U.S. House of Representatives; won in a special
election to fill a vacant seat
1979–1985: member of the U.S. House of Representatives; known for advocating
congressional term limits, strictly limiting the scope of the federal government,
ending the Federal Reserve System and the Department of Education, and
maintaining a gold monetary standard (which ended in the 1970s)
1997–2012: member of the U.S. House of Representatives; maintained strong
libertarian stances, returned to the Republican Party after joining the
Libertarian Party and being that party's presidential candidate in the 1988
election

EXECUTIVE EXPERIENCE   0
Never served in any executive capacity

MILITARY EXPERIENCE   4
1963–1968: served as a flight surgeon in the U.S. Air Force for two years, then
served in the Air National Guard until 1968

FOREIGN EXPERIENCE   4
Currently serves on the House Foreign Affairs Committee
[Not enough information on travel]

PRIVATE WORK EXPERIENCE   8
1968–2012: established a private medical practice near Houston, Texas,
specializing in obstetrics and gynecology; delivered babies periodically while in
Congress
1984–2001: established Ron Paul & Associates, a small family-run corporation
which created and distributed various newsletters including *The Ron Paul
Investment Letter*, *The Ron Paul Survival Report*, and *The Ron Paul Political Report*,
most typically written by aides or freelance libertarian writers

EDUCATION/INTELLECT   7
1953–1957: attended Gettysburg College; received a degree in biology
1957–1961: attended Duke University School of Medicine; received medical degree
1961–1963: completed residency training at the Henry Ford Hospital in Detroit

WRITING ABILITY   8
Strong and prolific writer, particularly on libertarian and other political topics
Publications include *Gold, Peace and Prosperity* (1981), *The Case for Gold* (1982),
Abortion and Liberty (1983), *Freedom Under Siege* (1987), *Challenge to Liberty* (1990),
The Party System (2007), *A Foreign Policy of Freedom* (2007), *The Revolution* (2008),
Pillars of Prosperity (2008), *End the Fed* (2009), and *Liberty Defined* (2011)

PUBLIC SPEAKING ABILITY   7
An accomplished public speaker and debater; delivered thousands of speeches
Always articulate with a straightforward presentation and consistent messaging

INTANGIBLES
Tea Party supporter; most conservative voting record in eighty years; age

JOSEPH ROBINETTE BIDEN, JR.   48

Election: 2012	**Party**: Democratic	**Opponent**: Uncertain
Age: 69	**Home State**: Delaware	**Running Mate**: Obama

LEGISLATIVE EXPERIENCE   14

1970–1972: member of the New Castle County Council in Wilmington, Delaware

1973–2009: member of the U.S. Senate; in 1973 was the sixth youngest Senator in history at 30 years old; long-time member and chairman of both the Foreign Relations Committee and the Judiciary Committee; became very influential

Resigned to become Vice President; 14th longest serving Senator in history

2009–2012: Vice President; exercises very few legislative duties

EXECUTIVE EXPERIENCE   4

2009–2012: Vice President; significant executive responsibilities including foreign policy advisor related to Afghanistan and Iraq and championing the stimulus bill

MILITARY EXPERIENCE   0

Never served in any military capacity; received student deferments from Vietnam

FOREIGN EXPERIENCE   14

1970s–2008: member and several times chairman of the Senate Foreign Relations Committee; met with hundreds of foreign leaders from dozens of countries

Dealt with issues surrounding the Cold War and arms control, NATO issues, and wars in Yugoslavia, Serbia, Croatia, Bosnia, Iraq (two wars), and Afghanistan

As Senator and Vice President, traveled to dozens of countries around the world

PRIVATE WORK EXPERIENCE   1

1969–1972: practiced law in Wilmington, Delaware, as a public defender and later as a partner of his own small firm, Biden & Walsh; minimal financial success

EDUCATION/INTELLECT   5

1957–1961: attended Archmere Academy; star football player; average student

1961–1965: attended University of Delaware; graduated in bottom 25% of class; double major in history and political science; played football for several years

1965–1968: attended Syracuse Law School; graduated in the bottom 15% of class

WRITING ABILITY   5

Respectable writing abilities; published hundreds of editorial articles and committee reports as a Senator, published the book *Promises to Keep* (2007)

Accused of plagiarism in a law school publication he wrote; received a grade of F

PUBLIC SPEAKING ABILITY   5

Thousands of speeches since the 1970s; known for being blunt and plainspoken

Respectable speechmaker and debater; overcame stutter as a child and young adult

Reputation for being longwinded; occasionally makes gaffes or off-color remarks

INTANGIBLES

Wife and daughter killed in 1972; survived two aneurysms in 1988; Roman Catholic

JAMES RICHARD PERRY 46
Election: 2012   **Party**: Republican   **Opponent**: Obama
Age: 62   **Home State**: Texas   **Running Mate**: Uncertain

LEGISLATIVE EXPERIENCE   2
  1984–1990: member of the Texas House of Representatives as a Democrat; pushed
    strongly for smaller state budgets; became one of the most effective state
    legislators; became a Republican in 1989
EXECUTIVE EXPERIENCE   15
  1990–1998: Texas Agriculture Commissioner; responsible for promoting the sale
    of Texas farm products to other states and foreign countries and supervising the
    calibration of weights and measures at gasoline stations and grocery stores
  1999–2000: Lieutenant Governor of Texas; became Governor at Bush's resignation
  2000–2012: Governor of Texas; longest serving Governor in the country; pushed
    for more healthcare and education funding, tough crime laws, and tort reform
  Served as chairman of the Republican Governors Association in 2008 and 2011
MILITARY EXPERIENCE   4
  1972–1977: served as a pilot in the U.S. Air Force; flew a C-130 while stationed in
    the United States, the Middle East, and Europe; resigned with rank of Captain
FOREIGN EXPERIENCE   7
  Served outside of the United States as a military officer
  2004–2010: as Governor made at least 23 trips to foreign countries to promote
    foreign investment in Texas industries and the sale and trade of Texas goods and
    services with foreign countries
PRIVATE WORK EXPERIENCE   3
  1977–1990: joined father as a small business cotton farmer
EDUCATION/INTELLECT   5
  Early education in Paint Creek, Texas; graduated from high school in 1968
  1968–1972: attended Texas A&M University; member of the Corps of Cadets; yell
    leader; graduated with a degree in animal science
WRITING ABILITY   6
  Writes occasional opinion editorials for various newspapers and magazines
  Has published two books: *On My Honor* (2008) and *Fed Up! Our Fight to Save America
    from Washington* (2012)
PUBLIC SPEAKING ABILITY   4
  Has become an adequate public speaker and debater since entering politics
  Known for being straightforward, plainspoken, and self-confident
INTANGIBLES
  Eagle Scout; social and fiscal conservative; fifth generation Texan; NRA member

WILLARD MITT ROMNEY   44

Election: 2012	**Party**: Republican	**Opponent**: Obama
Age: 65	**Home State**: Massachusetts	**Running Mate**: Uncertain

LEGISLATIVE EXPERIENCE   0

Never served in any legislative capacity

EXECUTIVE EXPERIENCE   10

2003–2007: Governor of Massachusetts; successfully turned a budget deficit into a
  budget surplus and passed a state universal healthcare law

Executive responsibilities as a successful businessman and major company CEO

MILITARY EXPERIENCE   0

Never served in any military capacity; high draft number kept him out of Vietnam

FOREIGN EXPERIENCE   4

1966–1969: lived in France for 30 months as a missionary; had a leadership role
[Not enough information on travel]

PRIVATE WORK EXPERIENCE   10

1975–1977: worked as a management consultant for the Boston Consulting Group

1977–1983, 1990–1992: worked as a management consultant at Bain & Company;
  returned as CEO to successfully manage a corporate restructuring

1983–1999: became the general partner of Bain Capital, a private equity investment
  firm helping start companies and perform leveraged buyouts

1999–2002: president and CEO of the 2002 Olympic Games organizing committee

2008–2012: Republican candidate for president; fund-raiser and speechmaker

EDUCATION/INTELLECT   8

1959–1965: attended the prestigious Cranbrook School; was an average student

1965–1966: attended Stanford University prior to a two-year mission in France

1969–1971: attended Brigham Young University; graduated with high honors;
  received a degree in English; was the student graduation speaker

1971–1975: attended Harvard Law School and Harvard Business School; graduated
  cum laude from law school and was in the top 5% in business school

WRITING ABILITY   6

A strong analytical writer; occasionally published editorials and other articles

Published two books: *Turnaround* (2004) and *No Apology* (2010)

PUBLIC SPEAKING ABILITY   6

Accomplished public speaker; formal, straightforward, business-like presentations

Fairly effective at extemporaneous speaking; considered stiff and lacking passion

INTANGIBLES

Personal wealth of over $200 million; physically attractive; devout Mormon

MITCHELL ELIAS DANIELS, JR.   43

Election: 2012   **Party**: Republican   **Opponent**: Obama
Age: 63   **Home State**: Indiana   **Running Mate**: Uncertain

LEGISLATIVE EXPERIENCE   2
1977–1982: Chief of Staff to Senator Richard Lugar of Indiana
1983–1984: executive director of the Republican Senatorial Committee

EXECUTIVE EXPERIENCE   13
1984–1987: Deputy Assistant for Intergovernmental Affairs and later chief political
adviser and liaison to state and local officials in the Reagan administration
2001–2003: Director of the Office of Management and Budget
2005–2012: Governor of Indiana; reduced the state budget and budget deficit,
promoted privatization projects, and supported other conservative measures
Executive responsibilities as a business executive

MILITARY EXPERIENCE   0
Never served in any military capacity; obtained student deferments during
Vietnam

FOREIGN EXPERIENCE   2
As the Director of the Office of Management and Budget from 2001 to 2003, was
also a member of the National Security Council and Homeland Security Council
[Not enough information on travel]

PRIVATE WORK EXPERIENCE   7
1971–1977: staff assistant to Indianapolis mayor Richard Lugar
1987–1990: CEO of the Hudson Institute, a conservative think tank
1990–2001: vice president of corporate affairs at Eli Lilly & Co.; promoted to
president of North American pharmaceutical operations in 1993; promoted to
senior vice president of corporate strategy and policy in 1997

EDUCATION/INTELLECT   8
1967: graduated from North Central High School in Indianapolis; student body
president; named Indiana's top male high school graduate by President Johnson
1967–1971: attended Princeton University; graduated with honors from the
Woodrow Wilson School of Public Policy and International Affairs
1976–1979: attended Georgetown University Law Center; graduated with honors

WRITING ABILITY   6
A good writer; publishes occasional opinion editorials and other articles
Published the book *Notes From the Road* (2005)

PUBLIC SPEAKING ABILITY   5
A respectable public speaker; not a powerful orator, but very articulate on issues
Has not delivered as many speeches as many other current candidates

INTANGIBLES
Arrested for marijuana possession in 1970; divorced; devout Presbyterian

MICHAEL DALE HUCKABEE 43

Election: 2012 **Party:** Republican **Opponent:** Obama
Age: 57 **Home State:** Arkansas **Running Mate:** Uncertain

LEGISLATIVE EXPERIENCE 0
Never served in any legislative capacity

EXECUTIVE EXPERIENCE 14
1993–1996: Lieutenant Governor of Arkansas; first Republican since the
Reconstruction Era
1996–2007: Governor of Arkansas; took strong pro-life positions; helped turn the
state budget from deficits to a surplus; worked to improve education in Arkansas
by hiring more teachers, raising teachers' salaries, and focusing on early learning

MILITARY EXPERIENCE 0
Never served in any military capacity

FOREIGN EXPERIENCE 0
[Not enough information on travel]

PRIVATE WORK EXPERIENCE 7
1976–1980: staff member for James Robinson's Christian broadcasting program
1980–1986: pastor of Immanuel Baptist Church in Pine Bluff, AR
1986–1992: pastor of Beech Street Baptist Church in Texarkana, AR; encouraged
racial integration of the congregation (previously was an all white congregation)
Started a 24-hour Christian television station in both towns; served as president
2007–2012: candidate for president in 2008; host of the television program
Huckabee on Fox News and host of a show on the ABC radio network

EDUCATION/INTELLECT 6
Attended Hope, Arkansas, schools; served as student council president; elected
Governor of the Boys State program; graduated from Hope High School in 1973
1973–1975: attended Ouachita Baptist University; received a degree in religion
1975–1976: attended Southwestern Baptist Theological Seminary; no degree

WRITING ABILITY 8
A strong and prolific writer; publishes frequent opinion editorials and other articles
Has published a number of books including *Character is the Issue* (1997), *Kids Who
Kill* (1998), *Living Beyond Your Lifetime* (2000), *Quit Digging Your Grave with a Knife
and Fork* (2005), *From Hope to Higher Ground* (2007), *Makes a Difference* (2007), *Do
the Right Thing* (2008), *A Simple Christmas* (2009), and *A Simple Government* (2011)

PUBLIC SPEAKING ABILITY 8
An accomplished public speaker since the 1970s; a smooth, comfortable delivery
Strong debater with the ability to connect with the audience; fluent and articulate
Delivered thousands of speeches and sermons; a great storyteller; exudes empathy

INTANGIBLES
Base guitarist in rock band; born in Hope, Arkansas (like Bill Clinton); Baptist

TIMOTHY JAMES PAWLENTY   42

Election: 2012   **Party**: Republican   **Opponent**: Obama
Age: 51   **Home State**: Minnesota   **Running Mate**: Uncertain

LEGISLATIVE EXPERIENCE   5
1980, 1982: summer clerk in the office of U.S. Senator David Durenberger
1991–1992: member of the Eagan City Council (suburb of Minneapolis)
1993–2003: member of the Minnesota House of Representatives; served as
    Majority Leader from 1999 to 2003; became an influential legislator

EXECUTIVE EXPERIENCE   9
2003–2011: Governor of Minnesota; focused on issues such as balancing the state
    budget, not raising taxes, education reform, and 24-hour abortion waiting period
Re-elected in 2006 while the Democratic party won big statewide and gained a
    majority in both houses of the state legislature
Held leadership positions as chairman of the National Governors Association
    (2007–2008) and chairman of the Midwestern Governors Association (2006)

MILITARY EXPERIENCE   0
Never served in any military capacity

FOREIGN EXPERIENCE   4
2000s: traveled outside the United States several times as governor on trade
    missions or to visit troops, including to Canada (2003), Bosnia (2003), Kosovo
    (2004, 2008), Czech Republic (2004), China (2005), India (2007), Israel (2008),
    Afghanistan, and Iraq; established working relationship with Mexican officials

PRIVATE WORK EXPERIENCE   6
1986–2001: labor attorney (first associate, then partner) at Rider Bennett law firm
    in Minneapolis; also lead counsel for the Minneapolis school district for ten
    years
2001–2002: vice president of Wizmo Inc., a Minnesota software company
2011–2012: speechmaker and candidate for the 2012 Republican nomination

EDUCATION/INTELLECT   7
1975–1979: attended South St. Paul High School; was an above average student
1979–1983: attended University of Minnesota; was an above average student;
    received a degree in political science
1983–1986: attended University of Minnesota Law School; was an above average
    student; worked summers at Rider Bennett

WRITING ABILITY   5
Respectable writing abilities; publishes occasional editorials and other articles
Published *Courage to Stand* (2011) and contributed to *Minnesota's Capitol* (2005)

PUBLIC SPEAKING ABILITY   6
An accomplished and effective public speaker; articulate; sometimes lacks passion
Delivered hundreds of speeches; hosted one-hour weekly radio show as Governor
Always speaks calmly and methodically; can be seen as a dull or uninspiring
    speaker

INTANGIBLES
Baptist with Catholic background; avid hockey player; social and fiscal
    conservative

JON MEADE HUNTSMAN, JR.   42

Election: 2012	**Party**: Republican	**Opponent**: Obama
Age: 52	**Home State**: Utah	**Running Mate**: Uncertain

LEGISLATIVE EXPERIENCE   0

Never served in any legislative capacity

EXECUTIVE EXPERIENCE   11

1987: served as a White House staff assistant to President Reagan

1989–1992: Deputy Assistant Secretary of Commerce for trade development and later for East Asian and Pacific affairs

2001–2004: Deputy U.S. Trade Representative, negotiated several dozen free trade agreements with numerous countries

2005–2009: Governor of Utah; promoted conservative tax and economic policies

Executive experience as a business executive and ambassador

MILITARY EXPERIENCE   0

Never served in any military capacity

FOREIGN EXPERIENCE   12

1979–1982: lived in Taiwan as a missionary; fluent in Mandarin and Taiwanese

1987–1988: lived and worked in Taiwan for the Huntsman Corporation

1992–1993: Ambassador to Singapore (youngest ambassador in 100 years)

2009–2011: Ambassador to China; confirmed unanimously by the U.S. Senate

Extensive travel to dozens of countries; foreign policy experience as Deputy Assistant Secretary of Commerce

PRIVATE WORK EXPERIENCE   4

1980s–2000s: worked as an executive in the multi-billion dollar family business, including as chairman and CEO of the Huntsman Corporation and as president of Huntsman Cancer Foundation; board member for various other organizations

EDUCATION/INTELLECT   5

Early education in California; dropped out to play keyboard in a rock band

Received G.E.D.; attended University of Utah before going on a two-year mission

1983–1987: attended University of Pennsylvania; degree in international politics

WRITING ABILITY   4

Respectable writer; not prolifically published; writes occasional opinion editorials

PUBLIC SPEAKING ABILITY   6

A personable and engaging public speaker; has given hundreds of political speeches

Delivered nominating speech for Sarah Palin in 2008 at the Republican convention

INTANGIBLES

Mormon; father of seven; very wealthy (father is a billionaire); was an Eagle Scout

DONALD JOHN TRUMP, SR.   39

Election: 2012   **Party**: Republican   **Opponent**: Obama
Age: 66   **Home State**: New York   **Running Mate**: Uncertain

LEGISLATIVE EXPERIENCE	0

Never served in any legislative capacity

EXECUTIVE EXPERIENCE	10

Significant executive experience as a billionaire businessman

MILITARY EXPERIENCE	0

Never served in any military capacity

FOREIGN EXPERIENCE	0

[Not enough information on travel]

PRIVATE WORK EXPERIENCE	10

1968–2012: first joined real estate developer father at the Trump Organization;
     became the chairman and CEO in 1971; personal worth of several billion dollars
Developer of real estate projects in New York City and around the world, including
     numerous casinos and hotels under the name Trump Entertainment Resorts
Emerged from financial difficulties in the 1990s caused by a recession and a poor
     real estate market to become profitable once again; also owns the Miss Universe
     Organization and other Trump-branded products and services
2004–2012: executive producer, host, and star of the hit television shows *The
     Apprentice* and *The Celebrity Apprentice*

EDUCATION/INTELLECT	6

1959–1964: attended New York Military Academy; was a strong student; a student
     leader; and a strong athlete in football, soccer, and baseball
1964–1968: attended Fordham University for two years, then Wharton School of
     Finance at the University of Pennsylvania; received a degree in economics and
     finance; strong student who was already involved in the real estate business

WRITING ABILITY	7

A prolific writer; publications include *The Art of the Deal* (1987), *Surviving at the Top*
     (1990), *The Art of Survival* (1991), *The Art of the Comeback* (1997), *How to Get Rich*
     (2004), *The Way to the Top* (2004), *Think Like a Billionaire* (2004), *The Best Golf
     Advice I Ever Received* (2005), *Why We Want You to be Rich* (2006), *Think Big and Kick
     Ass in Business and Life* (2007), *The Best Real Estate Advice I Ever Received* (2007),
     Trump 101 (2007), *Never Give Up* (2008), and *Trump Tower* (2011)

PUBLIC SPEAKING ABILITY	6

An accomplished and comfortable public speaker; given hundreds of speeches
Known for occasionally being blunt and somewhat provocative

INTANGIBLES

Tenuous party affiliation; divorced twice; celebrity; known for provocative remarks

HERMAN CAIN 39

Election: 2012 **Party**: Republican **Opponent**: Obama
Age: 66 **Home State**: Georgia **Running Mate**: Uncertain

LEGISLATIVE EXPERIENCE 0
Never served in any legislative capacity

EXECUTIVE EXPERIENCE 8
Significant executive responsibilities as a business executive for large companies

MILITARY EXPERIENCE 0
Never served in any military capacity

FOREIGN EXPERIENCE 0
[Not enough information on travel]

PRIVATE WORK EXPERIENCE 10
1967–1971: worked as a civilian analyst for the U.S. Navy
1971–1977: business analyst for the Coca-Cola Company
1977–1999: worked as a business executive, first managing over 400 Burger King restaurants in Philadelphia, turning the region from the least profitable to the most profitable; then as CEO of Godfather's Pizza, returning the company to profitability; then as CEO of the National Restaurant Association
1992–1996: served on the board of directors of the Federal Reserve Bank of Kansas City, acting chairman in 1995 and 1996
1992–2008: on the board of directors of Aquila, Inc., a Missouri utility company
Has held other executive positions at various organizations and companies

EDUCATION/INTELLECT 6
Received early education in Georgia schools
1963–1967: attended Morehouse College; graduated with a degree in mathematics
1971: graduated from Purdue University with master's degree in computer science

WRITING ABILITY 7
A strong and fairly prolific writer; frequently publishes a political opinion column
Published books include *Leadership is Common Sense* (1997), *Speak as a Leader* (1999), *CEO of SELF* (2001), and *They Think You're Stupid* (2005)

PUBLIC SPEAKING ABILITY 8
An accomplished and passionate public speaker; both a strong debater and orator
Beginning in the 1990s, has delivered hundreds of speeches and lectures focusing largely on business management, leadership, and politics
Associate preacher at the Antioch Baptist Church North in Atlanta, Georgia
Fox Business on-air commentator; daily radio show host since 2008

INTANGIBLES
Black race; cancer survivor; social and fiscal conservative; Tea Party supporter

RICHARD JOHN SANTORUM 36

Election: 2012 **Party**: Republican **Opponent**: Obama
Age: 54 **Home State**: Pennsylvania **Running Mate**: Uncertain

LEGISLATIVE EXPERIENCE 13

1981–1986: administrative assistant to a Pennsylvania Senator; served as the office
director of the local government committee and transportation committee
1991–1995: member of the U.S. House of Representatives; somewhat effective
1995–2007: member of the U.S. Senate; gained influence as the youngest member
of the Senate leadership, serving as chairman of the Republican Conference

EXECUTIVE EXPERIENCE 0

Never served in any executive capacity

MILITARY EXPERIENCE 0

Never served in any military capacity

FOREIGN EXPERIENCE 0

[Not enough information on travel]

PRIVATE WORK EXPERIENCE 4

1986–1990: associate attorney at the Kirkpatrick & Lockhart law firm in Pittsburgh
2007–2012: attorney at the Eckert Seamans Cherin & Mellott law firm, practices in
Pittsburgh and Washington, D.C., provides business and strategic advice
Currently a senior fellow with the ethics and public policy center in Washington

EDUCATION/INTELLECT 7

1976: graduated from Carmel High School in Mundelein, Illinois
1976–1980: attended Penn State University; received a degree in political science
1980–1981: attended the University of Pittsburgh; received an M.B.A.
1983–1986: attended Dickinson School of Law; received a J.D.

WRITING ABILITY 6

A respectable writer; publishes occasional opinion editorials and other articles
Published: *It Takes a Family* (2005), which addresses socially conservative views on
issues including same-sex marriage, homosexuality, and abortion; *Rick Santorum*
(2005), an autobiography

PUBLIC SPEAKING ABILITY 6

An accomplished public speaker; articulate and straightforward
Delivered thousands of speeches as a politician; frequently acted as a party
spokesman in the U.S. Senate during the 1990s and 2000; Fox News contributor

INTANGIBLES

Outspoken social and fiscal conservative; strong positions on abortion, gay rights

CHRISTOPHER JAMES CHRISTIE   32

Election: 2012   **Party**: Republican   **Opponent**: Obama
Age: 50   **Home State**: New Jersey   **Running Mate**: Uncertain

LEGISLATIVE EXPERIENCE   2

1994–1998: member of Morris County, New Jersey, Board of Chosen Freeholders
(the county legislature); sometimes mixed legislative with executive functions

EXECUTIVE EXPERIENCE   3

2010–2012: Governor of New Jersey; aggressively pursued fiscal reforms to reduce
the state budget deficit by, among other things, curtailing government spending
and public worker pensions

MILITARY EXPERIENCE   0

Never served in any military capacity

FOREIGN EXPERIENCE   0

[Not enough information on travel]

PRIVATE WORK EXPERIENCE   8

1987–2001: attorney at the Dughi, Hewit & Palatucci law firm in Cranford, NJ;
became partner in 1993; specialized in securities law, appellate practice, election
law, and government affairs

1998–2001: while still a law firm partner, registered as a lobbyist and lobbied on
behalf of an energy company, the securities industry, a state medical center, and
the University of Phoenix

2002–2008: U.S. attorney for the district of New Jersey; was the chief federal law
enforcement officer in New Jersey; worked to prosecute and reduce political
corruption, corporate crime, human trafficking, gangs, terrorism, and pollution;
oversaw an office of over 130 government attorneys

EDUCATION/INTELLECT   7

Received early education in Newark, NJ; graduated from Livingston High School
1980–1984: attended University of Delaware; received a degree in political science
1984–1987: attended Seton Hall University School of Law; received a J.D.

WRITING ABILITY   5

A strong writer; drafted hundreds of memos, motions, and briefs and an attorney
Occasionally publishes opinion editorials in various newspapers and magazines

PUBLIC SPEAKING ABILITY   7

An accomplished yet raw public speaker and debater; not a polished orator
Has received attention for speaking candidly and bluntly to the press and citizens
Honed advocacy skills as a trial and appellate lawyer; known for being a good
storyteller, showing passion, being sharp and articulate without being smooth

INTANGIBLES

Catholic; wife Mary was a Wall Street investment banker; fiscal reformer

MICHELE MARIE BACHMANN 29

Election: 2012   **Party**: Republican   **Opponent**: Obama
Age: 56   **Home State**: Minnesota   **Running Mate**: Uncertain

LEGISLATIVE EXPERIENCE   8

2001–2007: member of the Minnesota Senate; briefly held a leadership role
2007–2012: member of the U.S. House of Representatives; early supporter of the
    Tea Party movement; leader of the House Tea Party caucus; modest influence
Advocate for domestic drilling, fiscal reform, pro-life bills; opposed to bank bailout

EXECUTIVE EXPERIENCE   0

Never served in any executive capacity

MILITARY EXPERIENCE   0

Never served in any military capacity

FOREIGN EXPERIENCE   2

2007: traveled as part of a congressional delegation to Ireland, Germany, Pakistan,
    Kuwait, and Iraq

PRIVATE WORK EXPERIENCE   3

1988–1993: became a tax attorney for the U.S. Internal Revenue Service
1978–2007: occasionally assists husband in a small business (mental health care)

EDUCATION/INTELLECT   7

1970–1974: attended Anoka High School near Minneapolis; a good student
1974–1978: attended Winona State University; an above average student
1983–1986: attended Oral Roberts University Law School; received a J.D.
1987–1988: attended William & Mary Law School; received an LL.M. (tax
    specialty)

WRITING ABILITY   4

A respectable writer; publishes occasional articles and editorials

PUBLIC SPEAKING ABILITY   5

A respectable public speaker; quite articulate; speaks with great passion
Delivered frequent Tea Party speeches; delivered a Tea Party response to President
    Obama's 2011 State of the Union Address which was well-received

INTANGIBLES

Mother of five; fostered 23 teenage kids; early supporter of Tea Party movement

SARAH LOUISE PALIN 28

Election: 2012 **Party**: Republican **Opponent**: Obama
Age: 48 **Home State**: Alaska **Running Mate**: Uncertain

LEGISLATIVE EXPERIENCE 2
1992–1996: member of the Wasilla City Council (Wasilla population = about 5,500)

EXECUTIVE EXPERIENCE 6
1996–2002: Mayor of Wasilla, Alaska; cut taxes and built community sports center
2003–2004: chairwoman of the Alaska oil and gas conservation commission
2003–2005: director of a non-profit corporation that trains Republican women
2006–2009: Governor of Alaska; focused on natural gas and oil drilling issues, ethics reform, education, and reducing waste and spending; resigned mid-term

MILITARY EXPERIENCE 0
Never served in any military capacity

FOREIGN EXPERIENCE 2
Traveled several times to Canada and Mexico
2007: visited Alaska national guard troops in Kuwait, Iraq, and Germany

PRIVATE WORK EXPERIENCE 4
1987–1988: sportscaster and reporter for an Alaska news station and newspaper
1988–2012: assisted part-time in husband Todd's commercial fishing business
2010–2012: political commentator on Fox News; television show host for eight episodes of *Sarah Palin's Alaska* (2010); speechmaker and Tea Party supporter

EDUCATION/INTELLECT 4
1978–1982: attended Wasilla High School; star basketball player; average student
1982–1987: attended (for at least one semester) Hawaii Pacific University, North Idaho Community College, Matanuska-Susitna Community College, and University of Idaho; average student; graduated with a communications degree and an emphasis in journalism

WRITING ABILITY 5
An adequate writer; notable for publishing brief remarks on social media websites
Wrote (with help) and published *Going Rogue* (2010) and *America by Heart* (2010)

PUBLIC SPEAKING ABILITY 5
Respectable public speaker; always fluent, sometimes articulate and other times glib
Plainspoken; occasionally stumbles in extemporaneous speaking or press interviews
Widely praised for 2008 nomination speech; exceeded expectations in 2008 debate
2008–2012: delivered hundreds of public speeches at political rallies and events

INTANGIBLES
Mother of five; considered a "maverick" conservative Republican; attractive female

APPENDIX C
CORRELATION GRAPHS

APPENDIX C PROVIDES SEVERAL graphs that give readers a visual representation of the overall results and the results in each resume category. Also included on each graph is the average score each president received in the category, and the statistical significance for each category.

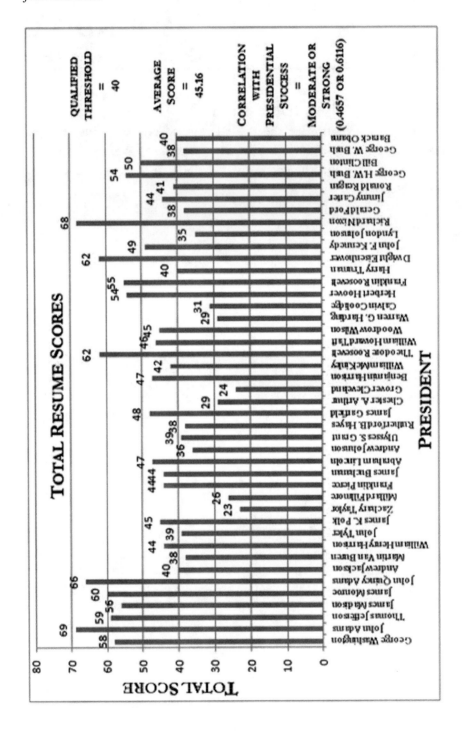

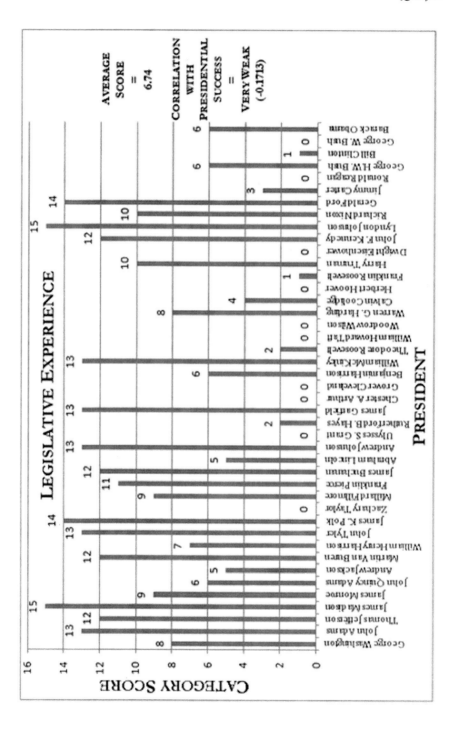

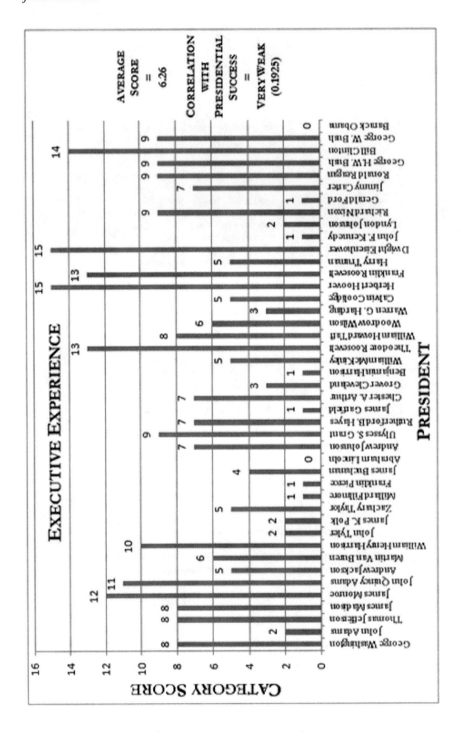

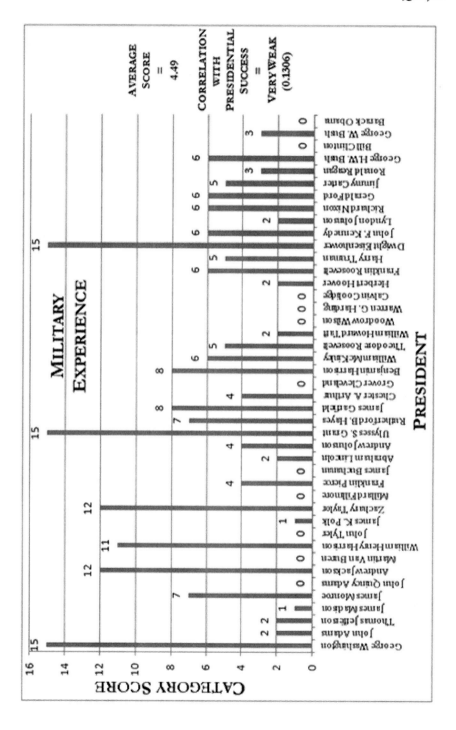

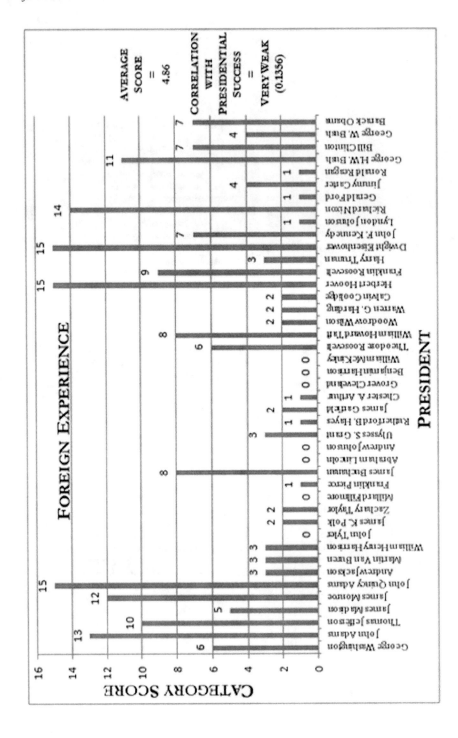

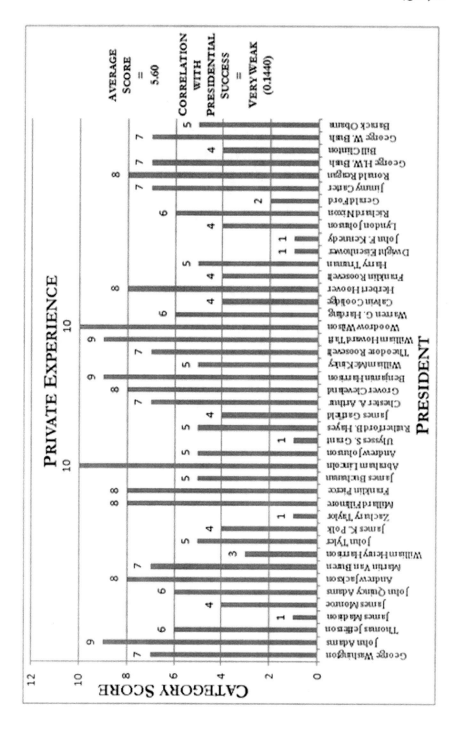

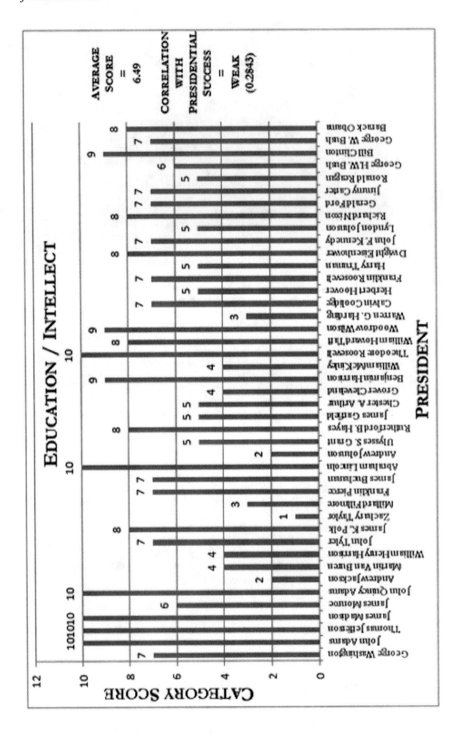

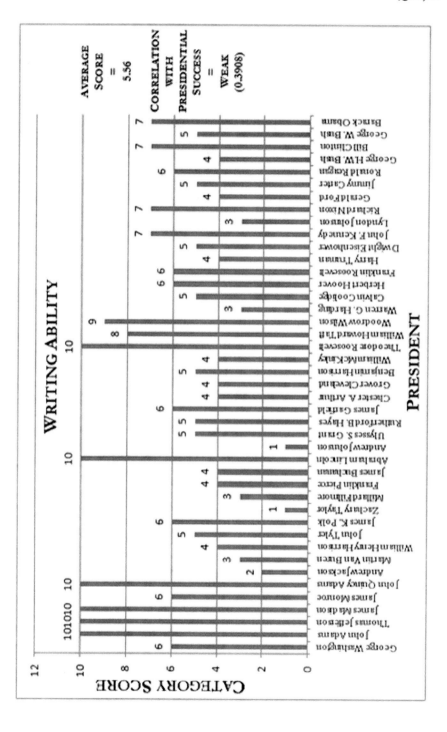

Jamin Soderstrom

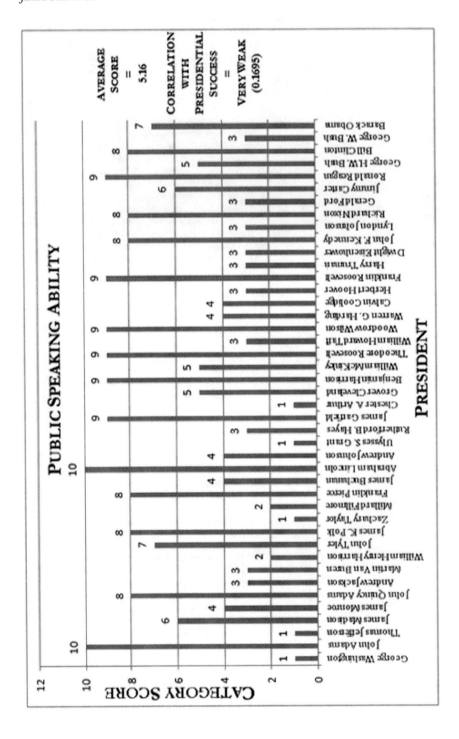

344

BIBLIOGRAPHY

Stephen E. Ambrose, *Eisenhower: Soldier and President* (New York: Simon & Schuster, 1990).

Judith Icke Anderson, *William Howard Taft: An Intimate History* (New York: W.W. Norton, 1981).

Harry Barnard, *Rutherford B. Hayes: And His America* (Newtown, Connecticut: American Political Biography Press, 1954).

K. Jack Bauer, *Zachary Taylor: Soldier, Planter, Statesman of the Old Southwest* (Baton Rouge, Louisiana: Louisiana State University Press, 1985).

Conrad Black, *Richard M. Nixon: A Life in Full* (New York: PublicAffairs, 2007).

Walter R. Borneman, *Polk: The Man Who Transformed the Presidency and America* (New York: Random House, 2008).

Peter G. Bourne, *Jimmy Carter: A Comprehensive Biography from Plains to Postpresidency* (New York: Scribner, 1997).

H.W. Brands, *The First American: The Life and Times of Benjamin Franklin* (New York: Anchor Books, 2000).

Alan Brinkley and Davis Dyer, eds., *The American Presidency* (Boston: Houghton Mifflin, 2004).

Douglas Brinkley, *Gerald R. Ford* (New York: Times Books, 2007).

David Burner, *Herbert Hoover: A Public Life* (Newtown, Connecticut: American Political Biography Press, 1978).

George W. Bush, *A Charge to Keep* (New York: William Morrow, 1999).

Charles W. Calhoun, *Benjamin Harrison* (New York: Times Books, 2005).

Robert A. Caro, *The Years of Lyndon Johnson: Master of the Senate* (New York: Vintage Books, 2002).

Ron Chernow, *Alexander Hamilton* (New York: Penguin, 2004).

Oliver Perry Chitwood, *John Tyler: Champion of the Old South* (Newtown, Connecticut: American Political Biography Press, 1939).

Hillary Rodham Clinton, *Living History* (New York: Simon & Schuster, 2003).

John Milton Cooper, Jr., *Woodrow Wilson: A Biography* (New York: Knopf, 2009).

Robert Dallek, *An Unfinished Life: John F. Kennedy 1917–1963* (Boston: Back Bay Books, 2003).

———, *Lyndon B. Johnson: Portrait of a President* (Oxford, England: Oxford University Press, 2004).

Burke Davis, *Old Hickory: A Life of Andrew Jackson* (New York: The Dial Press, 1977).

John Patrick Diggins, *Ronald Reagan: Fate, Freedom, and the Making of History* (New York: W.W. Norton, 2007).

Joseph J. Ellis, *American Sphinx: The Character of Thomas Jefferson* (New York: Vintage Books, 1996).

———, *Founding Brothers: The Revolutionary Generation* (New York: Vintage Books, 2000).

———, *His Excellency: George Washington* (New York: Knopf, 2004).

Alvin Stephen Felzenberg, *The Leaders We Deserved (and a Few We Didn't)* (New York: Basic Books, 2008).

James Thomas Flexner, *Washington: The Indispensable Man* (Boston: Back Bay Books, 1969).

Doris Kearns Goodwin, *Team of Rivals* (New York: Simon & Schuster, 2005).

Neil A. Hamilton, *Presidents: A Biographical Dictionary*, 3rd ed., revised by Ian C. Friedman (New York: Checkmark Books, 2010).

H. Paul Jeffers, *An Honest President: The Life and Presidencies of Grover Cleveland* (New York: Perennial, 2000).

Joseph Nathan Kane, *Facts About the Presidents: A Compilation of Biographical and Historical Information*, 8th ed., (New York: H.W. Wilson, 2009).

Doris Kearns, *Lyndon Johnson and the American Dream* (New York: St. Martin's Griffin, 1976).

Ralph Ketcham, *James Madison: A Biography* (Charlottesville, Virginia: University Press of Virginia, 1990).

Philip S. Klein, *President James Buchanan: A Biography* (Newtown, Connecticut: American Political Biography Press, 1962).

David Maraniss, *First in His Class: The Biography of Bill Clinton* (New York: Simon & Schuster, 1995).

David McCullough, *Truman* (New York: Simon & Schuster, 1992).

———, *John Adams* (New York: Simon & Schuster, 2001).

———, *1776* (New York: Simon & Schuster, 2005).

James M. McPherson, ed., *To the Best of My Ability* (New York: DK Publishing, 2000).

Jon Meacham, *Franklin and Winston* (New York: Random House, 2003).

———, *American Lion: Andrew Jackson in the White House* (New York: Random House, 2008).

Allan Metcalf, *Presidential Voices: Speaking Styles from George Washington to George W. Bush* (Boston: Houghton Mifflin Co., 2004).

H. Wayne Morgan, *William McKinley and His America* (Kent, Ohio: Kent State University Press, 2003).

Edmund Morris, *The Rise of Theodore Roosevelt* (New York: Coward, McCann & Geoghegan, 1979).

———, *Theodore Rex* (New York: Random House, 2001).

Timothy Naftali, *George H.W. Bush* (New York: Times Books, 2007).

Paul C. Nagel, *John Quincy Adams: A Public Life, a Private Life* (Cambridge, Massachusetts: Harvard University Press, 1997).

Stephen B. Oates, *With Malice Toward None: A Life of Abraham Lincoln* (New York: Harper & Row, 1977).

Allan Peskin, *Garfield: A Biography* (Kent, Ohio: Kent State University Press, 1999).

Norma Lois Peterson, *The Presidencies of William Henry Harrison & John Tyler* (Lawrence, Kansas: University Press of Kansas, 1989).

Robert J. Rayback, *Millard Fillmore: Biography of a President* (Newtown, Connecticut: American Political Biography Press, 1992).

Thomas C. Reeves, *Gentleman Boss: The Life and Times of Chester Alan Arthur* (Newtown, Connecticut: American Political Biography Press, 1975).

David Remnick, *The Bridge: The Life and Rise of Barack Obama* (New York: Knopf, 2010).

Francis Russell, *The Shadow of Blooming Grove: Warren G. Harding in His Times* (New York: McGraw-Hill, 1968).

Arthur M. Schlesinger, Jr., *A Thousand Days: John F. Kennedy in the White House* (Boston: Houghton Mifflin, 1965).

Robert Schlesinger, *White House Ghosts: Presidents and Their Speechwriters* (New York: Simon & Schuster, 2008).

Jean Edward Smith, *Grant* (New York: Simon & Schuster, 2001).

————, *FDR* (New York: Random House, 2007).

Robert Sobel, *Coolidge: An American Enigma* (Washington, D.C.: Regnery Publishing, 1998).

Theodore C. Sorensen, *Kennedy* (New York: Harper & Row, 1965).

James Taranto & Leonard Leo, eds., *Presidential Leadership: Rating the Best and the Worst in the White House* (New York: Free Press, 2004).

Hans L. Trefousse, *Andrew Johnson: A Biography* (Newtown, Connecticut: American Political Biography Press, 1989).

Harlow Giles Unger, *The Last Founding Father: James Monroe and a Nation's Call to Greatness* (Cambridge, Massachusetts: Da Capo Press, 2009).

Jack Valenti, *A Very Human President* (New York: W.W. Norton, 1975).

Peter A. Wallner, *Franklin Pierce: New Hampshire's Favorite Son* (Concord, New Hampshire: Plaidswede Publishing, 2004).

Ted Widmer, *Martin Van Buren* (New York: Times Books, 2005).

David C. Whitney and Robin Vaughn Whitney, *The American Presidents*, 8th ed. (Pleasantville, New York: Reader's Digest, 1996).

Garry Wills, *Lincoln at Gettysburg: The Words That Remade America* (New York: Simon & Schuster, 1992).

Other Sources

www.merriam-webster.com

www.wikipedia.com

www.biography.com

http://millercenter.org/academic/americanpresident

ABOUT THE AUTHOR

JAMIN SODERSTROM WAS BORN and raised in Ketchikan, Alaska. He then attended Pepperdine University in Malibu, California, where he played baseball for several years and graduated in 2002 with a degree in broadcast news. As an undergraduate student, he interned for a semester with the late night show *Politically Incorrect with Bill Maher.* During the summer of 2003, he also worked in the Capitol Hill offices of Senator Ted Stevens (Alaska). He then received a master's degree in business administration in 2004 from Grand Canyon University in Phoenix, Arizona.

Jamin returned to Malibu in 2005 to attend Pepperdine University School of Law. As a law student, he worked for two years as a research assistant for then-Dean Kenneth W. Starr, and for a semester as a legal extern in the chambers of Chief Judge Alex Kozinski in the United States Court of Appeals for the Ninth Circuit. He graduated magna cum laude in 2008, and was the student graduation speaker. Also in 2008, Jamin published *Back to the Basics: Looking Again to State Constitutions for Guidance on Forming a More Perfect Vice Presidency,* a scholarly article analyzing the constitutional and historical foundations of the American vice presidency.

After law school, Jamin joined the law firm Sullivan & Cromwell LLP in Los Angeles, where he worked on securities, mergers and acquisitions, and litigation matters. He currently works as a law clerk for Judge Harold R. DeMoss, Jr. in the United States Court of Appeals for the Fifth Circuit. He lives in Houston, Texas, with his wife Lisa and their Boston Terrier Moose.

ACKNOWLEDGEMENTS

I WANT TO EXPRESS my deepest thanks to a number of people who helped make my dream of writing *Qualified* a reality. First and most importantly, thanks to my wife Lisa, who offered more encouragement, support, and editorial advice that I could ever have hoped for.

Thanks also to my family (Sam and Donna Soderstrom, Jennie and John Holstrom, Donnie Soderstrom, Laurie Soderstrom, and Doug, and Peggy Trombly) and my friends and colleagues (Dane and Casey Ball, Jonna Stallings, Jake Lewis, Sharon Hicks, and Judge Harold R. DeMoss, Jr.), each of whom offered indispensable advice, assistance, and encouragement throughout the writing and editing process.

Finally, thanks to the editorial, production, and customer service teams at iUniverse, who helped turn my manuscript into a book of which I can be proud.

Each of you (and many other friends to whom I am also grateful) listened patiently to me talk about presidents, presidential candidates, and resumes for hours on end and never let me be discouraged during this three-year journey. Without you, my dream of writing *Qualified* never would have come true. Thank you for everything!

CPSIA information can be obtained at www.ICGtesting.com
Printed in the USA
LVOW072151211011

251631LV00003B/1/P